Issues in Higher Education

Series Editor: GUY NEAVE, International Association of Universities, Paris, France

SAGARIA
Women, Universities, and Change: Gender Equality in the European Union and the United States

SLANTCHEVA AND LEVY
Private Higher Education in Post-Communist Europe: In Search of Legitimacy (forthcoming)

The IAU

The International Association of Universities (IAU), founded in 1950, is a worldwide organization with member institutions in over 120 countries. It cooperates with a vast network of international, regional and national bodies. Its permanent Secretariat, the International Universities Bureau, is located at UNESCO, Paris, and provides a wide variety of services to Member Institutions and to the international higher education community at large.

Activities and Services

- IAU-UNESCO Information Centre on Higher Education
- International Information Networks
- Meetings and seminars
- Research and studies
- Promotion of academic mobility and cooperation
- Credential evaluation
- Consultancy
- Exchange of publications and materials

Publications

- International Handbook of Universities
- World List of Universities
- Issues in Higher Education (monographs)
- Higher Education Policy (quarterly)
- IAU Bulletin (bimonthly)

WOMEN, UNIVERSITIES, AND CHANGE
GENDER EQUALITY IN THE EUROPEAN UNION AND THE UNITED STATES

Edited by

MARY ANN DANOWITZ SAGARIA

palgrave
macmillan

INTERNATIONAL
ASSOCIATION OF
UNIVERSITIES
INTERNATIONAL UNIVERSITIES BUREAU

First published in 2007 by
PALGRAVE MACMILLAN™
175 Fifth Avenue, New York, N.Y. 10010 and
Houndmills, Basingstoke, Hampshire, England RG21 6XS
Companies and representatives throughout the world.

PALGRAVE MACMILLAN is the global academic imprint of the Palgrave Macmillan division of St. Martin's Press, LLC and of Palgrave Macmillan Ltd. Macmillan® is a registered trademark in the United States, United Kingdom and other countries. Palgrave is a registered trademark in the European Union and other countries.

ISBN-13: 978-1-4039-6844-9
ISBN-10: 1-4039-6844-6

Library of Congress Cataloging-in-Publication Data

Women, universities, and change : gender equality in the European Union and the United States / edited by Mary Ann Danowitz Sagaria
    p. cm.— (Issues in higher education)
  Includes bibliographical references and index.
  ISBN 1-4039-6844-6 (alk. paper)
    1. Women—Education (Higher)—Europe. 2. Women—Education (Higher)—United States. 3. Women college teachers—Europe. 4. Women college teachers—United States. 5. Women college administrators—Europe. 6. Women college administrators—United States. 7. Education, Higher—Europe—Administration. 8. Education, Higher—United States—Administration. 9. Sex discrimination in higher education—Europe. 10. Sex discrimination in higher education—United States. 11. Feminism and education. I. Sagaria, Mary Ann Danowitz. II. Title: Gender equality in the European Union and the United States.

LC2036.W65 2007
378.1'982—dc22   2006050875

A catalogue record for this book is available from the British Library.

Design by Newgen Imaging Systems (P) Ltd., Chennai, India.

First edition: February 2007

10 9 8 7 6 5 4 3 2 1

Printed in the United States of America.

Transferred to digital printing in 2007.

CONTENTS

List of Tables

LIST OF FIGURES

ACKNOWLEDGEMENTS

This book is the outgrowth of conversations about the need to identify the scaffolding of university change efforts towards gender equality that began at the Conference of the Consortium of Higher Education Researchers in September of 2002 in Vienna. The discussions continued at the European Higher Education Society Meeting in Prague with the symposium Gender Equity National Politics and Institutional Responses: Comparing Europe and the U.S. in which Judith Glazer-Raymo, Barbara Sporn, and I participated. It was there that the idea for a book emerged, but it was the help of many people that brought the project to fruition.

I would like to thank Guy Neave for his probing questions about the realities of gender equality in higher education and his encouragement to write a book to make the issue more public and visible.

I am also especially thankful to Barbara Sporn for her salient suggestions on frames and foci for the prospective contributors and for her support and encouragement during all phases of the project. My gratitude is also with Cynthia Secor, Tatiana Rents, and Linda Bernhard for their critical and constructive suggestions on parts of the manuscript.

I would like to acknowledge Pamela Van Horn's unwavering commitment to the publication of the book. Her painstaking work with the editing and preparing of the text is most appreciated.

This book would not have been possible without institutional support. Grants from Ohio State University's Office of International Education and the Critical Difference Program for Women provided funds to travel Europe to conceptualize the project. Funding from the University of Denver's College of Education, Office of Graduate Studies, and the Office of Internationalization enabled me to complete the project.

Women, Universities, and Change: Gender Equality in the European Union and the United States is the result of collaboration among 16 authors and me. We have tried to achieve coherence in theme and form as well as to maintain the diversity of our voices, perspectives, and experiences. What unifies the following chapters is the authors' deep commitment to leading and documenting change in higher education, especially that relating to gender equality and to recognizing the influence that women have in that process. While all of the contributors are academics, the lead author of each chapter is a feminist academic activist. Much of our professional lives have been devoted to creating scholarship in the areas of higher education, organizations, policy, employment, feminist sociology, and women's studies. We have written about what we have practiced, and we have practiced what we have written. It is not by chance that many of us have been asked to take on new leadership challenges and professional responsibilities during the three year gestation period of the book. Seven of the 11 lead authors have changed jobs with 5 of them changing universities as well. Our career changes reflect a reality of our lives as feminist academic activists as they also complicate both our individual writing projects as well as the dynamics of a collaborative volume. Most importantly, I would like to thank the contributors who have dealt with me kindly when I asked for 'one more change' and who made time from their over-committed schedules to write for this book. I have gained greatly from their generous colleagueship and wisdom in bringing this book to birth.

Mary Ann Danowitz Sagaria

CONTRIBUTORS' BIOGRAPHIES

Mary Ann Danowitz Sagaria is Professor and Director of the Higher Education Program at the University of Denver and a Fulbright Scholar at the Vienna University of Economics and Business Administration. She has held faculty positions at on Ohio State University and the College of William and Mary and administrative appointments at Penn State University, State University of New York at Geneseo, and the University of Minnesota at Morris. Mary Ann has been a Fulbright Scholar to Indonesia and a visiting scholar in Australia and Malaysia. Her research and publications focus on leadership and governance, the academic profession careers and human resources, and gender and racial equality and include *Empowering Women: Leadership Development on Campus*.

Lyndsay J. Agans is a doctoral student and research assistant in Higher Education at the University of Denver. Her research interests include organization and governance as they relate to change and reform in higher education, feminist educational policy analysis, and scholars and education for sustainable development.

Miriam E. David is Professor of Sociology of Education and Associate Director (Higher Education) of the Economic and Social Research Council's Teaching and Learning Research Programme, London University Institute of Education, and Professor Emerita at Keele University. She has also served in administrative and research positions at Keele, London South Bank University, and the Universities of Bristol and London. Miriam has been a Visiting Professor in Australia, Canada, New Zealand, and the United States. Her research and scholarship focus on gender, family (parents and children), education and social policy, professional and doctoral education. She is Chair of Council of the Academy of Social Sciences and her recent publications include (with Diane Reay and Stephen Ball) *Degrees of Choice: Class, Gender and Race in Higher Education* and *Personal and Political Feminisms: Sociology and Family Lives*.

Judith Glazer-Raymo is Lecturer and Fellow of the Higher and Postsecondary Education Program at Teachers College, Columbia University, and Professor Emerita of Education at Long Island University. She also chairs Scholars and Advocates for Gender Equity (SAGE), a standing committee of the American Educational Research Association. Her research and scholarship focus on gender and ethnic diversity in higher education, innovations in graduate education, and critical approaches to higher education policy analysis. Judith is the author of *Shattering the Myths: Women* *in Academe* and *Professionalizing Graduate Education: The Master's Degree in the Marketplace.*

Michaela Gindl is Research Fellow at the Department for Higher Education Research, University of Klagenfurt, Vienna location. Michaela is a sociologist and is active in projects researching the promotion of women and the implementation of gender-sensitive didactics at universities. Her research focuses on gender-specific issues in higher education and strategies towards gender equality at universities.

Liisa Husu is a Research Fellow in the Helsinki Collegium for Advanced Studies, University of Helsinki, and is Vice Chair of the Equality Committee of the University. Her research and scholarship focus on gender dynamics in science, academia, and higher education. Her publications include the book *Sexism, Support and Survival in Academia,* the co-edited book *Hard Work in the Academy,* and (with Louise Morley) a co-edited special issue on Academe and Change for the UNESCO/CEPES journal *Higher Education in Europe.* She has been National Coordinator of Women's Studies in Finland, is currently actively engaged in several European initiatives on gender and science, and is the moderator of the European Network for Gender Equality in Higher Education.

Louise Morley is a Professor of Education at the University of Sussex, United Kingdom. Her previous posts were at the Institute of Education, University of London, the University of Reading, and the Inner London Education Authority. She recently directed a DFID/ Carnegie funded research project on gender equity in Commonwealth higher education. Her research and publication interests focus on quality, equity, gender, power, and empowerment in higher education. Recent publications include *Researching Women: An Annotated Bibliography on Gender Equity in Commonwealth Higher Education* (with Annik Sorhaindo and Penny Burke); *Theorising Quality in Higher Education; Quality and Power in Higher Education; Organising Feminisms: The Micropolitics of The Academy; Breaking Boundaries: Women in Higher Education* and *Feminist Academics: Creative Agents for Change* both edited with Val Walsh.

Ursula Müller is Professor of Sociology and Women's Studies at the Bielefeld University and Faculty of Sociology where she has also served as Dean. She is the Director of the university's Interdisciplinary Center for Women's and Gender Studies. She has published on methodological and theoretical issues in women and gender studies with a special emphasis on the interference of theory and empirical research. Her research and publications have examined gendered labour markets, German men and their reactions towards the women's movement, sexual harassment, gender and organization in German police, diversity, violence, gender in higher education, and e-learning in gender studies. In addition, she has been active in international research networks, such as the EU-network *Critical Research on Men and Masculinities (CROME)* and *Co-ordination Action Human Rights Violations (CAHRV).*

Ada Pellert is Vice-Rector at Danube University, Krems. She also serves as Associate Professor for Organizational Development in Higher Education Institutions at the

Department for Higher Education Research, University of Klagenfurt, Vienna. Ada formerly was Vice-Rector for Instruction, Staff Development, and Affirmative Action for Women at the University of Graz where she led efforts to promote gender equality in university reform.

Teresa Rees is Pro Vice-Chancellor of Cardiff University in Wales, United Kingdom, and a Professor in the School of Social Sciences there. She is a long-term adviser to the European Commission on gender mainstreaming. She was a rapporteur for many of the reports of the Women and Science Unit of the European Commission's Research Directorate-General. These include *Science Policies in the European Union: Promoting Excellence through Mainstreaming Gender Equality*, the ETAN Report, *The Helsinki Group on Women and Science: National Policies on Women and Science in Europe*, and *Women in Industrial Research: A Wake Up Call for European Industry*. She was also co-author of the Greenfield Report on women in science, engineering, and technology in the United Kingdom. She is an Academician of the Academy of Learned Societies in the Social Sciences and was made a Commander of the British Empire for services to education and equal opportunities in 2003.

Suzanne Rice is an Associate Professor in the Department of Teaching and Leadership at the University of Kansas. Her interests include philosophy of education and educational policy studies. In addition to gender issues, her work focuses on ethics and moral education.

Christine Roloff is a member of the Center for Research on Higher Education and Faculty Development. From 1998 to 2003, she directed a project of the University of Dortmund's governing board linking organizational reform and quality assessment with gender equality. Christine has published on professional women in science and technology and on reform and gender equality strategies in higher education.

Terhi Saarikoski is the University of Helsinki Equality Adviser. She was earlier employed by the national gender equality authorities in Finland as the Secretary of its Subcommittee of Research. Her interests include equality policies and politics. She is the moderator of the European Network for Gender Equality in Higher Education.

Barbara Sporn is University Professor and Vice Rector for Research, International Affairs, and University Relations at the Vienna University of Economics and Business Administration. Her research and leadership activities focus on organizational adaptation, organizational culture, strategic planning, and university management from an international and comparative perspective. Barbara's publications include *Adaptive University Structures: An Analysis of Adaptation to Socio Economic Environments of US and European Universities* and *Emerging Patterns of Social Demand and University Reform: Through a Glass Darkly*.

Susan B. Twombly is Professor of Higher Education at the University of Kansas. Her research interests include women in higher education, women in Latin America, and community college faculty and administrators. She is co-author, with Lisa Wolf-Wendel and Suzanne Rice, of *The Two-Body Problem: Dual Career Couple Hiring Practices in Higher Education*.

Pamela S. Van Horn is pursuing her PhD in Quantitative Research Methods at the University of Denver. Her research interests lie in psychometrics, community-based research, equity in higher education, teacher education, and secondary English education.

Lisa E. Wolf-Wendel is an Associate Professor of Higher Education at the University of Kansas. Her research focuses broadly on equity issues concerning women and people of colour in higher education. She has conducted research on women's colleges, dual career couple-hiring concerns, and academic motherhood (or how women faculty with young children balance work and family).

CHAPTER ONE

REFRAMING GENDER EQUALITY INITIATIVES AS UNIVERSITY ADAPTATION

Mary Ann Danowitz Sagaria

Contemporary scholars of higher education change tend to overlook gender, and gender scholars tend to overlook higher education adaptation. In *Women, Universities, and Change: Gender Equality in the European Union and the United States*, we take a different approach because we are committed to promoting equality between women and men in our universities as well as enhancing the capabilities of our institutions to address other pressing social, political, and economic problems. Thus, the contributors to this book analyse how higher education's responses to sociopolitical and economic influences affect gender equality at the nation-state and university levels in the European Union and the United States. We do this by examining strategic responses to key contextual and environmental factors and their impact on gender equality in higher education and by identifying ingredients for promoting gender equality within the structures and cultures of universities.

The lack of gender equality in higher education is a global problem. It has been identified as a principal factor limiting research and development in Europe (Osborn et al., 2000; Rees, 2002), and it is a subtle but pervasive problem in the United States (Glazer-Raymo, 1999; Hornig, 2003) which was recently acknowledged at Duke and Princeton universities with the launch of major gender equity reforms (Zakian et al., 2003; Keohane et al., 2003). Yet, there has been a lack of cross-national analyses of gender as a dimension of higher education organizational adaptation. One of our goals in writing this book is to reframe and further analyse contemporary policy dynamics, organizational practices, and gender equality outcomes within different, political, historical, and cultural contexts. Our endeavours focus on the transnational level of the European Union and national and institutional levels of four EU countries – Germany, Austria, Finland, and Britain along with the United States to uncover some of the international patterns of gender inequalities that are affected by decentralization of decision making, entrepreneurialism, and reallocation of finances. We undertook this project to assist policy makers, university leaders, and gender activists at national and institutional levels to make informed policy decisions to improve gender equality.

In order to raise understanding of gender equality as a dimension of organizational adaptation, we focus on the relationship between the status of women (mainly academic staff faculty members) and external factors, such as governmental agendas, finances, market pressure, and competition. We do this on two levels. On one level, we analyse key gender equality, affirmative action, and higher education policies and practices of the European Union and the five nation-states. We include variables such as governmental-funding decisions, benchmarking and reputational ranking, accountability practices, and career and legal decisions as they relate to educational equality changes. On the other level, we examine changes in the status of women in relationship to adaptation strategies associated with leadership, management, and financing in six institutional case studies – Dortmund University (Germany), Vienna University of Economics and Business Administration (Austria), Helsinki University (Finland), and Keele University (Britain), and two U.S. public research universities, the Ohio State University and the University of Kansas.

These feminist case studies of higher education change provide new culturally and historically sensitive insights into gender equality and the challenges and opportunities to improve the status of academic women. Our research from Europe identifies facilitating and inhibiting practices that occur within the top-down model from the EU Commission to member-state education ministries and to the university level. Our research from the United States identifies public university responses within a political and economic context of decreased state funding and legal challenges to affirmative action. Each of the five nation-states and six universities studied has had both substantial improvements as well as setbacks regarding equality.

Gender as a Category of Analysis to Improve Higher Education

Research in the United States (Volk, Slaughter, & Thomas, 2001) and Australia (Currie, Theile, and Harris, 2002) indicates that unless higher education institutions factor in the potential results of adaptation strategies on gender, women will experience highly adverse consequences. Each of our 12 transnational, national, and institutional cases presents grounded analyses to inform and assist policy and decision makers and gender advocates about the gendered subtexts and unintended gender consequences of adaptation. These lessons from a variety of political and social settings present possible problems and issues to be considered prior to implementing a policy change, offering a greater possibility that future policy makers will avoid mistakes that have already been made and will instead adopt more realistic and successful strategies.

Gender equality in academe has been studied mainly from the perspective of organizational gendering (the presence of masculine principles and structures that lead to advantages for male staff and disadvantages for female staff). Universities have been analysed as sites of sexual discrimination (Aisenberg & Harrington, 1988; Clark et al., 1996; Glazer-Raymo, 1999), power relationships (Morley, 1999; Currie, Theile, & Harris, 2002), and male domination (Morley & Walsh, 1995; Brooks & Mackinnon, 2001; Hornig, 2003). Scholars have also studied interventions to reduce gender inequalities (Folgerberg et al., 1999; Wiedner, 2002; Blättel-Mink & Mischau, 2001). These studies have mainly employed cultural and feminist approaches to understand how power is structured and used in organizational life. Most writers employing organizational-gendering approaches, however, have not considered equality as an integral part of university adaptation and have tended to isolate gender equality rather than consider it enmeshed in organizational and environmental structures and actions. Consequently, the complexities associated with institutional gender reforms within a neo-liberal context often have been underestimated whereas the successes and failures have been overstated.

Likewise, most scholars of higher education organizations have not considered educational equality as a dimension of institutional adaptation. Gumport and Sporn (1999) analysed more than 150 studies of university adaptation to conclude that the societal environment, institutional environment, and university administration (the structure and processes within universities for implementing and executing decisions made by academic governance) must be considered the primary influences in higher educational organizational change. Noticeably absent from these studies, however, is attention to gender or the gendered nature of university adaptation. For example, only one study analysed by Gumport and Sporn considered the consequences of university adaptation on women. Similarly, Slaughter's (1993) analysis of retrenchment decisions at 17 U.S. universities found that those decisions had especially adversarial consequences for women. Institutions tended to cut the number of women faculty in inverse relationship to their growth in student enrolments and retrench fields that were likely to have a higher percentage of women and minorities than non-retrenched fields.

To offer a realistic picture of gender equality as a dimension of organizational adaptation, we build upon scholarship from educational equality, gendered organizations, organizational change, and feminist sociology. Our work extends but differs from much of the previous research on higher education by coupling topics that are intertwined in organizational adaptation but that are usually treated separately by researchers. For example, Barbara Sporn reframes and deconstructs new Austrian management and institutional autonomy policies from an organizational adaptation framework. She then examines the institutional consequences of this devolution on formal policies and structures as well as the culture of gender equality at the Vienna University of Economics and Business Administration.

Women, Universities, and Change: An Overview

Each chapter addresses some aspect of two following questions: How are governmental, social, political, and economic agendas, leadership, competitive market pressures, finances, and university structures and cultures influencing gender equality? And how are gender equality and women changing universities? We use a variety of social science methods including policy and documentary analysis, interviews, and secondary data analysis. Most chapters use demographic data as well to measure the progress of women across faculty ranks over time. Moreover, taken together, the chapters offer useful comparisons across several nations and universities. We do not suggest, however, that our approach is comprehensive; we caution against generalizing from the national case studies to other nations, especially the 11 EU nations not represented in the book. Political, economic, historical, and cultural differences are too great to do so. That being said, the work of the European Commission represents an innovative effort to address what policies are needed to ensure that gender ceases to be an insignificant organizing principle in the social construction of excellence.

Germany, Austria, Finland, and Britain represent diverse national models of governance steering (relationships between the nation-state and universities), including differences in funding, access, research and development practices, cultures (Neave, 2001), and diverse approaches to gender equality (Rees, 2002). The United States has decentralized governance steering with variations among the 50 states and was an early global leader in promoting gender equality. Each nation-state chapter analyses recent policies, practices, and demographic data to consider strategies, activities, and measures to advance the status of women within the context of governance, differentiation, and changes in key policies, finances, and the academic labour force.

Each of the university chapters demonstrates a different approach to gender equality by analysing a policy or practice at the university and its gender impact (consequences for gender equality and the status of women) to determine where and why change has or has not occurred and to describe the historical and cultural context of gender equality and university adaptation. Nation-state and university case studies are placed side by side in order to couple and highlight the relationship between government policies and economic conditions, and culture gender equality on the national level with conditions, issues, and changes within universities. The chapters that follow raise important considerations, issues, and questions about higher education in order to provide some insights and guidance to promote gender equality in our universities and their practices.

In chapter 2, 'Gender Equality in European Universities', Teresa Rees focuses on the emerging policy responses to the acknowledgement that there is a problem regarding gender equality in European universities. She lays a foundation for current EU policies by identifying antecedent events and reports, and she then contrasts the three current policy approaches to gender equality: equal treatment, positive action, and mainstreaming. She argues that if gender is to become less important in the allocation of positions in universities then equal treatment as a human right is fundamental to the process. Describing the European Commission's commitment to gender mainstreaming as 'the promotion of gender equality through its systematic integration into all systems and structures, into all policies, processes, and procedures, into the organization and its culture, into ways of seeing and doing' (in press 2005), Rees makes a compelling case for gender mainstreaming to be pursued in tandem with equal treatment and positive action. Following this framing of gender equality in Europe, each chapter explores issues of gender equality and university change in greater detail.

In chapter 3, 'Between Change and Resistance: Gender Structures and Gender Cultures in German Institutions of Higher Education', Ursula Müller describes structures and cultures of universities to explicate gendered subtexts and asymmetrical gender cultures. She raises questions about the frames of the Bologna Process, professorial careers, and entrepreneurialism for their future consequences for women and gender equality. In chapter 4, 'Gender Equality Challenges and Higher Education Reform: A Case Study of the University of Dortmund', Christine Roloff traces the role of institutional leadership and private funding to advance gender equality in teaching and learning. She also provides evidence of the importance of formalizing and increasing the transparency of a process to increase women's participation in PhD programmes. Ada Pellert and Michaela Gindl consider the need for mainstreaming in Austrian universities through an examination of social and historical roots and the changing nature of autonomy in chapter 5, 'Gender Equity and Higher Education Reform in Austria'. In chapter 6, 'University Adaptation and Gender Equality: A Case

Study of the Vienna University of Economics and Business Administration', Barbara Sporn applies a theoretical frame to elucidate how adaptation has occurred within the Austrian strategy for gender equity, revealing committed leadership, differentiated structure, professional management, clear mission and goals, and discretionary funding as critical factors in creating change. Lisa Husu in chapter 7, 'Women in Universities in Finland: Moving Closer to Gender Equality', focuses on the representation of women in universities to reveal both horizontal and vertical gender stratification through embedded norms in academe as influenced by policy measures and research priorities. In chapter 8, 'Promotion of Gender Equality in the University of Helsinki', Lisa Husu and Terhi Saarikoski provide a case study which evaluates the university's gender equality plan by examining the capacity of the agenda for diversity and identifying the successes and challenges encountered through gender equality promotion in an increasingly feminized environment. In 'Gender and U.K. Higher Education: Post-Feminism in a Market Economy', Louise Morley uncovers the need for gender mainstreaming in the wake of the silencing effect of the shifting U.K. economy on women in academe as she identifies opportunities for change in chapter 9. In chapter 10, 'Personal Learning on Professional Doctorates: Feminist and Women's Contributions to Higher Education', Miriam David investigates the role of personal values and reflective practice as an underlying element of higher education through learning and teaching, pedagogies, and research practices.

Chapter 11 turns a comparative lens towards equality practices in the United States. In 'Gender Equality in the American Research University: Renewing the Agenda for Women's Rights', Judith Glazer-Raymo traces the changing educational landscape in U.S. higher education through the shifting political ideology regarding equality frameworks. She goes on to identify the fallacy of women's majority representation in higher education and the fragility of the current diversity paradigm for achieving gender equality in the United States. Chapter 12, 'Academic Excellence and Gender Equality at The Ohio State University', a case study of the Ohio State University by Mary Ann Danowitz Sagaria and Pamela Van Horn, portrays the successes and tension of an organization with many formal structures for women but with a policy of directing funding to achieve selective excellence in the disciplines without regard to gender. In chapter 13, 'Helping or Hurting Women? The Case of a Dual Career Couple Policy at the University of Kansas', Suzanne Rice, Lisa Wolf-Wendel, and Susan Twombly document the development and implementation of a programme of innovative hiring strategies and practices. Finally, the concluding chapter 14, 'Frames, Changes, Challenges, and Strategies' by Mary Ann Danowitz Sagaria and Lyndsay Agans attempts to synthesize the various frames, tensions, and analyses of these chapters and offers current insights about how to promote equality as part of a university change process.

References

Aisenberg, N., & Harrington, M. (1988) *Women of academia: Outsiders in the sacred grove.* Amherst, MA: University of Massachusetts Press.

Blättel-Mink, B., & Mischau, A. (Eds.) (2001) From the bottom to the top in higher education: Women's experiences and visions in different parts of the world. *Special issue of international journal of sociology and social policy, 21*(1/2).

Brooks, A., & Mackinnon, A. (Eds.) (2001) *Gender and the restructured university*. Buckingham: Society for Research into Higher Education and Open University Press.

Clark, V., Garner, S. N., Higonnet, M., & Katrack, K. H. (Eds.) (1996) *Antifeminism in the academy*. New York: Routledge.

Currie, J., Theile, B., & Harris, P. (2002) *Gendered universities in globalized economies: Power, careers and sacrifices*. Lexington: Lexington Books.

Folgerberg, P., Hearn, J., Husu, L., & Mankkinen, T. (Eds.) (1999) *Hard work in the academy: Research and interventions on gender inequalities in higher education*. Helsinki: Helsinki University Press.

Glazer-Raymo, J. (1999) *Shattering the myths: Women in academe*. Baltimore: Johns Hopkins University Press.

Gumport, P. J., & Sporn, B. (1999) Institutional adaptation: Demands for management reform and university administration. In J. Smart (Ed.), *Higher education: Handbook of theory and research: Vol.14*. (pp. 103–145). Bronx, NY: Agathon Press.

Hornig, L. (Ed.) (2003) *Equal rites, unequal outcomes: Women in American research universities*. New York: Kluwer.

Keohane, N. et al. (2003) *Report of the steering committee for the women's initiative at Duke University*. Retrieved February 21, 2006, from http://www.duke.edu/womens_initiative/report_report.htm.

Morley, L. (1999) *Organizing feminisms: The micropolitics of the Academy*. Basingstoke: Macmillan.

Morley, L., & Walsh, V. (Eds.) (1995) *Feminist academics: Creative agents for change*. London: Taylor and Francis.

Neave, G. (2001) *The European dimension in higher education: An excursion into the modern use of historical analogues*. Amsterdam: IAU Press.

Osborn, M., Rees, T., Bosch, M., Hermann, C., Hilden, J., McLaren, A., Palomba, R., Peltonen, L., Vela, C., Weis, D., Wold, A., & Wennerås, C. (2000) *Promoting excellence through mainstreaming gender equality*. A report from the ETAN Network on Women and Science. Luxembourg: Office for Official Publications of the European Communities.

Rees, T. (2002) *The Helsinki group on women and science: National policies on women and science in Europe*. Luxembourg: Office for Official Publication of the European Communities.

——— (2005) Reflections on the uneven development of gender mainstreaming in Europe. *International journal of feminist politics*, 7(4):555–574.

Slaughter, S. (1993) Retrenchment in the 1980s. *Journal of higher education*, 64(3):250–282.

Volk, C., Slaughter, S., & Thomas, S. L. (2001) Models of institutional resource allocation: Mission, market and gender. *Journal of higher education*, 72(4):387–413.

Wiedner, C. (Ed.) (2002) *Sound changes: An international survey of women's career strategies in higher education*. Zurich: UniFrauenestelle `1University of Zurich.

Zakian, G., Drain, Buc, Ferrand, L., Girgus, J., Lee, R., Paxson, C., Rubenstein, D., Troian, S., Walker, S., & Ward, B. (2003) *Report of the task force on the status of women faculty in the natural sciences and engineering at Princeton*. New Jersey: Princeton University Press.

Chapter Two

Pushing the Gender Equality Agenda Forward in the European Union

Teresa Rees

Interest in and, indeed, concern about the issue of gender equality and universities in the European Union have been growing over the last decade. EU commissioners have been particularly alarmed by the failure of universities in the EU to recruit, retain, and promote women academics. Although women constitute over half the undergraduates in the European Union, they stubbornly retain only 14% of the professorships (EC, 2003). Universities present themselves as meritocratic, liberal institutions. However, even though gender equality may be a principle of academic life, statistics show that it is not the practice. The 'leaky pipeline', which haemorrhages women from academic careers, is a cause for concern largely because of the European Union's commitment to become a more economically competitive, knowledge-based global region. But gender equality is also driven partly by a commitment to the European 'social model' and hence to social justice. This commitment was manifested in the Amsterdam Treaty mandating that the European Union and all its member states provide equal treatment for all regardless of sex, race, and ethnic origin, sexual orientation, age, disability, and religious and political beliefs and that gender equality be mainstreamed in all EU policies (Commission of the European Communities, 1996).

This concern at EU level reflects growing attention paid to this issue by member states themselves. In the early 1990s, demographic trends, more precisely the decline in the number of students leaving school and the ageing of the workforce, led to an enhanced focus on recruiting and retaining women scientists in particular and attracting back those who had taken career breaks. In the United Kingdom, for example, the idea that women scientists were a 'wasted resource' began to emerge during the mid-1990s (Chancellor of the Duchy of Lancaster, 1993; Committee on Women in Science Engineering and Technology, 1994). Since then, a series of independent reports reviewing the U.K. university sector have drawn attention, albeit sometimes in passing, to the 'problem' of the position of women in the academy (National Committee of Inquiry into Higher Education, 1997; Independent Review Committee on Higher Education Pay and Conditions, 1999). In 2002, the secretary of state at the Department of Trade and Industry asked Baroness Professor Susan

Greenfield to investigate the issue specifically. Her report *SET Fair* revealed that in the United Kingdom as many as 50,000 women with science, engineering, and technology degrees no longer used their scientific education (Greenfield et al., 2002). Following her recommendations, the government invested in a number of measures to promote good practice among employers as well as to support women in their academic careers (Office of Science and Technology, Department of Trade and Industry, 2003). They included a Resource Centre for Women in Science, Engineering, and Technology (www.setwomenresource.org.uk). The United Kingdom is the third EU member state to have such a resource centre.

Over the last decade, similar reports have been commissioned and initiatives taken up by many of the original 15 EU [EU-15] member states (prior to enlargement in 2004), for example, in Finland, France, Germany, and the Netherlands, as well as by the European Commission itself (Academy of Finland, 1998; Ministère de la Recherche, 2002; Federal Ministry of Education and Research, 2001; Ministry of Research and Information Technology, 1997; Osborn et al., 2000). In the Central and Eastern European countries and the Baltic States, many of which are former communist countries but have now joined the EU, women in universities face different but equally intransigent problems. Whereas many universities have a better record of employing and retaining women, the sector is under-resourced, and men remain three times more likely to reach senior academic positions than women (Blagojević et al., 2004). Throughout Europe, then, the following questions can be asked: If universities select and promote academics simply on merit, then why is the proportion of women professors so low? If women constitute the majority of undergraduates in some subjects, for example, medical and biological sciences, then why are they still a diminishing minority among lecturers, senior lecturers, and professors? If membership of the learned societies is an indication of scientific excellence, then why is the proportion of fellows who are women so persistently miniscule?

It is clear from these and other figures and reports that the 'equal access' to an academic education and career that women have enjoyed for the past 50 years in Europe has not thus far led to 'equal outcome' in terms of positions, pay, research funding, or indeed scientific prizes. On the contrary, gender appears still to be a significant organizing principle in academic life, despite the rhetoric of objectivity and excellence that imbues scientific and university culture. If academic life is a competitive labour market where the currency is excellence, then how is it that women do so disproportionately badly in it? Could it be, as echoed in the provocative words of the authors of the European Technology Assessment Network (ETAN) Report, that exclusionary mechanisms allow mediocre men to take precedence over excellent women in recruitment and promotion (Osborn et al., 2000)?[1]

This chapter focuses on the emerging policy response to the growing acknowledgement that there is a problem regarding gender equality in European universities. The first section looks at initiatives at the EU level. The second focuses more on the member states and their attempts to recruit, retain, and promote women in the academy. The final section is concerned with evaluating these policy approaches.

Three contrasted policy approaches are considered: equal treatment, positive action, and mainstreaming gender equality. The principle of *equal treatment* is clearly an essential human right and has been underpinned by a series of directives in the European Union in the 1970s in particular. However, often, in practice, equal treatment means that women are treated the same as rather than equal to men. *Positive action measures*, targeting the *special needs* of women, popular in the 1980s, can contribute significantly to promoting good practice and unstopping blockages. However, they can attract accusations of tokenism and invoke backlash, and they tend to be temporary and piecemeal. Both these approaches are essential but remain severely limited in their effectiveness (Rees, 1998).

The third approach, *gender mainstreaming*, has yet to be tried systematically in universities and requires a more complex approach to *promoting* gender equality than either equal treatment or positive action. Gender mainstreaming is about integrating gender equality into processes, policies, and practices. This integration is accomplished by institutional arrangements and the use of such tools as developing a gender balance in decision making, using gender-disaggregated statistics, and constructing equality indicators in policy formulation, delivery, monitoring, and evaluation. It also involves using a transparent evidence base informed by gender studies for managing human resources. Gender mainstreaming moves beyond a concern with numbers and processes to the examination of such phenomena as the *gendering* of the institution and indeed of science itself. This move challenges ideas about the gender neutrality of the social construction of *excellence* and *merit*. Equally, it means engaging with the current, pervasive neglect of a gender dimension in some research projects and indeed in pedagogy and the curriculum.

Before considering policy approaches to gender equality in the universities in the European Union and its member states, some background context is provided on higher education policy in the European Union along with the statistical profile of women in universities.

The Context

Whereas member states retain control of policy developments for the higher education sector within their own countries, the EU plays a role in *value-added* policies for the European Union and indeed to some extent other European countries as an economic region. This role is manifested through policies currently being developed to create a European Research Area and a European Research Council. A significant commitment to increase financial investment in the Framework Programs in Research and Development (R&D) supports work undertaken by transnational groups of researchers from within the European Union and beyond. The European Commission encourages the international mobility of researchers (through the Marie Curie Programme inter alia) and students (through the ERASMUS Programme). Meanwhile, the Bologna Process is seeking to harmonize the currency and acceptability of undergraduate and postgraduate degrees across the European Union.[2]

All of these issues have a gender dimension. However, of particular significance here is the growing concern among member-state ministers about the European Union's economic competitiveness vis à vis other global regions. Consequently, in 2000, this concern led to the commitment to enhance the European Union as a knowledge-based economy and the goal of increasing the investment of gross domestic product (GDP) in R&D of the EU-15 member states from 1.9% in 2000 to 3% by 2010. This readjustment compares to the U.S. figure of 2.7% and Japan's 3%. It was calculated that for the EU-15 considerably more qualified researchers in science, engineering, and technology would be needed to realize this spending target (EC, 2003).

As the European labour supply both shrinks and ages, projected numbers of new graduates entering the labour market with science, engineering, and technology degrees are insufficient to meet this demand. Women make up the majority of undergraduate students in the biological and medical sciences but still remain a small minority in mathematics, chemistry, physics, and engineering. Women then proceed to fall out of the academic career system in disproportionate numbers, whatever the discipline, at every stage of the academic hierarchy, especially at the postdoctorate level, through the leaky pipeline. Hence, just as so many qualified women scientists drop out of academic careers at each level, in each discipline, in each country, they are identified as a major potential supply source (Blagojević et al., 2004; EC, 2005; Rübsamen-Waigmann et al., 2003).

The leaky pipeline is not, of course, just a European phenomenon (Etzkowitz, Kemelgor, ancl Uzzi, 2000; Glover, 2000; Schiebinger, 1999). However, the consistency of the pattern across such highly diverse countries and over time is remarkable. In 2000, in universities and research institutes throughout the EU-15, men were found to be selected for academic positions disproportionate to their numbers in the recruitment pool at every grade, in every subject, and in every country, irrespective of the equality policies of the country and whether or not women constituted a majority of the undergraduates in that subject (Osborn et al., 2000). Figure 2.1 shows the percentage of women among academic staff in 30 of the countries associated with the Framework Programs, including most of the EU member states, in 1999 and 2002. Among both the EU-15 states and the 25 member states, women occupied just 35% of all academic positions in 2002 while they comprised an average of 50% of all students.

However, as figure 2.1 shows, women held only 14% of the senior posts. In each of the countries, it is possible to see this pattern of loss, or 'the higher, the fewer' (Rees, 2002; EC, 2003).

One of the first large-scale attempts to make international comparisons revealed substantial differences among the countries, for example, in the way scientific disciplines are grouped for statistical analyses and in academic career structures (including what 'counts' as professorial status) (Osborn et al., 2000). This makes benchmarking highly invidious. This issue is now being tackled in Europe, and the improved availability of gender-disaggregated statistics and the development of equality indicators have been helpful to those at both the EU and member-state levels seeking to increase awareness of the issue and to improve gender equality in universities. Statistics and indicators are tools of the gender-mainstreaming approach to promote gender equality, not simply for benchmarking against policies but as an awareness-raising exercise.

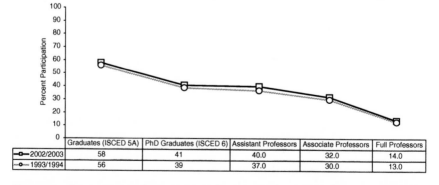

	Graduates (ISCED 5A)	PhD Graduates (ISCED 6)	Assistant Professors	Associate Professors	Full Professors
2002/2003	58	41	40.0	32.0	14.0
1993/1994	56	39	37.0	30.0	13.0

Figure 2.1 Representation of Women among Students and Academic Staff in EU Universities

Sources: European Commission. (n.d.) Research: Women and Science indicators and statistics. Brussels: Directorate-General Research, European Commission. Retrieved from http://ec.europa.eu/research/science-society/women/wssi/downindi_en.html.

The European Union and Gender Equality:
The Women and Science Unit

In 1996, the European Commission made a commitment to gender mainstreaming in all of its policies (Commission of the European Communities, 1996); in 1999, the Research Directorate-General published its communication detailing how it would respond to this commitment (Commission of the European Communities, 1999). The Women and Science Unit had already been set up in the Directorate-General to promote research 'for, by, and about women'.[3] It undertook a range of gender-mainstreaming activities that have had some influence on both the European Union and member states.

Specifically, the Directorate-General committed itself to a better gender balance in decision making, a key element of the gender-mainstreaming approach, both in decisions about research policy and in the construction of scientific excellence. *Science* here is very broadly defined to include the social sciences and the humanities as well as science, engineering, and technology. Hence, a 40% minimum target was set for its scientific committees, whose members are nominated by member states, and for the evaluation and monitoring committees of its Framework Programs on R&D. Even though these targets have not yet been reached, the proportion of women participating in both activities has increased. Nevertheless, figures from the ETAN Report commissioned by the Women and Science Unit demonstrated the extreme paucity of women seated on committees determining what science should be conducted, funded, and rewarded and by whom within individual countries across the world (Osborn et al., 2000). In addition, the ETAN Report found that most international prize committees have no female members and that a shortage of women exists among the fellows of learned societies. In the case of the United Kingdom's Royal Society, the proportion rose from 0.5% in 1945 (when women were first admitted) to only 4.5% in 2005. Research-funding bodies (with the exception of those in Portugal and Finland) are likely to have an overwhelming number of men among their membership (Osborn et al., 2000; EC, 2003).

The issue is more complex than simply one of numbers, however. Drawing on data from qualitative research in a university in the United Kingdom, Bagilhole and Goode (2001) identified an 'in-built patriarchal support system' that male staff are able to access and from which they benefit. They argue that women are not admitted into this support system. Similarly, Valian (1997) refers to a 'male bonus'. In Sweden, Wennerås and Wold (1997) demonstrated how the application of the much revered and allegedly 'neutral' peer-review system in a research council can be flawed through the gendering of networking. They showed how successful women applicants for medical research council fellowships had published two and half times as much as the successful male candidates had. Important variables determining success, as well as a standard measure of 'excellence' determined by publications, included being male and having worked with one of the committee members. The article, published in *Nature*, caused a scandal (Wennerås & Wold, 1997) and prompted other funding bodies to examine their practices (Blake & La Valle, 2000).

This revelation, that peer-review systems do not always operate fairly, provoked concern not simply about gender balance in decision making but also about the complex idea of the gendered construction of scientific excellence. The Women and Science Unit co-organized a workshop on this issue, inviting scholars from the

United States and Europe to discuss to what extent procedures, criteria, and definitions regarding 'scientific excellence' are in fact gender-neutral (EC, 2004).

Such discussion was to inform thinking about the design of research-funding evaluation for future Framework Programs that provide a considerable source of funding for research in the European Union. At the instigation of the Women and Science Unit, a gender impact assessment was conducted of some projects in the Fifth Framework Program to look especially at their treatment of the gender dimension (Laurila & Young, 2001). It was found that the projects did not necessarily pay appropriate attention to gender as a significant variable in many social processes. In the design of the Sixth and Seventh Framework Programs, guidelines stipulated not only that attention should be paid to the issue of a gender balance among the groups of partners that apply but also that proposals should have a 'gender action plan' to address how the gender dimension will be addressed in the research. In addition, a number of specific projects on the issue of gender equality in universities have been funded, including one leading to a *Manual on Gender Mainstreaming in Universities* (Stevens & Van Lamoen, 2001).

The Women and Science Unit held a series of conferences to facilitate the networking of women academics, including one designed to 'network the networks' of women in professional scientific associations (European Networks on Women and Science, 1999). These events acted to some extent as a consciousness-raising exercise across member states and indeed other European countries that participated in the Framework Program. They facilitated the work of feminists within various academic disciplines to organize and develop links across countries to promote gender equality. They also brought together social scientists and gender experts who worked on exclusionary mechanisms in the academy with women scientists, many of whom who did not necessarily acknowledge that such mechanisms existed (EC, 2001, 2002, 2005a).

The Women and Science Unit commissioned a series of reports to inform its work. The ETAN Report drew attention to the lack of good quality comparable statistics and gender equality indicators (Osborn et al., 2000). Similarly, the Women and Industrial Research Report addressed women researchers in science, engineering, and technology in the private sector, examining statistics, research, and good practice (Rübsamen-Waigmann, 2003; EC, 2005b). Both reports made recommendations for mainstreaming gender equality in policy and practice.

Finally, the Women and Science Unit brought together representatives from all the 33 countries participating in the Framework Programs for a benchmarking exercise on women in science. Known as the Helsinki Group, as the first meeting took place there during the Finnish EU presidency in 2000, most members were civil servants from science ministries and gender experts. The Helsinki Group met twice a year to exchange information and ideas on gender equality policies in universities. A report of their activities shows how some emerging patterns have been developing across very different countries in addressing the leaky pipeline, the gender balance in scientific decision making, and modernization of the academy (Rees, 2002). Part of the work of the Helsinki Group is to coordinate national statistics on women and science and to explore the development of gender equality indicators; a parallel group of national correspondents on statistics has also been set up (Glover & Bebbington, 2000). Because of its varied work, the Group enabled countries to learn from each other and to push the agenda forward more easily than they might otherwise have done. In addition, for members from the accession countries, joining the European

Union entailed ensuring that appropriate equal treatment legislation was on the statute books.

In sum, the Women and Science Unit has used a range of gender-mainstreaming tools, such as gender balance in decision making, gender-disaggregated statistics, equality indicators, gender impact assessments, gender studies and gender experts, networking, awareness raising, benchmarking, and good practice to promote gender equality in the universities of Europe. Woodward (2004) refers in her work on the European Union to a 'velvet triangle' of feminist civil servants and politicians, gender experts, and the women's movement working together to promote gender equality. This way of working can be more informal than some systems of governance, calling on expertise, political pressure, networks, and contacts to significant effect. The Women and Science Unit, it can be argued, has worked within this framework by utilizing politicians within the European parliament and governments of the 33 countries, the civil servants of the ministries of science and education, lobby groups and networks of women scientists and their organizations, and social science gender experts.

National Approaches to Gender Equality in European Universities

The Helsinki Group Report provides a snapshot of equality policies among the 33 member countries (Rees, 2002; and table 2.1). These include both national equality policies and initiatives specifically about women in science. At the time the snapshot was taken, the accession countries had not yet joined the European Union and therefore were in the process of implementing the equality infrastructure, such as equal treatment legislation, that membership of the EU requires. The Nordic countries stand out as having the most developed general gender equality policies.

There is, of course, considerable diversity among the Helsinki Group countries in terms of the scientific infrastructure itself and, more specifically, the climate for women pursuing scientific careers. Nevertheless, there are also some common factors, such as a lack of gender balance in the higher echelons of decision making about science policy and, indeed, among those who determine what constitutes 'good' science.

In terms of infrastructure, some countries have set up a national, cross-ministerial women and science committee to focus attention on these issues. Some, such as Germany, have set up their own Women and Science units in a relevant government department, either in Education or Science. These units can be sources of data and providers of examples of good practice that can be used by women's groups and equality organizations as well as the sector itself.

Practices of benchmarking, initiatives to attract women back to academia, and good practice guides on mentoring, childcare, work/life balance are also on the increase, made possible in part by the opportunities for learning about the state gender equality in other countries. Gender-mainstreaming tools, such as equal pay audits, gender impact assessments, gender budgeting, monitoring, developing equality indicators, and securing a gender balance on committees are being used or developed in some EU member states and to an extent at the EU level. Investment in gender studies as a research area to inform gender mainstreaming in universities is also important here.

Many countries have instituted positive action measures to address the barriers to women in science. These include supporting networks of women in science,

Table 2.1 Summary Table of Equality Measures

Equality Measures	*Countries:* BE$_{(1)}$	BE$_{(2)}$	DK	DE	EL	ES	FR	IE	IT	LU	NL	AT	PT	FI	SE	UK
											EU Member States					
Equal treatment legislation	X	X	X	X	X	X	X	X	X	X	X	X	X	X	X	X
Statutory Sex Equality Agency	X	X	X	X	X		X	X	X	?	X	X	X	X	X	X
Ministry for Women	X		X	X			X		X	X	X	X				X
Women and Science Unit in the Science Ministry				X			X		X		X	X				X
National Steering Committee on Women and Science	X	X	?		X	X	X	X	X		X	X	X	X	X	X
Commitment to gender mainstreaming	X	X	X	X	X		?	?	X	X		X	X	X	X	X
Sex-disaggregated statistics	X	X	X	X	X	X	?				X	X	X	X	X	
Gender balance quotas on public committees		X		X	X		?				X					
Gender balance quotas on university/ research institute ctees											NA					X
Gender balance targets on university/ research institute ctees				X	X				X	X	NA	X			X	X
Development of gender equality indicators	X	X	X	X	X	X	X	X	X	NA	X	X	X	X	X	X
Women's studies taught at universities	X	X	X	X	X		X	X	X	NA	X	X	X	X	X	X
Gender studies taught at universities	X	X	X	X	X	X	X	X	X	NA	X	X	X	X	X	X
Universities/research institutes produce equality plans			X	X				X	X	NA	X	X	X	X	X	X

Note: X = equality measure; blank cell = no measures; NA = not applicable; ? = no answer

BE$_1$ = Belgium (French-Speaking)
BE$_2$ = Belgium (Flemish-Speaking)
DK = Denmark
DE = Germany
EL = Greece
ES = Spain
FR = France
IE = Ireland

IT = Italy
LU = Luxembourg
NL = Netherlands
AT = Austria
PT = Portugal
FI = Finland
SE = Sweden
UK = United

Source: Rees, T. (2002) *The Helsinki group on women and science: National policies on women and science in Europe.* Luxembourg: Office for Official Publication of the European Communities, page 32.

encouraging the development of role model and mentoring schemes, and in some cases, establishing targets and quotas. A few countries have experimented with earmarking chairs (Sweden) and allocating fellowships for returners and 'trailing spouses' (United Kingdom), all of which are aimed at women but, for legal reasons, are not exclusively for women.

Some countries, in particular Nordic ones, are using gender-mainstreaming tools in order to embed equality into the systems and structures of science. Such tools include more transparency in appointment processes, equality training for those on recruitment panels, examination of the pedagogy of science education to eliminate biases, and support for gender studies. Measures also include good employment practices that facilitate a reasonable work/life balance and programmes accommodating women re-entering scientific careers after a period at home with childcare responsibilities. Three EU member states (Finland, Sweden, and France) now have legislation to ensure a gender balance on public bodies, including research bodies and universities.

The Helsinki Group is determined to see that science is modernized using a range of approaches, such as ensuring that the highest standards prevail in peer review, addressing the portrayal of science and scientists in the media, and exploring what gender studies has to offer to our understanding of the gendering of science and its culture and institutions. Group members also share an interest in modernizing scientific careers by ensuring that merit is transparently the dominant criterion in selection and promotion processes and in the allocation of grants and prizes. Modernization also encourages flexibility, work/life balance, and support for dependents while studying abroad. Such measures should open up opportunities for scientific careers to a more diverse population, in particular, to more women. Monitoring and evaluation are considered vital because the story of women in science is not all one of progress. In some countries, the situation has worsened because of particular policies, for example, the backfiring of a positive action measure designed to encourage the appointment of more women professors in Austria. It is also important to recognize that what works in one context might not succeed in another.

Policy Approaches to Gender Equality

If gender is to play less of a role in the allocation of positions in universities and elsewhere, then the consideration of *equal treatment* as a human right is essential to the process. Equal treatment as a principle was enshrined in the Treaty of Rome that set up what we know as the European Union in 1957. It is essentially about providing a legal framework that ensures the equal treatment of men and women. Originally, the principle was about equal pay and access to employment and training, but a series of directives (EU legislation that is binding on member states) has been introduced to extend this right to pensions, social security, and other areas (Rees, 1998).

However, what we tend to see in equal treatment practices is that women and men are not in fact treated *equally*, but they are treated the *same*. More specifically, women are treated *the same as men* are treated. In effect, crudely put, women can succeed in academic life provided they behave like men; hence, for example, the difficulty arises for women scientists who take career breaks to get back into the system.

In equal treatment, the underlying androcentricity of the organization of science and of the culture of universities is not acknowledged and is therefore ignored.

Consequently, aspects of the organization of scientific careers are allowed to benefit men rather than women. For example, privileging an unbroken career over one marked by career breaks benefits men more than it benefits women because men are less likely to take career breaks. The acceptance that unlimited hours are needed to ensure a successful scientific career rather than one with a better work/life balance penalizes those who make a greater contribution to domestic and caring responsibilities, primarily women. The unequal gendered pattern of domestic division of labour remains extraordinarily robust despite significant changes in women's economic activity. Equal treatment, then, is an essential legal right but is insufficient to ensure gender equality. In many European countries, the breadwinner/homemaker gender contract still informs the organization of cultural and organizational settings with profoundly different consequences for men and women whatever their individual domestic circumstances.

Positive action measures, by contrast, are based on an acknowledgement that there are differences between women and men, and they seek to address the disadvantages that women experience because of these differences.[4] Such measures are intended to compensate women for the consequences of those disadvantages and create a level playing field. Like equal treatment, positive action also carries a health warning because it can be viewed as a mechanism to make women more like men. Nevertheless, many individual women in science have benefitted from positive action initiatives. Networking and mentoring schemes, for example, have gained some ground for women scientists in U.K. universities.

Gender mainstreaming was identified at the Beijing 1995 United Nations Conference on Women as one of ten agenda for action items. But even though gender mainstreaming is gathering momentum in Europe as an approach that has some potential in achieving gender equality, there is considerable confusion about the term. *Gender mainstreaming* can be described as 'the promotion of gender equality through its systematic integration into all systems and structures, into all policies, processes, and procedures, into the organization and its culture, into ways of seeing and doing' (Rees, 2005). It is a meta-approach based on principles and utilizing tools and addresses designed to tackle cultural and organizational discrimination (Rees, 1998).[5]

The principles of gender mainstreaming focus on respect and dignity for the individual both as a professional, which means sexual harassment and bullying are clearly off limits, and as a whole person, which means promoting an organizational culture that discourages excessive hours of working and encourages a better work/life balance. It also includes principles of justice, fairness, and equity, which are manifested in democratic decision making, open recruitment and promotion procedures, and clear equality policies (Rees, 2005). In this instance, a gender-mainstreaming approach seeks to address the *gendering of science* or the silent ways in which the culture and organization of science, while purporting to be gender-neutral, are imbued with gender.

This issue of gender mainstreaming has been addressed by Glover (2000) in a convincing comparison of women in science in the United Kingdom, France, and the United States. The total number of women in a discipline does not appear to be related to the proportion of women professors. However, Glover points out that even if there are more women in science, neither the agenda nor the methodological approach necessarily changes. She has drawn attention to the fact that most of the rhetoric and debate about women in science has focussed on 'getting in' (recruitment) whereas the real difficulties lie in 'staying in' (sustaining an academic career) and in 'getting on' (securing promotion). She argues that whereas human capital, such as qualifications, is clearly significant for advancement in science, the importance of reputational capital, and more particularly cultural capital, is underestimated. The importance of networking and the phenomenon of invisible women scientists are both well known, but Glover's analysis sheds considerable light upon how the gendering of accumulating patterns of cultural capital works for men and against women in the sciences. Human capital, in terms of appropriate qualifications, may be needed for entry, but for progression, cultural capital appropriate to the habitus is essential. This principle governs the differences between the genders in the sciences in terms of women getting in, staying in, and getting on. Glover pays particular attention to physics, the science where women have made the least progress. She argues first that the lack of a cadre of junior staff undertaking data entry or routine analysis has made it more difficult for women to gain access. However, she also draws attention to a historic link between science and religious orders, both being engaged in a quest for a theory to explain creation. She argues that Western science has produced a male, celibate, homosocial, and misogynous culture that has had little experience of women. Glover makes the case for ethnographic studies of physics departments to be undertaken to explore these ideas further.

The ETAN Report on women and science concluded that many European universities and research institutes are highly old-fashioned in their employment practices (Osborn et al., 2000). They purport to be liberal institutions, privileging 'merit' in their recruitment and promotion, but in fact use male networks and personal sponsorship in preference to modern assessment techniques. Many posts are not advertised; rather, existing senior academics secure succession lines through their own networks. Alternatively, recruiters are used. Evidence from Finland shows that women are much more likely to be appointed if a post is advertised rather than filled through recruiting efforts (Academy of Finland, 1998). Because existing members of academic societies nominate new members, networks are important in the allocation of opportunities that facilitate the visibility and career building of an academic, such as delivering keynote addresses, joining editorial boards, and external examining.

The ETAN Report advocated mainstreaming gender equality in the culture and organization of universities in order to ensure that merit really does take precedence over gender in the allocation of positions and opportunities. The main challenge of this endeavour is to move beyond tokenism. Gender mainstreaming is a long-term strategy requiring organizational and cultural change. It is not a quick fix. That is why it needs to be pursued in tandem with measures of equal treatment and positive action. Another challenge to mainstreaming gender equality is the all-pervasive lack of understanding of it except in the Nordic countries; this is why research, awareness raising, and training in gender-mainstreaming issues is essential. Making the case for business is also important. Universities need to understand that in order to achieve their mission of excellence in research and teaching, they need to attract the best candidates, whatever their gender. Policies that are good for women are good for promoting excellence. No well-qualified, excellent male scientist has anything to fear from fair competition with women.

Conclusion

It is possible to identify all of the categories of individuals that Woodward (2004) refers to as 'velvet triangles' of people working to promote gender equality in the work of the Women and Science Unit and in many of the countries in the Helsinki Group. The combination of an agenda of equality and social justice with the more powerful agendas of economics and labour has fostered more progress in securing gender equality in European universities than have efforts in previous decades. However, the picture remains extraordinarily bleak, and hence this progress is slow. The biggest hurdle facing women pursuing academic careers in Europe is no longer direct but indirect discrimination. As Schiebinger (1999) has observed, science is both a profession and a body of knowledge. However, it may be some time before the language (e.g., *bachelors'* and *masters' degrees* and *fellows*), the work culture, and the organization of science in the academies of Europe allow women to develop their careers and their scientific agendas on an equal footing with men.

In the first instance, there are institutional requirements for embedding a gender-mainstreaming approach. These include commitment from the top, mechanisms to achieve buy-in from middle and junior management tiers, awareness raising, training, and expert advice. Second, the gender-mainstreaming tools of statistics, indicators, impact assessments, gender budgeting, and gender balance in decision making need to be used, and a gender dimension must be built into monitoring, evaluation, and reporting processes. Third, the institution needs organizational and cultural change to ensure that it is promoting gender equality in its organization and practices.

The Women and Science Unit has achieved a considerable amount in connecting those concerned with the issue of women in European universities and mobilizing networks to exchange experience and good practice. There is a danger that the momentum may be lost as other agendas are pursued. It is critical that the current focus on the European Research Area, the European Research Council, the expansion of the Framework Programs, and the machinations of the Bologna Process embed the gender dimension.

Notes

1. The influential ETAN Report (2000) on women in science, engineering, and technology in Europe was commissioned by the Women and Science Unit of the Research Directorate-General of the EC.
2. The European Commission's Framework Programme enables it to invest in research and development through consortia of universities, and others partner from different countries in projects on integrated projects and in networks of excellence on a range of themes. Applicants from 33 countries are eligible. The Marie Curie Programme supports researchers wanting to conduct research in other countries while the ERASMUS Programme allows students to undertake degrees made up of modules from universities in different countries. The Bologna Process is designed to enable a better understanding of qualifications across Europe by harmonizing what is expected, for example, from a bachelor's and masters' level degree in participating countries.
3. The Women and Science Unit is an integral part of the Research Directorate-General and focuses on collecting statistics, developing indicators, publishing research, documenting policies and exchanging good practice on women and science in the 33 countries that take part in the Framework Programmes. It has been in existence for over ten years. See http://europa.eu.int/comm/research/science-society/women-science/women-science_en.html, retrieved October 16, 2005.

4. The European Commission's positive action measure is known as the Community Program on Gender Equality (2001–2005), the purpose of which is 'to ... co-ordinate, support and finance the implementation of horizontal transnational activities under the fields of intervention of the Community framework strategy on gender equality. The Programme is complementary to the other EU programmes and grants, which ... shall equally aim to eliminate inequalities and to promote equality between men and women'. The objectives are to '(1) promote and disseminate the values and practices underlying gender equality, (2) improve the understanding of issues related to gender equality, including direct and indirect gender discrimination and multiple discrimination against women, by evaluating the effectiveness of policies and practice through prior analysis, monitoring their implementation and assessing their effects, and (3) develop the capacity of players to promote gender equality effectively, in particular through support for the exchange of information and good practice and networking at Community level'. See http://europa.eu.int/comm./ employment_social/equ_opp/gender_equality/actions/index_ en.html, retrieved October 16, 2005.

5. The official EC definition of gender mainstreaming is as follows: ' Gender mainstreaming is the integration of the gender perspective into every stage of policy processes – design, implementation, monitoring, and evaluation – with a view to promoting equality between women and men. It means assessing how policies impact the life and position of both women and men – and taking responsibility to re-address them if necessary. This is the way to make gender equality a concrete reality in the lives of women and men creating space for everyone within the organizations as well as in communities – to contribute to the process of articulating a shared vision of sustainable human development and translating it into reality'. See http://europa.eu.int/comm./ employment_social/equ_opp/gender/gender. equality/gender_mainstreaming/ general_overview_en.html, retrieved October 16, 2005.

References

Academy of Finland (1998) *Women in academia.* Report of the Working Group appointed by the Academy of Finland. Edita: Academy of Finland.

Bagilhole, B., & Goode, J. (2001) The contradiction of the myth of individual merit, and the reality of a patriarchal support system in academic careers: A feminist investigation. *European journal of women's studies,* 8(2):161–180.

Blagojević, M., Bundele, M., Burkhardt, A., Calloni, M., Ergma, E., Glover, J., Groó, D., et al. (2004) Waste of talents: Turning private struggles into a public issue. In *Women and Science in the Enwise Countries.* Brussels: Directorate General for Research, European Commission. Retrieved August 31, 2005, from the European Commission Community Research Website, http://europa.eu.int/comm/research/science-society/pdf/enwise_report2_fulltext-120704.pdf.

Blake, M., & La Valle, I. (2000) *Who applies for research funding? Key factors shaping funding application behaviour among women and men in British higher education institutions.* London: Wellcome Trust and the Research Councils.

Chancellor of the Duchy of Lancaster (1993) *Realising our potential: A strategy for science, engineering and technology,* Cmnd. 2250. London: Her Majesty's Stationary Office.

Commission of the European Communities (1996) *Communication from the Commission: Incorporating equal opportunities for women and men into all community policies and activities (The mainstreaming communication),* COM (96) 67 final. Luxembourg: Office for Official Publications of the European Communities.

——— (1999) *Communication of the Commission Women and Science: Mobilising women to enrich European research,* COM (99) 76 final. Luxembourg: Office for Official Publications of the European Commission of 17.

Committee on Women in Science Engineering and Technology (1994) *The rising tide: Women in science, engineering and technology.* London: HMSO.

Etzkowitz, H., Kemelgor, C., & Uzzi, B. (2000) *Athena unbound: The advancement of women in science and technology.* Cambridge: Cambridge University Press.

EC (European Commission) (2001) Women and science: Making change happen. In *Proceedings of the Brussels conference* (April 3–4, 2000). Luxembourg: Office for Official Publications of the European Communities.

———— (2002) *Proceedings of the European Commission Gender and Research Conference, 2001.* Luxembourg: Office for Official Publications of the European Communities.

———— (2003) *She Figures 2003: Women and science, statistics and indicators.* Luxembourg: Office for Official Publications of the European Communities.

———— (2004) *Gender and excellence in the making: Minimising gender bias in the definition and measurement of scientific excellence.* Report of the European Commission/Joint Research Centre/European University Research Institute Workshop. Luxembourg: Office for Official Publications of the European Communities.

———— (2005a) *Women and science: Excellence and innovation—Gender equality in science.* Retrieved March 5, 2005, from the European Commission Website, http://europa. eu.int/comm/research/science-society/pdf/documents_women_sec_en.pdf.

———— (2005b) Women in industrial research: Speeding up changes in Europe. In International Conference Proceedings. Luxembourg: Office for Official Publications of the European Communities.

European Networks on Women and Science (1999) *Declaration of networks active in Europe.* Brussels: European Commission, Research Directorate-General.

Federal Ministry of Education and Research (2001) *Women in education and research.* Germany: Federal Ministry of Education and Research (BMBF), Public Relations Bureau 53170 Bonn. Retrieved August 31, 2005, from http://www.bmbf.de.

Glover, J. (2000) *Women and scientific employment.* Basingstoke: Macmillan.

Glover, J., & Bebbington, D. (2000) *Women and scientific employment: Mapping the European data.* Brussels: Women and Science Unit, Research Directorate, Commission of the European Communities.

Greenfield, S., Peters, J., Lane, N., Rees, T., & Samuels, G. (2002) *SET fair.* A report on women in science, engineering and technology from the Baroness Susan Greenfield to the secretary of state for Trade and Industry. London: Department for Trade and Industry. Retrieved August 30, 2005, from the Department for Trade and Industry Website, http://www.dti.gov.uk.

Independent Review Committee on Higher Education Pay and Conditions (1999) *The report of the Independent Review Committee on higher education pay and conditions (The Bett Report).* London: HMSO.

Laurila, P., & Young, K. (2001) *Gender in research: Gender impact assessment of the specific programmes of the Fifth Framework Programme – An overview.* Brussels: European Commission Directorate General for Research.

Ministère de la Recherche (2002) *Les femmes dans la recherché Française: Livre blanc.* Paris: Ministère de la Recherche.

Ministry of Research and Information Technology (1997) *Women and excellence in research (The Hilden 11-point plan).* Copenhagen: Statens Information.

National Committee of Inquiry into Higher Education (1997) *Higher education in the learning society (The Dearing report).* London: NCIHE.

Office of Science and Technology Department of Trade and Industry (2003) *A strategy for women in science, engineering and technology: Government response to SET Fair.* A report from Baroness Greenfield CBE to the Secretary of State for Trade and Industry. London: Department for Trade and Industry.

Osborn, M., Rees, T., Bosch, M., Ebeling, H., M., Hermann, C., Hilden, J., McLaren, A., et al. (2000) *Science policies in the European Union: Promoting excellence through mainstreaming gender equality.* A report from the ETAN Network on Women and Science. Luxembourg: Office for Official Publications of the European Communities. Retrieved August 30, 2005, from http://europa.eu.int/comm/research/science-society/documents_en.html.

Rees, T. (1998) *Mainstreaming equality in the European Union.* London: Routledge.

———— (2002) *The Helsinki group on women and science: National policies on women and science in Europe.* Luxembourg: Office for Official Publications of the European

Communities. Retrieved August 31, 2005, from http://www.cordis.lu/improving/women/policies.htm.

———— (2005) Reflections on the uneven development of gender mainstreaming in Europe. *International journal of feminist politics, 7*(4):555–574.

Rübsamen-Waigmann, H., Sohlberg, R., Rees, T., Berry, O., Bismuth, P., D'Antona, R., De Brabander, E., et al. (2003) *Women in industrial research: A wake up call for European industry.* Luxembourg: Office for Official Publications of the European Communities. Retrieved August 31, 2005, from the Women in Industry Website, http://europa.eu.int/comm/research/science-society/women/wir/pdf/wir-ulb_en.pdf.

Schiebinger, L. (1999) *Has feminism changed science?* Cambridge: Harvard University Press.

Stevens, I., & Van Lamoen, I. (2001) *Manual on gender mainstreaming at universities.* Leuven: Apeldoorn Garant. Retrieved August 31, 2005, from http://awi.vlaanderen.be/documenten/Gender_Manualongendermainstreamingatuniversities.pdf.

Valian, V. (1997) *Why so slow? The advancement of women.* Cambridge, MA: MIT Press.

Wennerås, C., & Wold, A. (1997) Nepotism and sexism in peer review. *Nature, 387*(5):341–343.

Woodward, A. E. (2004) Building velvet triangles: Gender and informal governance. In T. Christiansen & S. Piattoni (Eds.), *Informal governance in the European Union* (pp. 94–113). Cheltenham: Edward Elgar.

CHAPTER THREE

BETWEEN CHANGE AND RESISTANCE: GENDER STRUCTURES AND GENDER CULTURES IN GERMAN INSTITUTIONS OF HIGHER EDUCATION

Ursula Müller

This chapter offers information on recent developments in German higher education following the Bologna Protocol, reflects on the processes of implementation of new regulations into the universities as organizations, discusses gendered subtexts and asymmetrical gender cultures as relevant factors of change or obstinacy, and provides some empirical evidence on German institutions of higher education regarding gender equality measures.

Theoretically, the chapter draws on the debate of *gender and organization*; Joan Acker's (1991) thesis about the *gender subtext* in seemingly gender-neutral formal settings is relevant here as is, for instance, Halford, Savage, and Witz's (1997) transfer of Foucauldian thoughts to the analysis of gender, organization, and segregation. Viewed from the theoretical ground of organizational analysis and gender research, institutions of higher education are complex organizations. Their level of structure is important, but an evaluation of gender developments remains incomplete without consideration of universities' level of culture, which means analysing the discourses that accompany structural changes, commenting on them, and sometimes foregoing or even contradicting them. Drawing from neo-institutionalist theory, especially in Meyer and Scott's (1992) elaborated version, organizations are both self-steering and simultaneously sensitive to their environments. The level of discourse on gender developments in higher education itself will be contextualized by some aspects of gender discourses in Germany that may be described as *strategical de-thematization*. The chapter concludes that there are some chances for more gender equality through structural change but that a prevailing asymmetrical gender culture has to be taken critically into account because it is deeply involved in the newly established criteria for success, excellence, and market orientation. *Gender mainstreaming* as a 'pervasive' concept is confronted with Meyer and Rowan's thesis that formal regulation and routines of action are only loosely coupled in institutionalized organizations.

The Frame: The 'Bologna Process' and
Its Impact on German Higher Education

German higher education is under reconstruction. With the signing of the Bologna Protocol in 1999, 29 European states have agreed to redesign their diversified university systems into a homogenous space of European higher education, where students can move freely from one European university to another, safely guarded by regulations ensuring that their credits will be transferred to any European university of their choice. For this reason, the traditional European systems of exams, diplomas, and credits will be abolished and reformed as a system of BA, MA, and PhD. By 2005, already 45 European states, including the Russian Federation, were participating in the Bologna activities, and European conventions obliged the member states to complete these processes by 2010. The huge impact of this political process of integration and homogenization may be measured in light of the participation of the Russian Federation, which is not a member of the European Union. As one of the European Union's most important and powerful neighbours, the Russian Federation has decided to join the Bologna Protocol and to reform its graduate system according to it, even though it had just finished a first round of redesigning its graduate system according to the former standards of Western Europe[1] (Bologna Protocol, 1999).

These reform processes also aim to support competition and profiling. According to the prevailing neo-liberal thinking of the majority of the European Commission, European universities compete for students, research money, and scholars. In Germany, although the payment of professors is differentiated, the differences are not as large as are those in the United States or United Kingdom. A possibility for more differentiation among the academic staff in Germany lies in the creation of the position of lecturer. Even though the division between research universities and teaching universities or colleges has been raised as an issue only occasionally, the most visible differentiation in Germany is the one between the universities and the universities of applied sciences (*Fachhochschulen*). Whereas the regular time limit of a course of study for university students has been no fewer than five years, the regular time limit for students in the universities of applied sciences has been three years. With the new scheme, each time limit for a course of study is three years, regardless of the institution in which it is situated. After that, according to selection criteria that are not yet clear, MA studies may follow for one or two years for some students. Therefore, the former 'normal' university time limit is split into two unequal halves, and the first academic degree for all students has been reduced to the lower of the two existing norms.

The broad and foreseeable impact of these reforms is publicly debated with a considerable amount of controversy. The critics argue that this system will strengthen the high selectivity that characterizes Germany's educational system as a whole, according to PISA results.[2] They suspect that the general aim of these reforms is to legitimize tremendous cutbacks of state funds for the institutions of higher education by drastically reducing the number of students that transgress the time limit of three years, which indeed is part of significant plans to reduce state activity (see below). The predicted consequences are the decline of the general standards of higher education and the increase of still more inequality within levels of education and the social opportunities connected to them. The supporters welcome the curtailment of the time limits because, in an international comparison, German graduates are older on average when leaving the university, and many students do not graduate at all. Furthermore, the new system promises more flexibility because, in principle, it allows students to finish their MAs in disciplines different from their BAs. This development allows for more *interdisciplinarity* and *trans-sectionality* in higher education, which is thought to prepare students more adequately for the complexities of the problems that they could face in the future.[3]

For the academic teachers, a reform of the payment schemes and the trajectories of the academic staff accompany the new scheme of study. The general payment scheme for professors now provides a split between 'basic' income and 'performance' income. *Performance* is not yet defined – thus inviting power-plays on the definition in which gender aspects may play a role – but it will certainly contain the elements of number of graduates, publications (in certified fields and high-impact publications), and, of course, fund-raising for research. This reform does not concern the professors who are active today, except when they accept a call to another university; in this case, they will have to negotiate their conditions according to the new law. But it does affect each 'newcomer' to the level of tenure and will slowly turn around the relative equality among German professors with regard to payment and equipment.

Referring to career tracks, the new position of a *junior professor* has been established, which is similar to the assistant professor in the United States. The candidate may be promoted in his or her 'home' faculty, which has been the rare exception in German tradition. The new professor will be evaluated after three years, and after another three years, their temporary position may become a permanent one. Critics argue that these new elements of the academic career track create many disadvantages: the junior professors carry the same teaching load as advanced assistants (four hours per week), but unlike them they work under the high pressure of fund-raising while writing the 'second book' after their PhD and presenting themselves as valuable members of the faculty. Furthermore, they are not entitled to receive the equipment equivalent to a professor. Supporters suggest that academic career paths in Germany have been excessively time-consuming and indeterminate and, therefore, may have discouraged many promising people. They further underline that junior professors now pursue their scholarly work freely unlike former advanced assistants who were dependent on their assigned professors.

As of yet, there is no consensus that the habilitation, accused of being one decisive factor prolonging academic apprenticeship and dependency, will vanish; the general law allows both junior professors or PhDs with habilitation to obtain a tenured chair. According to some experts, this regulation will lead to the curious fact that junior professors, who figure as the model for abolishing the habilitation, will write one as well because the tacit (or even overt) evaluation cultures in academia still advantage candidates with habilitation.[4] Add gender considerations to these changes. Critics argue that the pressure to build careers increases for women just as they are building families. In fact, demographic forecasts predict continued low birth rates in Germany: 25% of the younger cohorts of women will never become mothers, among them female academics of whom up to 40% are predicted to remain childless (Wirth & Duemmler, 2004).[5]

Generally, a tendency to enforce differences and hierarchies among universities has developed over the years. German universities have not been accustomed to evaluation and ranking on a whole or with respect to their various disciplines. This process has been changing dramatically since the 1990s and has been accelerating in recent years. Rankings by research institutes, published annually or biannually, always provide well-received headlines in the weekly journals and daily newspapers, and they guide students in their decisions regarding where to study and which disciplines to pursue. The debate also continues on the methods and criteria of evaluation and the neutrality of the referees. Nevertheless, the rankings seem to have established themselves; they have managed to develop from a means of external observation to a means of self-observation, giving important hints for the self-steering of the universities (Wirth & Duemmler, 2004).

Implementation and Resistance

The implementation of the new federal regulations varies among the Laender governments. Like culture and police, education is decentralized in German – a historical consequence of the conformity in Nazi totalitarianism that shall never happen again (Müller, 1999b). Generally, conservative Laender (governed by Christian democratic majority) will accelerate the process of turning universities into marketplaces and will decide on disciplines according to their *commodifiability*. They will also be the first to introduce fees for the courses. Until now, university education has been tuition-free in Germany. Experience also shows that the Laender tend to cut back or even eliminate disciplines, such as sociology, and will retreat from active gender equality policies. Social democratic majorities, on the other hand, do not differ in many respects from the conservatives; in fact, strong support for the introduction of neo-liberal thinking comes from this party, as the reorientation of German social and labour market politics show, but they tend to keep university education tuition-free in order to facilitate equal opportunities for students from all social classes and to maintain sociology and active gender politics. Nevertheless, the social democrats will require the universities to decide for themselves which disciplines they will promote in the future and which shall be abandoned. To obtain this goal, a new routine of negotiating *goal contracts* for a certain period, three years for instance, and developing *university profiles* has been introduced.[6] Until now, most of the German universities have been 'full' universities, which means that a comprehensive spectrum of disciplines may be studied, regardless of the place of study, for example, Berlin, Bielefeld, or Munich.[7] This system will be changed radically; only a few universities will continue to offer the full range of academic disciplines, and the majority will become more restricted and specialized. Universities that have taken up these processes of defining their profiles and negotiating their goals have come to realize, however, that the ministry administration, which is backed by ratings, rankings, and evaluation boards, on whose expertise universities may draw or not, has already developed in advance a profile scheme of its own that will be advanced in the form of financial cutbacks. One might call this practice *negotiating from unequal backgrounds*, remembering the feminist critique on contract theory.

The *entrepreneuralization* of universities has many consequences for gender relations in these organizations and for the educational system as a whole. Yet, to discuss these consequences is not simple because they are diverse and not free of ambivalence.

The reforms in question are contextualized in a general discourse on the withdrawal of the state to its core tasks. Without doubt, the *core tasks* are a debatable field. Referring to gender questions, however, it has hitherto been important that equal opportunities officers (EOOs), women's groups from inside the universities, and academic associations of women have had the opportunity to apply to the Ministry of Science for reconsideration of the university's decisions. This possibility is now abolished; any debate on distribution of resources or on filling positions is transferred to the universities and modified – again – into an internal issue of the organization.

The impact of reassigning the power of decision making to the universities is not easy to forecast; it will be intricate. Optimistically, it could be argued that general laws on gender equality have been elaborated over the years and have gained structural power; therefore, gender mainstreaming as a guideline will more or less 'automatically' force the university organizations to evaluate any decision with consideration for gender perspectives. Gender is said to have become a routine criterion in budgeting, promoting, evaluating, and the like. In fact, nobody would deny that gender has progressed in these realms; the central ministry of science and education, for instance, has taken up a *gender concept* as a distribution criterion for any research funds they promote, and the government of Northrhine Westphalia has demanded a *gender profile* from any university in the recent goal negotiations. On the other hand, experience shows – and organization theory agrees – that any formal regulation can be counteracted informally.

Inherent in these processes are questions of gender play that are rarely addressed in public debates, in expert discourses, or in administrative acts that push those processes forward, regulate them, and evaluate them. Gender is routinely addressed in the beginning stages because the general guideline of gender mainstreaming in the European Union calls for it to be observed in every policy and measure that is adopted. In most cases, gender mainstreaming needs the organized attention of the federal and regional EOOs who certify that gender questions have been answered adequately. Nevertheless, the permanent conference of the ministers of education released a resolution in 2004 that 'the gender mainstreaming concept of the Amsterdam treaty and the respective national regulation will be recognized and implemented in the process of accreditation (of the new BA/MA curricula, UM)' (KMK, 2004). Furthermore, universities have partially introduced gender criteria into their audit systems, which could be used as a point of reference to introduce a gender audit as an element of quality assurance.

Before moving on to the discussion of the possible impact of these university changes on gender relations, we look at the more recent statistical developments.

Gender Developments in Academe: Some Statistical Evidence

German institutions of higher education do not appear to face any gender-related problems in recruiting students: the annual rate of new entries of young women into the universities has been 50% or above for decades (Müller, 1999b, 2000). This rate may indeed be taken as a proof for the thesis of *de-institutionalization of gender* in the sense that no formal barrier prohibits women from entering the system of higher education just as no informal barriers bar women because such barriers are normatively prohibited.

The picture changes significantly when switching from a quantitative to a qualitative perspective. German institutions indeed face a gender problem in recruiting women because there is a clear segregation between disciplines chosen by women and disciplines chosen by men. The 'female' disciplines are the languages mostly, but, since the 1990s, the field of medicine has also comprised more than 60% female beginners. Economics, social sciences, and law show gender parity, but the technical disciplines and the sciences, except 'female' biology, are 'male' in their majorities. Although the gender percentages within the sciences differ and female percentages continue to grow, it is necessary to point out that German institutions of higher education have yet to solve the problem of how to attract young women to the sciences and to technical disciplines. This problem and its resolution differentiate German universities from universities in other countries (Mischau et al., 2004).

From the first grade to the PhD and afterwards the habilitation, German universities lose many capable women who could contribute excellently to the further development of all disciplines. In the research literature, we have found a variety of reasons that are presumably responsible for this loss: the difficulties of combining career with family, the devaluation of scholarly work by powerful actors and gatekeepers (Krais, 2000), the number of men in powerful positions, and a general lack of acknowledgement of women's performance in academia (Müller & Stein-Hilbers, 1996; Krais, 2000; Majcher, Schenk, & Zimmer, 2003). The 'leaky pipeline' in German academia has been associated with the *old* system that provided a basic degree after five years of study, which entitled one to progress to a PhD. It is imaginable that the reform under process, which schedules *two* stages, BA and MA, before earning the right to try a PhD, may render the pipeline even 'leakier' with regard to young female talents; however, it is not unforeseeable that the contrary may happen as well.

There are indeed some positive changes. Figure 3.1 shows that the number of female beginners in academia has reached and even exceeded the 50% level. Although there is a slight decrease in participation of women graduates to 46.9%, which should be analysed more, this figure nevertheless represents a clear amelioration compared to 1990 levels.

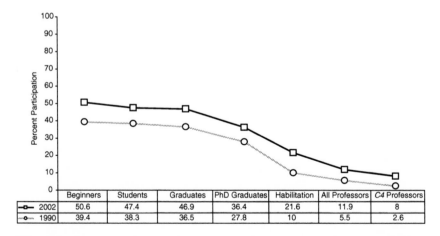

	Beginners	Students	Graduates	PhD Graduates	Habilitation	All Professors	C4 Professors
2002	50.6	47.4	46.9	36.4	21.6	11.9	8
1990	39.4	38.3	36.5	27.8	10	5.5	2.6

Figure 3.1 Representation of Women among Students and Academic Staff in German Universities

Source: Statistisches Bundesamt, Hochschulstatistik (Federal Bureau of Statistics, Statistics Higher Education), calculation by J. Loewen.

The numbers become more dramatically differentiated with the higher grades, however. Though better than 1990's figures, that only one-third of German's PhDs are earned by women in 2002 indicates a real problem, and so does the figure that just over one-fifth of all habilitations are completed by women even though this rate has doubled since 1990. Similarly, the rate of female professors shows both development and detainment.

The figure for 1990 shows a percentage of 5.5% for female professors. That percentage remained stable from the 1970s to the 1990s even though a steady increase in female students and graduates since the end of the 1960s should have given enough reason to increase the numbers of female professors in the 1980s (Müller, 2004, 1995). Therefore, it can be said that *without* gender equality policies in German higher education, figures would not have doubled in the span of a decade; these policies have been brought forward by a very active process of networking and organizing by women in higher education, which has led to a nationwide net of EOO grassroots organizations at the universities and many programmes to support women in higher education in various ways (for an overview, see Kirsch-Auwaerter, 2002). On the other hand, the number of habilitations among females is still twice as high as the number of female professors; therefore, the pipeline between first graduation and nomination for a chair remains leaky, steadily losing highly qualified women. This situation indicates that the female potential is not at all fully utilized and points to factors that may lie beyond political regulations. Therefore, a closer look into the cultural context of promoting or not promoting women follows.

Overall, scholars with special qualifications in gender issues have been installed on chairs with no explicit gender designation. Furthermore, such disciplines as the sciences, which are generally very reluctant to consider gender questions, are beginning to discover the relevance of gender for their fields. This recognition is evidenced by installation of a chair for gender questions in science and technology at Munich Technical University, one of the highest-ranking German universities, and comparable processes in other universities (Ihsen, 2005).

Meritocratic Principles and 'Gendered Subtexts'

Generally, feminist critique has always had good reasons to point out that the meritocratic principles that promise rewards to excellent performers have primarily favoured men. As Husu (2001) and many others (e.g., Wennerås & Wold, 1997; Kirsch-Auwaerter, 1996) have shown, gender-related hidden criteria for promotion and career have greatly influenced women's trajectories inside academia. This violation of the proclaimed meritocratic rules and the performance principle would never have been justified if it had not been based on a traditional gender ideology that has denied women the opportunity to do scholarly work in the full range of disciplines.[8] This is not the place to revisit the history and sociology of the development of science and its feminist reconstruction, but from this historical background, it is intriguing to note that the complete implementation of the performance principle within equal and just conditions is an important demand promoted by feminism in academia.

But even if criteria are elaborated and seem perfectly clear, the power to determine a valid *interpretation* still has to be considered as long as there are signs of a gendered subtext in an organization. Drawing from her work on Finland, Husu (2001) gives further insight into the actual contradictions within the meritocratic criteria and how design decisions emerge. In one of her case studies, we find a catalogue of criteria to measure merits in a particular competition for chair (p. 152). The respective faculty council agreed on a list of 'relatively unequivocal criteria' for candidate selection, such as publishing activity, teaching and supervising merits, merits in graduate education, success in one's own postgraduate studies. A second list of the faculty council listed 'evaluative criteria, including aspects of style and preference' and addressed 'feasibility and usefulness of the candidate in the activities of the department', 'visibility of the candidate in the disciplinary and broader field research and discussion', and 'the impact/significance of the research orientation of the candidate' (p. 153). Judging by the criteria used in this case study and drawing on empirical evidence from many others, it may prove very difficult for a more highly qualified woman to finally obtain the chair over a lower qualified male candidate. An intervention of the EOO is needed to effect the meritocratic principle when candidates compete for chairs.

Yet, the criteria themselves, although seemingly reasonable and adequate, will most likely function properly only in a situation where no asymmetrical gender culture is prevailing. As a criterion, *visibility*, for instance, will automatically exclude feminist scholars from a competition where a selection committee denies that feminist critique makes a relevant contribution to the department. Visibility may also exclude scholars who have been doing research in women's and gender studies from competing for posts where gender is not the main issue. In my personal experience, this exclusion occurred often in my own department of sociology in the past. 'Being identified with women's or gender studies may be hazardous to your career prospects' could be written on some of those procedures. Of course, this is not the whole truth as there indeed has been a remarkable increase in numbers of female professors in Germany (see figure 3.1). But in their study on grant applications in sociology, Allmendinger and Hinz (2002) give reasons for wondering about who has fallen off the career tracks and why.

In processes of distributing and reallocating resources, of opening and closing spaces for recognition and impact, peer review has established itself as *the* scholarly procedure to produce legitimate decisions. Although there has been some criticism that peer review may lead to an unwanted conformity instead of productive diversity, the peer-review procedure itself remains unquestioned. However, since the study by Wennerås and Wold (1997), it has become widely known that gender is one of the possible criteria that may subvert peer review. According to Allmendinger and Hinz (2002), peer review of articles for mainstream journals of sociology and applications, instead of shortlists for chairs in sociology, can still be used to undermine gender concerns. For example, the least successful applications to the German Research Foundation DFG (Deutche Forschungsgemeinschaft) turned out to be those in women's and gender studies, especially when female scholars had applied. Generally, the rates of success for applications were 60.4% for male applicants and 48.7% for females. An advantage for male authors became visible as well in acceptance rates for the two most highly respected German journals in sociology (ZfS and KZSS): 32.2% of submissions by male authors were accepted compared to 26.9% of the submissions by female authors. The acceptance rate of papers by female professors was lower than that of contributions by male professors, and contributions by female and male assistants fared the worst. Fortunately, the number of applications for chairs and the final placement on a shortlist did not differ for men and women; the success quota was 11% for both. However, a difference existed between being shortlisted and finally receiving/accepting the call: only 31% of shortlisted women finally received/accepted the call compared to 36% of the shortlisted men.[9]

Decisions made by using criteria lists as well as peer-review lists are elements of the process of *legitimation by procedure*, Niklas Luhmann's (1983) phrase for the ways organizations obtain legitimation, acceptance, and the willingness on the part of their members to comply with their decisions. The basic concept of consensus building, Luhmann says, is not to agree on the issues but to agree *beforehand* on the procedures as to how decisions shall be constructed. By agreeing on the *prerequisites* of a decision, any participant has also accepted the prospective, and yet unknown, *outcomes* of the decision. One may not like the result, but he or she will be unable to deny that it has been decided by an agreed-upon procedure. Any critique of the decision has to be transformed into a procedural question; if not, the argument cannot pretend to be serious. Of course, critique is always possible from 'outside' the procedure, for instance, to point to equal opportunities regulations or to openly question whether important actors inside the procedural routines have acted out of prejudice, but members of the organization who take this position run the risk of becoming marginalized by confronting the organization with the ways it actually functions.[10]

Yet, organizational theory and the ongoing process of creating gender-sensitive constituencies in higher education have made clear that the question of legitimation is double-sided: it is not only the representatives of the marginalized or excluded groups who may face the problem of legitimation when criticizing the outcomes of decisions; it is also the excluding organization itself that will face such a problem over time. This is especially the case if there are *relevant environments* (e.g., a state legislation, a women's movement, etc.) that are connected to constituencies inside the organization. Therefore, it has to be remembered that gendered prejudices and marginalization do not reveal the whole picture in Germany.

As I have tried to argue, because meritocracy has not been liberated from its gender blindness, hopes for gender justice have been only partially realized. According to Kirsch-Auwaerter (1996), the anti-discrimination discourse has attacked the self-constructed image of the universities by revealing the criteria according to which they factually function. Reactions against the anti-discrimination discourse, in this view, are only superficially problematic when the process of organizational development as a whole is taken into account. Even the most conservative institution of higher education has had to face the anti-discrimination discourse as a changed frame condition. For Germany in the 1990s, refusal and repudiation could therefore be interpreted as a paradoxical form of acceptance: it expresses the acknowledgement that active anti-discrimination has become an issue that can no longer be de-thematized by those institutions (Müller, 1999a). Yet, from this general background, very different 'coping strategies' can be observed.

Change and Obstinacy: Some Empirical Evidence

In my evaluation study of all 27 institutions of higher education in Northrhine-Westphalia (Holzbecher et al., 1998), the implementation and impact of the first general guideline on promoting women, released in 1993, was evaluated after five years. The results showed that those institutions could be roughly divided into three types.

One quarter of the institutions in question represented type one. They had developed gender equality policies that had been implemented on the structural and cultural level. They had formally integrated gender equality aspects into their fundamental order and into the regulations of recruiting and had presented gender equality programmes with some explicitly defined goals. These institutions also employed EOOs who were totally or partially exempted from their 'normal' duties in the institution with substitutes available who would assume EOO duties in case of task overload; in addition, the EOOs were equipped with basic resources, such as secretary, telephone communications, office equipment, email, and Internet access. The presence of an EOO was generally regarded as relevant for the self-evaluation and further development of the institution. Furthermore, this type of institution regarded gender-related acts of discrimination as events that may well happen inside their realm, yet they indicated the necessity for institutional action. The university heads would regularly commission reports on the quantitative development of gender relations in every position, level, and department and would transfer the results to be discussed to an internal constituency, such as the academic senate or the rectorate. Consequently, they had no difficulty providing these differentiated statistics to outsiders on the gender developments in each positional level and department in any discipline. Moreover, institutions of this type did not articulate significant difficulties in finding excellent female candidates for high positions in their administrations because they paid gender-sensitive attention to the development of both the scholarly qualifications and qualifications of the administrative personnel. Therefore, it can be said that they had already provided ground for continuous self-observation.

With regard to the implementation of gender equality policies into their organizational routines, this type of institution of higher education could be considered well developed, especially when compared to another group of institutions approximately the same size, which distinguished itself by structurally and culturally preventing the implementation of efficient gender equality measures. At the time of the study, these institutions had implemented few if any elements of gender equality policies into their fundamental orders or recruitment regulations, and if they had, they had implemented them past the compulsory time limits of the state regulations. No programme of measures to increase gender equality had been released, and the EOOs were not exempted from their 'normal' duties except to a minimal degree. The EOOs did not have any substitutes nor were they equipped with email or telephone-answering machines; therefore, they were difficult to contact. A tremendous part of their time was spent securing adequate working conditions for their jobs. The position of EOO as a permanent element of the organization was non-desirable in the eyes of this group's university heads because in every case they contended that the decisions of individual persons involved would make the difference rather than the EOO. They reasoned further that an inappropriate person serving as EOO would destroy rather than facilitate chances for promoting women and that a rector or chancellor who was enlightened on women's issues would more effectively promote gender equality than would any bureaucratic guideline. The university heads in this type of institution agreed that equality policies were lacking in their universities because gender discrimination did not play any role in recruiting, that is, the only criterion for decision was 'quality'. In this type of institution, it was difficult to obtain gender-differentiated statistics; for example, the allegations that quite a few women had been recently appointed often turned out to refer to one or two cases in one year. These institutions still lacked any ground for continuous self-observation that would enable them to plan their development in a self-steering way, at least with respect to gender questions.

The third type, which comprised about half of the cases, was characterized by partial openings to gender equality measures by maintaining principal reservations simultaneously. A contradictory picture emerged of objectively observable structural strategies referring to gender questions and cultural patterns of responses to them in organizational discourse. State regulations promoting women in academia were principally agreed to, and most had been implemented into the fundamental order, but powerful actors often forestalled their efficiency. A programme of measures to promote women was often lacking, and internal discourses on the subject were not yet widely developed. But there were female constituencies inside those institutions that wanted to accelerate the progress of these discourses. In this type of institution, the attitudes of university heads towards gender equality measures differed. Some rejected measures as too bureaucratic, without knowing much about them in detail, while others called for more 'consistency' in the ministry's equality politics (implying that the ministry should transfer more financial resources for gender equality measures because the universities could not proceed without them). The accommodation of EOOs in most of the cases differed with respect to their equipment, their participation in decisions, and their right to receive full information in a reasonable timeframe. In many cases, the EOOs were perceived in a personalized way rather than as a new element of the organizational structure. Nevertheless, contrary to the 'official' announcements, many of these institutions featured innovative elements of gender equality policies, such as providing childcare and hiring female heads in administration areas formerly considered 'male', for instance, in the supply department with its huge budget. Some institutions even made surprising decisions in selection processes. After an EOO had intervened, some institutions revised the criteria for adequate candidate qualifications for chair, resulting in the invitation to a broader range of female scholars to participate in the competition and shortlisting them afterwards with high rankings. University heads in this type of institution tended to perceive discrimination against women as a historical relic, which would dispose of itself in due time. Most of them verbally engaged themselves in purposive promotion measures of encouragement to young female talents, and some of them took practical initiatives in this direction. The methods of self-observation in these institutions varied with respect to their grade of development. The picture emerged that those institutions that elaborated professional methods of evaluation and planning more easily integrated gender equality guidelines and measures into their procedures and routines of decision making.

These findings support the view that gender equality guidelines serve as an important innovation to the further organizational development of institutions of higher education, even if these institutions themselves are only reluctantly becoming aware of it. In this field, a variety of critical issues are intertwined, as seen from the perspective of organizational theory. First, the unwillingness of all organizations to change has to be taken into account, which may result in strategies that answer to innovative strategies from 'outside' that are not actively oriented to gender policy formation. Second, gender conservatism is inherent not only in academia but also in the society as its 'environment', which draws support from the quantitative male dominance inside academia and the questioning of gender equality policies as such; this is a hint for the prevalence of an asymmetrical gender culture in which anti-discrimination measures are reinterpreted as an unjustifiable advantaging of the objectively disadvantaged. And third, subtle cultural asymmetries between the genders become apparent each time formal barriers are removed.

Nevertheless, the findings also show the presence and the impact of *cultural agents* inside the institutions of higher education, some of which have already learned to *thematize* practices of structural or discursive exclusion and marginalization and to make transparent the hitherto denied problems of the status quo of gender relations (Eckart, 1995). Additionally, at the structural level, some Laender parental leaves, additional qualifications, research abroad, and other reasons are not counted, so they do not account for people who are outside the time limits of 'normal' career tracks. In former times, young women who already had families upon entering the university or became mothers afterwards and took parental leaves had been automatically sorted out of further career tracks. To inhibit these losses by changing law is a big success; however, that 40% of the younger female academic cohorts will not become mothers shows that the culture of academe is still hostile towards motherhood (Krais, 2000).

Recent Developments: Gender Mainstreaming as a Pervasive Concept

In a study of some Northrhine Westphalian universities, Metz-Goeckel and Kamphans (2002b) analysed the discourses of equality policies. These policies themselves have changed significantly compared to the first regulations, whose impact and discursive treatment has been discussed above. They too see universities as complex organizations, which are not homogenous and closed but divided into many subunits with a relative autonomy; these subunits are bound together by formal regulations and by spontaneous communication (Metz-Goeckel & Kamphans, 2002).[11]

Referring to processes of gender sensitization and active construction of gender justice, Metz-Goeckel and Kamphans (2002) differentiate between three phases that partially overlap but are characterized by different features of gender awareness:

- Phase 1 (the early1980s) is a period of providing a frame of law that opens up a space for action in the field of gender justice.
- Phase 2 (from the mid 1980s to the mid 1990s) is a period of measures for affirmative action that attempts to promote women with special programmes.
- Phase 3 is the present period of gender mainstreaming (from end of the 1990s until the present), which can be named as a period of *cultural counter-steering*.

Gender mainstreaming appears as a policy of cultural counter-steering because the process of equally integrating women into academia can no longer be regarded as self-supporting but is pursued actively. The concept of gender mainstreaming does not address the exclusion of women as a 'repair task' but as an organizational task that will optimize the recruitment of personnel in order to activate potentials. It demands a change in perspective because the powerful actors in the university question what they *themselves* do to either exclude or welcome women into the university. This is a relevant item because, in former times, they generally presented themselves as persons with very little influence when asked about gender gaps in promotion and career inside the organization when they themselves were steering the decisions (Holzbecher et al., 1998).

Agreeing with Etzkowitz et al. (1994), Metz-Goeckel and Kamphans suppose that in order to achieve a change in the culture of steering, there has to evolve a critical mass of women in academia, close to 30% (an important figure in Kanter's 1977 work), which may be generated by redistributing resources and symbolic power. Second, the cultural resistance of the university against female intellectuality must be overcome; this cultural resistance does not present itself as a conscious and purposeful prohibition of women but as a tacit strangeness moulded by tradition and customs.

Partially, a cultural turn has already been recognized. As Metz-Goeckel and Kamphans say from their study of rectors and chancellors, women's right to participate in high positions has become widely accepted. Women are regarded as a new resource of scholarly development (Baltes, 1997).[12] The reception of the notion of gender mainstreaming among chancellors and rectors is not enthusiastic, but it seems more discursively acceptable to them than the language of 'promoting women' or 'gender equality programme' or 'anti-discrimination' has been.

Whereas Metz-Goeckel and Kamphans found that chancellors and rectors agreed on gender mainstreaming as a routine-changing initiative that should make sense, some of them overtly admitted that, in the 1990s, 'double talk' was needed to routinely include gender equality programmes on the agenda. While 'on stage', gender equality had been a normal important goal of interior and exterior constituencies; 'off-stage', which means inside the rectorate or in confidential deliberations with the department heads on shortlists for chairs, gender equality had been treated as negligible. Later, some chancellors and rectors perceived a rapprochement of *official text* and *subtext*: they acknowledged showing more respect for the EOOs or for gender equality regulations the more they were realized. Along with this recognition, however, came a definite *historization* of the first pioneering EOOs as really difficult people to deal with, who with their aggressive behaviour were said to have caused more damage than good; in contrast, today's EOOs were evaluated as 'reasonable' and 'competent'. The change in attitude towards gender equality seems to have emerged from the university heads. The first generation of EOOs, whose hard fights had forced the university organization to open itself to gender questions, are discursively expropriated and depicted as agents of the former problem, not as the pioneers of solution. They are institutionally forgotten (Douglas, 1986), which shows that an asymmetrical gender culture is still working, even though it has become riddled.

Gender Discourses as Cultural Frames: Asymmetries and Reinterpretations

With these examples, I have tried to show that structure and culture are related in complex and sometimes even contradictory ways when organizations have to change, especially with respect to gender. A discourse of gender equality generally prevails, framed by the newly developing discourse of competitiveness. Equal chances for both genders, equal abilities, equal performances, as well as equal prospects and aspirations for life are elements of this discourse of equality. Principally, this discourse of equality is de-legitimizing any type of discrimination. Feminism is said to have become a historical phase and therefore obsolete; gender inequality is said to have more or less lost its power to segregate and has been refigured as mere gender differences. But underneath this discourse, a subtext of inequality is still continuing, a discourse of devaluation, diminishing and belittling women's performances, giving them very little encouragement, little radiant recognition, and few promotions. An empirical hint of this phenomenon is provided by a study on female PhD candidates at the

University of Bielefeld (Holzbecher, Kuellchen, & Loether, 2002). On the whole, women showed worse self-perceptions and more insecurity about their performances than did male PhD candidates. To interpret this, at least two possibilities are discursively legitimate: 'Blame it on the women' and send them to counselling in order to develop their self-consciousness or use institutional self-reflection to reveal how these results may be linked to the dominant gender culture in the department, that is, to show the 'colour' of gender discourses. It seems that equality discourse, theoretically underpinned by the thesis that gender differences have become de-institutionalized, has lost its legitimation. Despite the idea that still-perceivable gender-linked inequalities will disappear over time, it is not easier to assume that asymmetrically gendered cultures in academe as a severe source of discrimination and exclusion will also vanish. According to some public opinion makers, gender is losing its structural and structuring power. On the other hand, others subscribe to the thesis that academia is still inherently deeply gendered.

One hint for this thesis lies in an empirical project on organizational learning about overt and hidden asymmetrical gender culture at the University of Bielefeld (Müller, Holzbecher, & Meschkutat, 1999). After analysing and using some interventions to initiate organizational learning, five departments with varying gender relations (physics, law, literature and languages, educational science, and biology) and the university administration as a whole were confronted with controversial elements of gender discourse. It turned out that on many crucial issues, for instance, sexual harassment or stalking, there was a prevailing gender consensus whereas such a consensus did not prevail in other controversial issues.

Gender-Neutral Language. The use of gender-neutral (or gender-inclusive) language is now compulsory for all official university documents, but in practice, many university teachers do not respect this regulation in their personal documents. The female university members in the study were very sensitive to this fact, but they wondered if they should thematize these offences at any time because they feared they could marginalize themselves in many contexts.

Indirect Discouragement of Female Students. This issue immediately made sense to females but only rarely to males. The latter could not imagine what indirect hints of exclusion could be perceptible to women but not to themselves.

Women's Colleges. Since research in the 1980s found that female German informational scientists and chemists graduated much more often from girls' schools (which are a rarity today in Germany), and owing to public debates on Hillary Clinton and other graduates from women's colleges in the United States in the 1990s, women's colleges have become an issue of public and scholarly interest. To our amazement, every respondent knew about this discourse and recapitulated the theme that women's schools are good for women: they learn better in the women-only environment, and they develop interests in a broader range of disciplines. The female respondents consistently approved of women's colleges as a good space for development of women but were sceptical about the acceptance of those graduates' certificates in male-dominated working life. The male respondents, although aware of the advantages for women's development, rejected the vast majority of mono-educational institutions because they sheltered students from the 'real', or 'serious', world, that is, the one in which they themselves lived; furthermore, men felt that universities would become too boring without female students.

Prevention. The question whether universities could do more to reduce the dropout rate of females climbing up the academic ladder was answered positively by female respondents, who named many measures that universities could adopt. The majority of male respondents saw neither the necessity nor possibility of such strategies. They relied on competitiveness ('Excellent women will be successful; see example xyz') and the passage of time to let self-steering processes heal discrimination; they blamed the rest on the women's own traditional behaviour: choosing traditional partners and interrupting their own careers to follow their partners' paths or to care for children.

These results show that as gender transitions (in each gender group are some who do not agree with their respective majorities) and gender boundaries become visible, females still experience the university as much more asymmetrically gendered than do males. For example, 'women-only' spaces are welcomed by females but are still distrusted and devalued by males.

Karin Zimmermann (2000) also shows this impact of gender discourse in her analysis of the usurpation of East German departments of sociology by West German sociology. She shows that, during the process of transforming East German universities, gender justice had never been constructed as a general question of the new structures but as a particularity. To act responsibly for the 'common good', for instance, to establish new chairs quickly, to install newly selected professors, and so on did not require gender equality criteria or chairs in women and gender studies, for example – those circumstances were not 'common' but 'particular'. Any attempt to address gender questions had to build its arguments in answer to the rhetorical barrier of pursuing particular interests instead of common ones. Together with an almost entirely male representation on all boards making decisions, 'bringing gender questions back in' has been a slow and laborious process. Because the discourse is taking place in a discursively active asymmetrical gender culture, the discourse must acknowledge the threat of gender equality policies and gender studies to excellence. Consequently, the successes of gender equality policies are belittled and discredited; some discourses confirm that those successes have come about *despite* gender equality measures and not *because* of them.

Conclusion

Today, Germany's institutions of higher education have developed with respect to their structural gender policies. They have developed some routines in self-observation and have established influential tools for observation from the 'outside' with regard to gender relations inside academia (BMBF, 2001; BuKoF, 2002; BLK, 2004; CEWS[13]). On the cultural level, there are also some changes towards more openness and recognition of gender questions, representation of females in the faculties, and gender studies; on the other hand, strong anti-feminist discourses that take the form of negative historization and maginalization are still active in academic constituencies as well as in public. More market orientation and competitiveness, together with a politics of clearer differentiations and distinctions among the scholarly personnel and students in academia, may have effects in two directions: they may promote women because of the merits of their performance, but they may also disadvantage them because the interpretation of selection criteria has a gendered subtext.

Gender mainstreaming as a new form of gender equality politics is a pervasive concept: every layer of institutional structures, routines, and decisions has to be evaluated according to their impact on gender relations in the institution. This seems to be an enormous step forward compared to the measures in the past that were oriented more towards persons and situations and less towards structures and routines. But organizational theory questions whether complex organizations can be expected to change pervasively at all.

Meyer and Rowan's (1992) thesis on organizations and change is that, of course, organizations react to changes in their environments by incorporating elements that are legitimated externally, thus demonstrating that they are acting on collectively valued purposes in a proper and adequate manner (1992, p. 30). The incorporation of such institutionalized elements as gender equality regulations provides an account of the organizations' activities that protects them from having their conduct questioned. By incorporating socially legitimated rationalized elements into their formal structures, organizations maximize their legitimacy and increase their resources for survival in their exchange relations with their environments (e.g., ministries who require universities implement and monitor gender equality policies). But organizations also have to take care of their internal and boundary-spanning relations. Categorical rules may conflict with other logics, and putting them through by control and sanctions may lead to conflicts and loss of legitimacy as well. Therefore, as Meyer and Rowan (1992) suggest, inside organizations, a process of *decoupling* elements of structure and activities has begun. With this strategy, many problems can be redefined in advantageous ways. Internal adversity against gender equality policies, for instance, can be maintained, and realms of traditionalism may exist further, as the internal constituencies are segregated from one another and oriented towards diverse segments of structural elements.

This view shows that organizations may answer to pervasive strategies with strategies of building up internal flexibilities by decoupling and therefore may cushion themselves against pressure from the outside. This again raises interesting questions concerning the relationship between structure and culture. To analyse the change of structure, for instance, changing legislation in order to change gender inequality or establishing more competition among higher education institutions, is very important, but changing practices and cultures is a process that may develop independently. How those processes forgo or follow behind one another may facilitate, hinder, or even ignore one another, and the consequences lie in a presently unresearched field of organizational analysis, higher education, and gender relations.

Notes

1. Furthermore, it has to be noted that the majority of European states did not have a system of BA/MA/PhD but used Diploma, Magister Artium, and various types of state exams for certain disciplines instead. In place of a PhD that enables to go further with an academic career, both a dissertation and subsequent habilitation had to be written in the German-speaking countries. Of course, some countries, such as the United Kingdom and the Netherlands traditionally have had a system that resembles the U.S.-American system, but many other countries have not.
2. PISA = Programme for International Student Assessment is an OECD-driven comparative international panel study that shows that using characteristics of class and ethnicity to select students for higher education has a particularly great impact in the German education system.

3. On the level of implementation, however, restrictive admission criteria on the MA level may in fact inhibit the chances for developing more interdisciplinarity; here, the fear of losing disciplinary excellence, as well as losing 'space' for the respective specialties inside a discipline, seems to work against it.

4. There are other critical arguments as well that cannot be discussed more fully here; one argument stresses that academic freedom in teaching and research is in danger when finances and academic fields are increasingly oriented towards something called 'the market' (Blomert, 2005; Nida-Ruemelin, 2005).

5. This is not a new phenomenon but has been recognized as consternating news for two years by both the Ministry of Family, Seniors, Women, and Youth and the association of employers in German industry (BMFSFJ/BDI/IW, 2005).

6. This is a general trait of administrative reform in Germany. In the author's project on gender constructions in German police, for instance, it turns out that, in the course of introducing new management strategies, all police stations in Northrhine-Westphalia shall now define their 'goals' for the next season, such as increasing the rate of robberies solved to 70%, preventing traffic accidents involving children, or increasing the number of parking tickets. Citizens become 'customers' along with the state agencies co-operating with the police.

7. Of course, there are also differences. Not every university disposes of a department of medicine, and some universities specialize in fields that others do not. Dortmund University, for instance, developed from a former technical university and therefore has disposed of some engineering departments and a department of statistics, which is an exception in Germany. The disciplines in each university may be represented in very different sizes; 'big' sociological departments are, for instance, in Bielefeld and Frankfurt with more than 20 chairs, whereas all the other sociological departments in Germany are distinctively smaller. But the fact remains that, in the last 50 years, sciences, literature, arts, humanities could all be found in almost any German university.

8. In West Germany, these misogynous attitudes in academia were still prevalent among the majority of German professors, as Anger (1960) found out. Even the very few female professors that existed at that time agreed that *generally* women were not able to do scholarly research.

9. This may be interpreted in two ways: tradition and change. In the 'tradition' line, it may seem that women become short-listed but de-valued afterwards by peer review from outside. In the 'change' line, it may seem that women often are short-listed on quite a variety of lists at several universities and finally decide on the best offer.

10. This happened to many equal opportunities officers in German higher education in the late 1980s and early 1990s (see Holzbecher, Mueller, & Schmalzhaf-Larsen, 1998).

11. As Pellert also has pointed out, universities are not only characterized by their formal structures but also by their respective disciplinary cultures and generally by an academic culture based on expertise and excellence (Pellert 1999; Müller 1999a).

12. Also on the structural level, developments cannot be denied. The increase in the percentage of female professors is not large and differs considerably among the disciplines but is continuous, although, from an international perspective, the reluctance of German universities and big research institutions against women at the top continues to persist.

13. The CEWS, Centre of Excellence for Women in Science, was established in 2000 by the BMBF (Ministry for Education and Research) to report regularly on the developments of gender relations in science and research. It has established a ranking of its own that compares the gender policies in institutions of higher educations and their respective outcomes (www.cews.org).

References

Acker, J. (1991) Hierarchies, jobs, bodies. In J. Lorber & S. Farrell (Eds.), *The social construction of gender* (pp. 162–179). Newbury Park: Sage.

Allmendinger, J., & Hinz, T. (2002) Die Verteilung wissenschaftlicher Gueter. Publikationen, Projekte und Professuren zwischen Bewerbung und Bewilligung. *Zeitschrift fuer Frauenforschung und Geschlechterstudien.* Bielefeld, *20*(3).

Anger, H. (1960) *Probleme der deutschen Universitaeten. Bericht ueber eine Umfrage unter Professoren und Dozenten.* Tuebingen: Mohr.

Baltes, P. (1997) Foerderung von Frauen in der Wissenschaft. In S. Lang & B. Sauer (Eds.), *Wissenschaft als Arbeit – Arbeit als Wissenschaftlerin.* Frankfurt/Main: Campus.

Blomert, R. (2005) Effizienz ist das Ende der Universitaet. Die Hochschulen sind gefaehrdet: mit der Anpassung an wirtschaftspolitische Ziele verlieren sie ihr groesstes Potential. *die tageszeitungs* July 2.

BLK (Bund-Laender-Kommission fuer Bildungsplanung und Forschungsfoerderung) (2004) (Ed.), *Frauen in Fuehrungspositionen,* 7. Fortschreibung des Datenmaterials, Bonn.

BMBF (Bundesministerium fuer Bildung und Forschung) (2001) *Frauen in Bildung und Forschung, Gender mainstreaming.* Bonn.

BMFSFJ/BDI/IW (Bundesministerium für Familie, Senioren, Frauen und Jugend/ Bundesverband der deutschen Industrie/Institut der deutschen Wirtschaft Köln) (2005) *Bevoelkerungsorientierte Familienpolitik – Ein Wachstumsfaktor,* Berlin. Retrieved November 27, 2005, from www.bmfsfj.de/Kategorien/Publikationen/Publikationen,did= 21864.html.

Bologna Protocol (1999) *Der Europaeische Hochschulraum. Gemeinsame Erklaerung der Europaeischen Bildungsminister 19.* Juni 1999. Retrieved November 27, 2005, from http://www.bmbf.de/pub/bologna_deu.pdf.

BuKoF-Kommission Hochschulplanung, Hochschulsteuerung (2002) *Stellungnahme zum Gender mainstreaming an Hochschulen.*

Douglas, M. (1986) *How institutions think.* Syracuse: Syracuse University Press.

Eckart, C. (1995) Feministische Politik gegen institutionalles Vergessen. *Feministische Studien, 13*(1):82–90.

Etzkowitz, H., Kemelgor, C., Neuschatz, M., Uzzi, B., & Alonzo, J. (1994) The paradox of critical mass for women in science. *Science, 266*:51–54.

Halford, S., Savage, M., & Witz, A. (1997) *Gender, careers and organizations.* Basingstoke: Macmillan.

Holzbecher, M., Kuellchen, H., & Loether, A. (2002) *Fach – und Fakultaetsspezifische Ursachen der Unterrepraesentanz von Frauen bei Promotionen.* Bielefeld: IFF-Forschungsreihe 14.

Holzbecher, M., Müller, U., Schmalzhaf-Larsen, C., & Krischer, B. (1998) *Evaluierung der 'Grundsaetze zur Frauenfoerderung an den Hochschulen des Landes NRW'.* Abschlussbericht: Universitaet Bielefeld.

Husu, L. (2001) *Sexism, support and survival in academia: Academic women and hidden discrimination in Finland.* Social Psychological Studies 6. Helsinki: University of Helsinki.

Ihsen, S. (2005) 'Was interessiert Sie denn als Frau and er Technik?' Professur fuer 'Gender Studies in den Ingeniuerwissenschaften' an der TU Muenchen. *Neue impulse, 1*(2):3–4.

Kanter, R. M. (1977) *Men and women of the corporation.* New York: Basic Books.

Kirsch-Auwaerter, E. (1996) Emanzipatorische Strategien an den Hochschulen im Spannungsverhältnis von Organisationsstrukturen und Zielvorstellungen. *VBWW-Rundbrief, 12*:51–55.

——— (2002) Gender mainstreaming als neues Steuerungsinstrument? Versuch einer Standortbestimmung. *Bielefeld Zeitschrift fuer Frauenforschung und Geschlechterstudien, 20*(3).

Krais, B. (Ed.) (2000) *Wissenschaftskultur und Geschlechterordnung. Uber die verborgenen Mechanismen maennlicher Dominanz in der akademischen Welt.* Frankfurt: Campus.

KMK (Kultusministerkonferenz) (2004) Eckpunkte fuer die Weiterent wicklung der Akkretierung in Deutschland. Beschluss Der KMK vom 15.10.2004. Retrieved August 26 2006, from http://www.kmk.org/doc/besch/eckpunkle_akk.pdf.

Luhmann, N. (1983) *Legitimation durch Verfahren.* Frankfurt/Main: Suhrkamp.

Majcher, A., Schenk, A., & Zimmer, A. (2003) Frauen in Wissenschaft und forschung: ein Literaturbericht. *Zeitschrift fuer Frauenforschung und Geschlechterstudien, 21*(4):6–17.

Metz-Goeckel, S., & Kamphans, M. (2002) *Gender mainstreaming in Hochschulleitungen von NRW.* Mit gebremsten Schwung und alter Skepsis, Hochschuldidaktisches Zentrum der Universitaet Dortmund.

Meyer, J. W., & Rowan, B. (1992) Institutionalized organizations: Formal structures as myth and ceremony. In J. W. Meyer & R. W. Scott (Eds.), *Organizational environments: Ritual and rationality* (rev. ed) (pp. 21–44). Newbury Park: Sage.

Meyer, J. W., & R. W. Scott (1992) (Eds.), *Organizational environments: Ritual and rationality* (rev. ed). Newbury Park: Sage.

Mischau, A., Blaettel-Mink, B., Daniels, J., & Lehmann, J. (2004) *Doing gender in mathematics: Indications for more gender equality in German Universities?* IFF-Forschungsreihe Band 16.

Morley, L. (1999) *Organizing feminisms: The micropolitics of the Academy.* Basingstoke: Macmillan.

Müller, U. (1999a) Asymmetrische Geschlechterkonstruktionen in der Hochschule. In A.Neusel & A. Wetterer (Eds.), *Vielfaeltige Verschiedenheiten. Geschlechterverhaeltnisse in Studium, Hochschule und Beruf* (pp. 135–159). Frankfurt.

——— (1999b) Making gender visible: Affirmative action programs in German Universities. In P. Fogelberg, J. Hearn, L. Husu, & T. Mankinnen (Eds.), *Hard work in the academy: Research and interventions on gender inequalities in higher education* (pp. 51–66). Helsinki: Helsinki University Press.

——— (2000) Gender equality programs in German institutes of higher education: The North Rhine-Westphalia Case. *Higher education in Europe, 25*(2):155–161.

——— (2004) SIGMA Women's and Gender Studies in Germany (1995). In R. Braidotti, E. Just, & M. Mensik (Eds.), *ATHENA, advanced thematic network in European women's studies: Vol. 5. THE making of European women's studies* (pp. 196–217). Utrecht: ATHENA.

Müller, U., & Stein-Hilbers, M. (1996) Arbeitsplatz Hochschule – kein Ort fuer Frauen? In E. Kleinau & C. Opitz (Eds.), *Geschichte der Maedchen – und Frauenbildung, Bd. 2: Vom Vormaerz bis zur Gegenwart* (pp. 487–496). Frankfurt: Campus.

Müller, U., Holzbecher, M., & Meschkutat, B. (1999) *Asymmetrische Geschlechterkultur an der Hochschule und Frauenfoerderung als Prozess.* Bielefeld: Projektbericht Universitaet Bielefeld.

Nida-Ruemelin, J. (2005) Auf dem Irrweg. Die Universitaet zwischen Humboldt und McKinsey – Perspektiven der wissenschaftlichen Bildung. *Sueddeutsche Zeitung,* May 3.

Osborn, M., Rees, T., Bosch, M., Hermann, C., Hilden, J., McLaren, A., Palomba, R., Peltonen, L., Vela, C., Weis, D., Wold, A., & Wennerås, C. (2000) *Promoting excellence through mainstreaming gender equality.* A report from the ETAN Network on Women and Science. Luxembourg: Office for Official Publications of the European Communities.

Pellert, A. (1999) *Die universitaet als organisation.* Wien: Boehlau.

Wennerås, C., & Wold, A. (1997) Nepotism and sexism in peer review. *Nature, 387:*314–343.

Wirth, H., & Duemmler, K. (2004) Zunehmende Tendenz zu spaeteren Geburten und Kinderlosigkeit bei Akadem ikerinnen. Eine Kohortenanalyse auf der Basis von Mikrozensusdaten. *Informationsdienst Soziale Indikatoren, 32.*

Zimmermann, K. (2000) *Spiele mit macht in der wissenschaft: Passfaehigkeit und geschlecht als kriterium fuer berufungen.* Berlin: Sigma.

Chapter Four

Gender Equality Challenges and Higher Education Reform: A Case Study University of Dortmund

Christine Roloff

With the expansion of higher education, women have gained access to German universities and are seeking the opportunity to learn and ascend the professional ranks. It is still in dispute whether their access to higher education has developed owing to democratic expectations of cultural forces or to market strategies responding to the demand for a highly skilled labour force (Morley, 1999; Scott, 1999). Both factors attest to modernization and social change. Within these developments, it seems as if German higher education has taken over the role of social stratification. The universities' knowledge, traditions, cultural codes, and hierarchy of decision making have remained unchanged in spite of the differentiation of students and their educational needs. Thus, the German higher education system has not integrated the new student groups in a qualitative way; instead, it produces and perpetuates inequality by sorting out rather than integrating non-traditional ideas and aspirations as students pursue their academic careers. Consequently, a great amount of human resources, creativity, and potential to further scientific and university development are lost. This wasteful trend threatens the goals of science in achieving excellence (Osborn et al., 2000).

Germany is one of the countries with the lowest participation of women in higher education careers as well as in the fields of science and technology. At the same time, the numbers of female undergraduates and graduates and women in professional work are constantly rising. Many women have become agents in the development of higher education by being employed in new fields such as evaluation, organizational development, and controlling (Hanft, 2000). Highly qualified women, among them young mothers, are deeply engaged in their careers, yet the universities and the research institutes are not prepared to integrate these highly motivated women into their respective hierarchies. Thus, to realize gender equality in German higher education and science careers is to achieve a new equality that no longer restricts the hopes of women by supporting the traditional target group of white males.

The gender debate must be seen as part of the postmodern debate questioning the epistemological tradition of unified science (Weiler, 2002). From the start, feminist theory has been criticizing categories such as objectivity, certainty, or truth and pointing out the limitations of knowledge based on the scientific culture of men. The new means of producing knowledge must synthesize interdisciplinary perspectives and multicultural experiences as well as interests of various agents in order to be able to find adequate definitions of social problems and democratic solutions (Gibbons et al., 1994; Pellert, 1999). Feminist research and gender studies contribute to the critique of science and to a new relationship between scientific knowledge and society. That is why gender equality and adequate participation of women in academia favour not just women in particular but the general development of a democratic society as well. Although feminist research and gender studies contribute to successful scientific production and to the education of young female researchers in Germany, the acceptance and reputation of such theoretical platforms within scientific communities are inadequate.

Strictly speaking, German universities are institutions of human resources development, but there is little institutional understanding of this purpose thus far. To reform higher education, the universities must take more responsibility at the level of the institution in order to be able to increase their performance standards, to compete with one another, and to rise to and/or maintain international standards. Improvements and new challenges are strongly dependent on the agency of involved people. The universities can no longer afford to individualize the attention given to the new academic generation or to ignore innovative administrative staff. Instead, German universities must implement systematic and transparent management of human resources. Academic work and learning processes must be organized in such a way that all students and employees are able to optimize their potential talents and invest their gained competence in the improvement of the institution's performance while they advance their individual careers. The universities must create a personnel development strategy that recruits undergraduate students and optimizes the quality of their learning conditions. This strategy must also devise suitable methods of supervising and supporting students, graduates, and employees. Mentoring and career guidance by professors and administrative and staff leaders are essential, especially in assisting students and employees as they consider various academic and professional career tracks. In addition, qualified academic lecturers and professors should demonstrate competence in personnel development and diversity management and should possess knowledge of distinct gender equality strategies. Most importantly, they should show respect for people of different origins and backgrounds, for their views of problems and solutions, and for their motivations and capabilities.

Combining gender questions with higher education reforms is therefore more than just a matter of equal rights in a given world. It aims at structurally and comprehensively qualifying science, academia, and society. This reciprocal relationship between gender equality and general improvements is basic to the implementation of the gender perspective into the reform processes in the University of Dortmund. The following text will present (1) information about the academic career track in Germany; (2) the characteristics and structure of the University of Dortmund; and (3) the steps to qualify the situation of women academics as well as to improve the performance and competitiveness of the University of Dortmund.

Characteristics of the Career Track and the Lack of Personnel Development Strategies

The German system of academic career track (assistantship, *habilitation*, co-optation) shows systematic weaknesses that work against the adequate participation of women through a highly individualized promotion process. Furthermore, freedom of research and teaching – the legal right of the German professor – is mostly misunderstood as one of individual freedom rather than institutional freedom. Therefore, students receive very little institutional career guidance, and neither the administration nor faculty embraces a sense of institutional responsibility to govern the recruitment and encouragement of future generations of academics. Guidance and mentoring are dependent on the motivation of each individual professor ('Die Situation der Doktoranden in Deutschland', 2004).

Undergraduate Studies

German undergraduate students usually do not receive substantial systematic feedback about their academic performance to encourage them to pursue graduate studies or academic careers. Students normally take an examination in several subjects to conclude their basic courses in order to be admitted to the advanced courses, yet each exam is assessed and graded by a professor or assistant.[1] Thus, students receive neither feedback on their overall performance nor a transcript that documents their academic progress. Because the system lacks a faculty-mentoring system to encourage students to continue their studies or to help them consider an academic career, informal encouragement tends to happen by chance from individual professors. What informal communication on performance does occur, however, furthers the informal male-mentoring system (Krimmer et al., 2003).

Admission to Graduate Studies

All vacancies for academic posts are formally announced, at least within the University of Dortmund. In reality, the official announcement is often merely a formality, and an informal process determines who is appointed, even before the official announcement of the position is made (according to the author's experience as the university equality representative). Therefore, one begins an academic career at the invitation of a professor to serve as his or her assistant for three to six years and asks him or her to write a dissertation during that time. The criteria for selection of graduate students vary greatly from post to post because the qualifications for a post in a chairgroup (i.e., the working section of a professoriate) are defined by one professor. Because approximately 90% of the professors are men, this process disadvantages women, a finding that is supported by Allmendinger et al.'s (1999) research showing that the more formalized the hiring processes in the research institutes the better the chances for advancement by women. Thus, in an extreme situation, one professor can 'make or break' a student's academic career in German higher education (Kavka & Wiedmer, 2001).

Steps to Obtaining Professorship

German universities have required passage of the examination of *habilitation* in addition to the PhD in order to obtain professorship. It requires another phase of assistantship of up to six years, an elaborate scholarly document, and a disputation with the faculty, which as a whole will decide to give or refuse the *venia legendi* (permission to read or teach). In order to improve the career track of graduate students, attempts have been made to weaken the requirement of habilitation. For example, the German Research Association (DFG) created the Emmy Noether Program in 2000 in order to open a new track to professorship.[2] It is a five-year programme for young academics with a PhD. Another attempt of the government to alter the career track is the newly created position of a junior professorship, which lasts for a period of six years. It gives young postdoctoral academics more flexibility and responsibility in their research and teaching activities.[3] Both career modules are temporary, which means that young academics cannot continue their careers in these positions. With the exception of tenured professorships, academic posts are normally temporary and restricted; after the postdoctoral lecturing qualification of habilitation, it is necessary to apply for a professorship in a different university in order to be offered a chair. Rarely does an individual receive a chair in the faculty where the assistantship has been completed. The qualified academics in both the Emmy Noether Program and the junior professorship must also be offered a chair after having completed the programme; however, they are allowed to continue their career in the same university if they have already transferred to another university after the PhD examination. In both programmes, it is still quite uncertain whether the respective faculties will respect these special career steps by the selection boards because, among professors, the abolition of the postdoctoral lecturing qualification is very controversial. Thus, it is not certain that, even after having completed habilitation or one of the programmes, a candidate will be successful in an application process. The German individualistic career system very often depends on connections and old-boy networks. In fact, there are rules and regulations as well as criteria for applying for and being offered chairs, but the whole system depends on co-optation. This means that the professional colleagues in a faculty have the greatest influence on the new faculty members. They not only negotiate the necessary qualifications, but they also decide whether the candidates fit into the faculty and whether qualifications should be reinterpreted in order to make certain candidates suitable (see, e.g., Zimmermann, 2000).

Whereas it is indispensable to do elaborate research and to publish when on the career track to professorship, the teaching capabilities of young academics are neither furthered nor evaluated systematically. Quite often women academics like to teach and in their early years and invest a great amount of time in teaching without obtaining official acknowledgement or documentation (Arnold & Bos, 1996) or much systematic instruction or evaluation of their teaching. At the University of Dortmund, for example, such instruction and evaluation are voluntary.

In sum, no clear promotional principle exists to make an academic career predictable and systematic. In addition, the German system tends to reproduce the status quo in all respects, including gender balance. Within this framework, male professors tend to further and select male students and applicants more frequently than they select females (Krimmer et al., 2003). Not only is the statistical probability very small for female newcomers to become professors when compared to male counterparts, but there are still strong cultural stereotypes against the expectation of either female professorships or academic careers. In addition, German universities do not generally provide childcare for students and academics. Consequently, only a few encouraging female role models do exist.

The University of Dortmund: Short History, Disciplinary Structure, and Gender Relations

The University of Dortmund is one of the 360 institutions of higher education in Germany. Among these, one-third are universities, including technical universities (Technische Universitäten/Hochschulen) as well as teacher training and theological colleges (Pädagogische Hochschulen, Theologische Hochschulen); more than half are universities of applied science (Fachhochschulen), and about 14% are colleges of art, music, and sport (Kunsthochschulen, Musikhochschulen, Sporthochschulen).

Approximately 1.9 million students are enrolled in these institutions. While three quarters of them study in universities, about one quarter attend universities of applied science, and a little more than 1% of the students study in colleges of art, music, or sport. The German higher education system has experienced considerable growth during the past 35 years. The growth has occurred, in part, because of the increase in the number of the universities of applied science (from 0 to more than 180 since 1970) and even more so because of the considerable expansion of the old universities and the establishment of new ones.

The University of Dortmund, located in the Ruhr region of the Bundesland Northrhine-Westfalia, is one of the large new universities, founded in 1968 during the phase of the educational expansion at the peak of the student movement. It was intended to be a technical university with faculties of science and engineering, including spatial planning, economics, and business management, in order to provide skilled workforce for the industrial firms of the region (Reininghaus, 1993). In 1980, it was united with the Pedagogical College Ruhr, the predecessors of which go back to the sixteenth century (Kirchhoff, 1993). And thus, the University of Dortmund has included faculties of educational theory, rehabilitation, social sciences, languages, and arts.

More than 90% of the University of Dortmund's, 21,244 students, come from the Bundesland Northrhine-Westfalia area, while the remaining 10% come from other German *Länder* (states) or from abroad (Universität Dortmund, 2002a). The University of Dortmund still has a somewhat twofold profile of science and technology as well as departments in educational theory, rehabilitation, social sciences, languages, and arts. All of these departments offer teacher-training studies but not exclusively; there are also a few diploma or BA/MA studies. This profile makes for an unequal distribution of gender according to subjects, exams, position, and staff.[4]

In October 2002, 2,337 people were employed by the University of Dortmund, half academic (1,164) and half administrative and technical staff (1,163). Another 1,096 persons were funded by research or industrial financing; half of the latter were students and the other half were auxiliary personnel (511). At that time, the proportion of women academics was 23%, and the proportion of women administrators and technicians was 54% (Universität Dortmund, 2002). For example, between 1995 and 2000, the *Kanzler*, or vice-chancellor, was a woman. In 2004, the central administration was comprised of six departments, two of which were led by women.[5] The proportion of women in leadership positions within the departments was 20% (4 of 20), including the head of the library. Otherwise, women were concentrated in lower ranks.

The constitutional organization of the University of Dortmund is based on a traditional rectorship (*Rektoratsverfassung*). The rector, or chancellor, is nearly always a professor from within the institution, a so-called primus inter pares. He or she is elected by colleagues – or more precisely by the academic senate – and after the end of the period of office (four or eight years), he or she continues as an ordinary member of the faculty.[6] The governing board of the University of Dortmund is chaired by the chancellor (*Rektor*), currently male, and consists of the vice-chancellor (*Kanzler*) and four vice-rectors (*Prorektor*), each of whom serves for two years. Currently, the vice-rector for study and curriculum reform is female. Each vice-rector is entrusted with responsibilities such as study and curriculum reform, research and promotion, finance, organization and personnel development, and infrastructure and media.

The participation of women at the University of Dortmund across subjects and academic levels is similar to the general distribution in Germany as well as that throughout Europe (Osborn et al., 2000). However, some characteristics should be mentioned in detail. Between 1995 and 2002, the percentage of women undergraduates was over 40%, but this rose by 3.5%. Even greater was the percent change for graduate (13.6%) and PhD students (10.7%). Women completing habilitation saw the greatest increase from 10 to 30%. In less than a decade, women students increased their participation to approximately half of undergraduates and graduates, one quarter of PhD students, and one-third of habilitation students (see figure 4.1). However, in October 2004, the proportion of female students enrolled at the University of Dortmund (45.2%) was slightly below the overall representation of women in German institutions of higher education: 47.9%. This overall participation of women varies greatly by subject with science and technology being dominated by men. Mathematics, with 32% female students, and natural sciences, with 35% female students, also continue to be male-dominated whereas women constitute the majority in pedagogy, languages, and cultural studies (70% women), and art, music, and sport (67% women).

The pattern of participation rates through the academic career at the University of Dortmund is similar to that of German higher education: 'the higher the position, the more male' it is, although some exceptions to the pattern exist. It is remarkable that 15.6% of the professors are women, which is 4.3% higher than the average of 11.2% for German universities (see figure 4.1).[7] The rate for the highest faculty position (*C4*) at the University of Dortmund at 13.5% is nearly twice the German average at 7.7%. Of course, there are higher rates of participation by women in pedagogic and language studies as well as cultural studies. However, the proportion of 10.9% in engineering's highest ranks is significant when compared to the average in Germany of about 3% (BLK, 2002). Four of these six female professors with the highest status are in the department of spatial planning, one in chemical technology, and one in building and construction. These are also the engineering fields with the greatest number of female students (above 30% each). This participation rate by women can most likely be attributed to the creation of spatial planning and building and construction as interdisciplinary departments when the university was founded and during its first phase of reform in the 1960s.[8]

Compared to the number of women in its faculties, the University of Dortmund has fewer female assistants than do other German universities. Women hold only 24.7% of assistant posts as compared to the 31.9% average for Germany. In all subject groups, female participation as academic assistant staff is lower than the proportion of women as students at the University of Dortmund. This phenomenon shows that, on

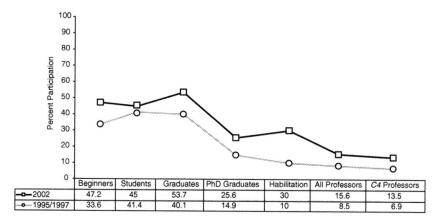

	Beginners	Students	Graduates	PhD Graduates	Habilitation	All Professors	C4 Professors
2002	47.2	45	53.7	25.6	30	15.6	13.5
1995/1997	33.6	41.4	40.1	14.9	10	8.5	6.9

Figure 4.1 Representation of Women among Students and Academic Staff at the University of Dortmund

Sources: Universität Dortmund Zahlen, Daten, Fakten 2002. Statistisches Jahrbuch der Universität Dortmund und Studierendenstatistik Wintersemester 2002/03. Dez. 2.

one hand, the faculties tend to privilege men when appointing assistants. On the other hand, the lower rates are due to the university's subject structure with only a few assistant posts in the subjects where there are many female graduates and, by comparison, many posts where only few women applicants exist.

Holding an assistant post does not mean one is pursuing a doctorate and striving for an academic career. In winter 2002/2003, 35% of the doctoral students were women, but only 25% of them held assistantships; thus, they pursued their doctoral studies as extern members or were funded by grants more often than men were. From 2000 to 2002, the average proportion of females who completed their PhD examinations was 23.2%. In each subject other than engineering, the females who completed their PhD exams exceeded the proportion of women in assistant posts. In engineering, the reverse was true: the rate of doctorates was only half of the proportion of assistant positions (Universität Dortmund Studierendenstatistik, 2002b). The difference in types of female participation within the subject groups or fields is accounted for by the environmental and structural variables within each field, such as the traditional cultures of these professional disciplines as well as the departmental attitudes and decisions about academic promotion.

Furthermore, the reasons for the differing figures and rates compared to Germany in general are (1) the historical development of the University of Dortmund as a technical university; (2) the relative rareness of female students and applicants in the departments of science and technology whereas, in the pedagogical departments, the competition for the best jobs is higher with males tending to win more often; and (3) the equality activities of the past years to explain the higher rate in the category professors. For example, the equality representative is a member of every selection board, and she has succeeded in several cases to promote women professors.[9] In addition, during the past 15 years, seven professors have been appointed for gender studies in several subjects, according to a special ministerial programme of Northrhine-Westfalia.[10]

Integrating Gender Equality in Reform Processes
at the University of Dortmund

Restructuring these and other aspects of German higher education requires a comprehensive perspective of human resource management. To improve structures and organization, the University of Dortmund is incorporating gender equality into reform strategies. For example, the university is examining the motivations and unequal participation of male and female students and academics.

In order to implement the perspective of gender equality into the reform processes in the university, the relationship between gender equality and general improvements must be reciprocal. The asymmetrical participation of women in study fields and higher education careers is a symptom of the structural problems in the system of higher education generally and at this university specifically. These structural problems are evidenced by the following:

- The drop in the number of students in science and engineering and the inability of these departments to attract new target groups, especially females;
- Subjects with curricula that do not lead to a distinct profession (such as spatial planning where professional employment is variable) and lack of guidance counselling for students – in these fields, female graduates have greater problems finding jobs; (Wasgien, 2002)
- A relatively high average dropout rate of 30% – the dropout rate of female students is higher in engineering; (Brendel & Metz-Göckel, 2001)
- The individual prolongation of the period of time of study until the first professional qualification is gained[11]
- The gap between qualification and the demand of the labour market
- The contingency of academic careers as indicated above
- The lack of appreciation for the teaching qualifications of lecturers by the scientific communities as well as the selection boards in universities

As one of the first universities to introduce new strategies of quality assessment and performance-based financing to improve these and other problems, the University of Dortmund responded to the change in government funding that gave institutions more freedom in financial decisions and increased accountability by emphasizing output criteria. In 1992, the governing board presented its first report on the teaching quality in different courses of studies one year before the government of Northrhine-Westfalia made this a legal requirement. In 1994, the university implemented an indicator-based system for the internal distribution of money to the academic faculty departments. It included such output criteria as completed examinations and research grants obtained. In 1995, when the government gave the universities more freedom in budget decisions, the governing board and the senate passed a concept of principles for these decisions; for example, surplus money should be spent to raise the quality of teaching and to support applications for research grants. In addition, in 1995, the university started a review procedure in order to assess performance in teaching, research, and organization in every faculty department. The method included both a self-evaluation based on a questionnaire, a peer assessment, and a reform process based upon faculty and other expert recommendations.

From 1994 on, there have been efforts to integrate gender equality criteria in these reform instruments. The equality representative recommended integrating gender monitoring into the evaluation, and the faculty departments were asked to report on the progress towards equality. In 1997, the first financial incentive to support gender equality was given. The governing board decided that surplus money should be spent supporting 'innovative personnel and intelligence resources' (resolution of the governing board in 1997), which spoke to efforts furthering women as academics and providing financially based incentives to support the progress of gender equality. Nevertheless, several years passed before systematic incentives became possible.

The most important step during this early phase of reform was not just integrating gender equality into the new public management instruments, such as evaluation and financing by performance criteria; rather, it gave the equality representative the platform to point out and to sharpen the argument that gender equality can be realized only within the context of reform by enlarging the talent pool, taking up personnel development in academia, and contributing to new means of knowledge production.

In 1996, an opportunity to realize the integration was launched with the Volkswagen Foundation 'Efficiency by Autonomy'. This programme was created to encourage and support ten German universities that implemented significant higher education reforms in organizational structure and management by reallocating funds as well as the modernizing both study programmes and quality assessment in research and teaching (VolkswagenStiftung, 1998). At the suggestion of the equality representative supported by other female academics of the university, the University of Dortmund participated in the programme with its project 'Quality and Innovation: Gender Equality Challenges Higher Education Reform', which documented the university's progress towards integrating gender equality within the subject of university reform. The Volkswagen Foundation required the chancellor (*Rektor*) to be responsible for the 767,000 Euro project. Although he and one of the vice-rectors chaired the internal steering group, a project team was responsible for mobilizing the co-operation of the governing board, the administrative departments, and the faculties. The Volkswagen Foundation sent several higher education reform experts to consult on and evaluate the project, which enhanced the status and importance of the project. Furthermore, the project was supported by the Science and Research Ministry of Northrhine-Westfalia with the sum of 130,000 Euros. The ministry was interested because they acknowledged the innovative ideas of adapting the frame of the equality law to the new situation in higher education management, giving more responsibility and autonomy to the individual institutions. The regulations dated from 1985 but were revised in 2000 with respect to the new public management instruments (University Law of Northrine-Westfalia).

The Processes of Change

In November 1998, the University of Dortmund started the five-year project with two foci: (1) to reform strategies and instruments of the governing board and the administration; and (2) to improve quality and performance within the faculty departments. Within these two foci was the intention to implement gender criteria into daily decisions about work (see figure 4.2). The centralized strategies and goals of the decentralized agency levels were gradually interrelated as the work progressed. The results mutually supported both the decisions and steering instruments of the governing board and the initiatives of the faculty departments, such as the decision of financing and rewarding gender equality progress.

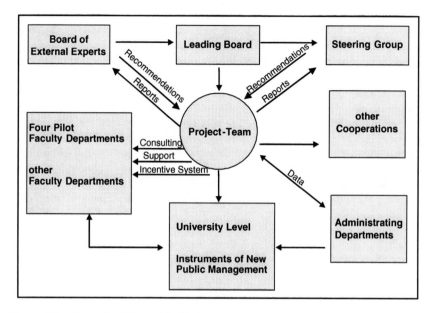

Figure 4.2 Organizing Chart of the Project

Source: Roloff, C., & Selent, P. (Eds.) 2003 *Hochschulreform und Gender Mainstreaming.* Bielefeld: Geschlechtergerechtigkeit als Querschnittaufgabe, p. 40.

The Reform Strategies and Structural Decisions

At the top level of the institution, the project team recommended and endorsed the systematic integration of gender equality into the reform instruments and prepared guidelines for the responsible administrative departments. These guidelines included (1) the questionnaire for self-evaluation within the review system that had been started in 1995; (2) the financial allocation system; (3) the data information and control system; (4) the goal-setting processes and primary objectives; and (5) the profile structure of the university.

External factors have delayed implementation of some measures. For example, the integration of gender criteria into the review and the allocation systems has yet to be completed owing to a delay in the implementation of the systems themselves pending ministerial decisions.

Centralized Decisions

The initiative 'Quality and Innovation: Gender Equality Challenges Higher Education Reform' has brought about significant changes in gender equality at the University of Dortmund. Currently, funds for teaching and research are distributed among the faculty and departments according to an indicator system where one criterion measures the adequate qualification of women. Faculties with both female undergraduates and graduates who have discontinued PhD have to spend a certain amount of their annual money to improve gender equality. It will be up to the equality representative as well as to the equal rights commission to continue these efforts under the new conditions.[12] Furthermore, more work is needed to complete monitoring of equal gender inclusion. The administration regularly produces data on students and personnel by gender, but new monitoring indicators should be introduced, such as statistics on the working conditions, the duration of short-term contracts, and pay and resource gender gaps as well as data on successful applications for awards and research grants and the provision of childcare facilities at the university.

German higher education reform has resulted in structural decisions intended to create a distinctive image and profile of each university. Within this process, the governing board of the University of Dortmund has recently begun to consider and include feminist research and gender studies. These fields have been quite traditional at the University of Dortmund (seven gender studies chairs and many more gender research publications), but thus far they have received little acknowledgement. With the support of the project, gender research was successfully positioned as one of the important factors in the future research structure of the university. In addition, an interdisciplinary centre for research on the dynamics of gender constellations was founded. The involved professors and academics have gained research grants, have started research projects, and are organizing workshops on feminist theory. The centre includes graduate education and a programme for international visiting scholars. Feminist and gender studies have gained importance for study programmes, too. According to the Bologna Process, the governing board decided that all newly created bachelor and master's programmes must include gender studies modules. One of the professors of the centre is head of an internal commission whose purpose it is to advise the faculty departments on how to accomplish this task. In 2002, the University of Dortmund and the Ministry of Science and Research of Northrhine-Westfalia officially agreed to these objectives and developments. Furthermore, the University of Dortmund promised to continue and expand the measures of academic personnel development that were implemented by the gender equality reform project.

Decentralized Decisions: Processes within Faculty Departments

At the decentralized level, the main focus of 'Quality and Innovation: Gender Equality Challenges Higher Education Reform' was to create four pilot departments representing different disciplines: chemistry, mechanical engineering, spatial planning, and the teacher-training faculty for social/philosophical/theological studies. The strategic initiative in each faculty was to analyse and verify organizational data on the situation of women and the state of reforms. Relevant agents, such as the dean, professors, students, assistants, and advisers were interviewed, and a network of contacts with the project team was established. Each faculty analysed the results and suggested improvements. Two faculties established working groups, and the other two welcomed project members on the respective boards of the proposed working subjects, for example, promoting commissions to improve study information. An incentive system was launched to give impetus to the activities. In order to establish special measures, the pilot faculties could apply for surplus money given by the governing board. Thus, each faculty appointed project groups working out special subjects on their own authority, for example, improving female enrollment, improving students' guidance and mentoring, and providing labour market information. They were supported and guided by the project team and advised by the steering group.

Five other units eventually joined the project: pedagogy, languages and cultural studies, the Building and Construction Department, the Department of Arts and Music, and the Center for Research on Higher Education and Faculty Development. They chose to participate in the incentive system and received surplus money to integrate improvements of gender equality into their reform strategies. They were also advised by the project team.

Activities at the level of the faculty departments included modernization and improvement of academic advise and study programme reforms; improvement of study conditions; guidance and mentoring of students; academic career guidance; career advice for academic professionals outside the university; integration of gender competence training in higher education didactics; and media instruction for research teams, including secretaries and student assistants.

Financial incentives were used to initiate the activities, but faculties and institutes had to contribute one quarter of their surplus funds in order to sustain the activities. They also had to promise to implement the new actions or procedures in order to continue funding. In principle, measures and improvements were aimed at both genders in that the departments dealt with general problems of higher education reform. But financial incentives were leveraged to create an awareness of gender regarding unequal conditions, participation, and opportunities for women and men that then became a starting point for general improvement.

Project Outcomes: An Example

As the project name 'Quality and Innovation: Gender Equality Challenges Higher Education Reform' suggests, reform in higher education is ongoing and systemic. Incorporating gender equality into reform initiatives often begins by changing existing programmes in which gender equality is not readily apparent. For example, the Faculty of Social, Philosophical and Theological Studies offers teacher-training programmes on three levels: primary, lower secondary, and high school. Only the high school level graduate is permitted to continue studies for a PhD. Primary and lower secondary school graduates principally have no other choice other than to leave the university to teach school. In times when school-teaching jobs are rare, these graduates have limited employability after having completed their traineeship in a school. Notably, many of these graduates pass their exams with great success and write final papers that often deal with school problems and didactics of the disciplines for which research is necessary. However, because of this system, many qualified graduates are disbarred from continuing an academic career even though a market exists for them in the university. Researchers with teaching experience are rare, and the professors would like to have more PhD students. Not surprisingly, 70–90% of these students are women. Intensifying the development of the new generation of academics in teacher-training disciplines is a matter of both institutional improvement and individual advancement, especially of women.

In response to this institutional oversight and its inherent implications regarding gender equality, the project supported the implementation of a graduate school for graduates of primary and lower secondary school levels. It offers a one-year study programme comprised of scientific theory and research methods as well as special subject fields. Upon completing the programme, the student is awarded a certificate, which allows her or him to begin a PhD study. Not only are the students able to begin advanced studies, but they are also able to circumvent the informal process of individually contacting a professor to assume an advisory role. Before this programme was introduced, it was possible for graduates of primary and lower secondary levels to find a professor who was willing to accept a dissertation, but then the students had to make individual arrangements regarding the additional credits to take. This current official and transparent programme generally meets the needs of graduates better than the former informal process did, and it addresses the particular needs of women. The programme has been positively evaluated and has been included in the university's internal grant system so that students can apply for grants.

Soon after the implementation of the new study programme, the number of participating students grew from 3 to 28, and now more than 50 students are enrolled; 75% of them are women. The participation of women in a regular PhD programme in the Faculty of Social, Philosophical and Theological Studies has also grown. Whereas in winter 1997/1998, 43% of the PhD students were female, in winter 2001/2002, women accounted for 61%.

The example given demonstrates that in order to increase participation by women, optional or qualitative improvements are basic. For example, without the graduate programme created specifically for the teacher-training graduates of primary and lower secondary levels, many would not have chosen the career path to a PhD. However, not every change or measure increases the number of women's participants.

Initiating Optional Qualitative and Quantitative Improvements

The perspective of a gender-equal personnel development process used by the project 'Quality and Innovation: Gender Equality Challenges Higher Education Reform' led to improvements in a variety of reform situations and institutional environments. Because these diverse and complex tasks were executed in subtly differentiated ways and through individual measures, much time passed before their completion. When change aims at thinking and awareness, at agency and decision making, and not at technical or organizational matters alone, those involved must consistently generate communication, argumentation, and acceptance in dialogue and negotiation. Thus, success is not easily measured. Three interrelated dimensions of improvement are (1) increased participation of women according to staff counts or exams; (2) expanded activities of women and extension of their career options and decisions; and (3) greater acknowledgement by the faculty and university members of women's potential, motivations, and performance.

Regardless of the discipline, when integrating feminist and gender studies into the programmes, the improvement is not measurable but is defined by the programmes' potential for engendering personnel development on the part of its participants. Sometimes reform efforts are delayed and struggles ensue despite efforts to infuse gender equality into the curricula. For example, the Faculty of Arts, Music, and Textile Design incorporated gender studies into the curriculum with a series of lectures by different speakers. The faculty did not continue the lectures, but because the governing board decided that the new bachelor and master curricula must contain gender studies modules, they will have to consider such studies in gender in the future and give feminist researchers more support.

Conclusion

The strategy at the University of Dortmund can be seen as part of the gender-main-streaming 'movement' of the European Union, which is the systematic integration of equal opportunities for both genders into organization and culture. The concept was adopted by the German central government in 2000 as one of the leading principles of the common standing orders of the federal ministries. The University of Dortmund was ahead of other universities on this development, and the initiative was judged promising by the Northrhine-Westfalian Ministry of Science and Research. In 2000, the university law was amended and now requires that *progress in gender equality* be added to the criteria governing the reallocation of financial resources. Furthermore, the law requires gender-equality criteria in quality assessment and gives the representative for equal rights admittance to the meetings of the governing board.

With the project 'Quality and Innovation: Gender Equality Challenges Higher Education Reform', the University of Dortmund has taken a leading position. With regard to the project's start, the idea of integrating gender questions into higher education reform strategies has disseminated into the reform efforts of other universities and the national higher education and research institutions and boards. Other universities' reform efforts are keeping pace or even overtaking those of the University of Dortmund. The Federal Ministry of Research supported the offering of a 'Total-E-Quality-Award', and various universities have already gained the rating. The German Research Council, the Science Council, and the Conference of the Federal and States' Governments for Educational Planning and Research recommend the inclusion of gender criteria in evaluation processes, award of financial incentives, and assessment of universities and research institutes (Wissenschaftsrat, 1998; BLK, 2000; 'Gleichstellung …', 2002). For the Federal Conference of University Leaders, the subject 'Women in Science' has become a 'matter of the bosses' (idw, 2003).

It is the non-stop interaction of women's claims and movements in each higher education institution and scientific community with the political lobby of government intended to change legislation that brings change gradually. I locate change within an action, interaction, and conflict theory: Social and organizational change is possible only by interference of those who want it. That is what has happened in the University of Dortmund, and what happens, actually, in higher education in general.

The incorporation of gender equality questions in the reform process at the University of Dortmund has been made possible in a historical situation wherein women are participating in higher education as students, lecturers, professors, and more rarely as leading administrative staff, such as vice-rectors, vice-chancellors, and chancellors. That women are present in these roles in universities is the result of the women's movement in the 1960s and 1970s and the efforts of the equality representatives during the past 15 years. As agents of higher education reform, women academics have greatly needed and now are able to use an infrastructure of networking and lobbying, which was established during those years. Furthermore, higher education structures are being reconstructed and are therefore somewhat vulnerable and susceptible to new ideas. In this situation, gender equality, when seen as a reciprocal concept, has something to offer: Women academics bring competence and potential; they also think and act with respect to the general quality of higher education and social development – and not simply with respect to their own advantage, a reproach with which many of them are confronted. The achievements of the project 'Quality and Innovation: Gender Equality Challenges Higher Education Reform' supporting the overall performance of the University of Dortmund have been acknowledged by the governing board and by the funding foundation.

However, for the University of Dortmund, the task has not finished. In reality, the university has taken only its first steps in creating gender-equal personnel development and amending structural decisions to accommodate gender equality. Before concluding the project, one of the last initiatives was to establish a commission for human resource development chaired by the vice-rector for finance, organization, and personnel development.[13] The commission was formed to further an institutional understanding of human resource development, including equality and equal opportunities. To the members of this commission belongs the equality representative as well as persons teaching didactics, organizing further education courses, or being entrusted with staff administration. These persons form a cooperative network all over the university. For example, the Center for Research on Higher Education and Faculty Development, which traditionally offers courses in teaching qualities, is now offering seminars on organizational and personnel development as well as workshops on gender competence for academics (Wildt, 2002; Metz-Göckel & Roloff, 2002; Metz-Göckel, Roloff, and Sattari, 2003). Structural decisions have been made in order to guide and support individual engagement and agency. It is up to the future agents to continue the task.

Notes

1. The German diploma courses are divided into *Grund* – (basic) and *Haupt* – (advanced) studies. In order to begin the *Hauptstudium* students have to pass a *Zwischen* – (interim) examination.

2. The programme (for men and women) is called Emmy Noether Program after the famous mathematician who earned her postdoctoral lecturing qualification (habilitation) in 1918 at the University of Göttingen two years before women were officially admitted to such an examination. Students in this programme will begin with a research stay in a university abroad, and afterwards they will be given the opportunity to establish a research group of their own in a German university. There they should become a member of a faculty and be fully integrated into the teaching programme. After five years in the programme, they should be ready to accept a chair as a professor.

3. Academics in the Junior Professorship Programme are members of faculty; they are not assistants of individual professors. A junior professor is evaluated after three years, and the position will only be prolonged for another three years if the junior professor receives a positive evaluation. The position of the junior professor is controversial among the German *Länder*, e.g., it is accepted in Northrhine-Westfalia but not in Bayern and Thüringen.

4. The proportion of female students in mathematics, natural sciences, and engineering is about 25%, whereas in pedagogics, languages, cultural studies, and art/music/sport, it is up to 70%. The same structure can be seen in examinations. Among the academic staff, only 23% are women and in the administrative staff, 54%. In the highest position of professor (*C4*), 13% are women, and in the leading positions of administration, about 20% are women.

5. The six departments are as follows: academic and students' affairs/legal section, planning and controlling, staff administration, organization and personnel development, budget and research affairs, technical and construction affairs.

6. The academic senate is an elected board, consisting of 13 professors, 4 assistants, 4 students, and 4 administrators. The chair of the senate is the chancellor (*Rektor*).

7. Note: Women PhDs were not counted in 1995. The figure shown, 14.9, was the percentage for 1997.

8. Many research findings state that women are more attracted by interdisciplinary studies in engineering. They have broader interests even in school (e.g., mathematics as well as languages) whereas boys, who choose engineering later on, already tend towards mathematics and physics in school (Roloff & Evertz, 1992; Minks, 2000).

9. The office of the equality representative has existed since 1988 at the University of Dortmund. The equality representative is a member of the university staff, either academic or administrative. She is elected by the women of the university. She is released from her usual tasks, but she does not receive extra pay for the job.

10. The subjects include sociology, spatial planning, rehabilitation, romance languages and literature, German language and literature, and cultural studies.

11. E.g., a period of time within which a student should complete his or her studies is 9 semesters, but the actual average duration of study time is 12 semesters.

12. Board of elected representatives consists of 2 professors, 2 assistants, 2 students, and 2 administrators; the chair is the equality representative.

13. Until September 2001, the responsibilities of this vice-rector were planning and finance only. When the basic order of the University of Dortmund was amended during the project, his area of work was extended to personnel and organization.

References

Allmendinger, J., Brückner, H., Fuchs, S., & von Stebut, J. (1999) Eine Liga für sich? Berufliche Werdegänge von Wissenschaftlerinnen in der Max-Planck-Gesellschaft. In Aylâ Neusel & / Angelika Wetterer (Eds.), *Vielfältige Verschiedenheiten. Geschlechterverhältnisse in Studium, Hochschule, Beruf.* Frankfurt/New York: Campus, pp. 193–222.

Arnold, E., & Bos, W. (1996) Geschlechtsspezifische hochschuldidaktische Orientierungen bei Assistentinnen und Assistenten. *Das Hochschulwesen, 44*(3):162–172.

Brendel, S., & Metz-Göckel, S. (2001) Das Studium ist schon die Hauptsache … Bielefeld.

BLK (Bund-Länder-Kommission für Bildungsplanung und Forschungsförderung) (2000) Frauen in der Wissenschaft – Entwicklung und Perspektiven auf dem Weg zur Chancengleichheit, *Materialien zur Bildungsplanung und zur Forschungsförderung, 87*(100). Bonn: Seschste Fertschreibung des Datenmaterials.

——— (2002) Frauen in Führungspositionen an Hochschulen und außerhochschulischen Forschungseinrichtungen – Sechste Fortschreibung des Datenmaterials, *Materialien zur Bildungsplanung und zur Forschungsförderung.*

'Die Situation der Doktoranden in Deutschland' (2004) Deutsche Universitätszeitung duz Special Magazin-Heft 12, December 3, Berlin. Retrieved http://www.duz.de/docs/duz_spezial.html.

European Commission/Research Directorate-General (2000) *Science policies in the European Union: Promoting excellence through mainstreaming gender equality.* A Report from the ETAN Expert Working Group on Women and Science, European Communities, Bruxelles.

Gibbons, M., Limoges, C., Nowotny, H., Schwartzman, S., Scott, P., & Trow, M. (1994) *The new production of knowledge: The dynamics of science and research in contemporary societies.* London: Sage Publications.

'Gleichstellung von Männern und Frauen in der Wissenschaft' – Satzungsänderung. Besprechungsgrundlage der Ordentlichen Mitgliederversammlung der DFG am 3. July 2002. Bonn: German Research Foundation, Kennedy allee 40, 53175.

Hanft, A. (Ed.) (2000) *Hochschulen managen? Zur Reformierbarkeit der Hochschulen nach Managementprinzipien.* Neuwied.

idw (Informationsdienst Wissenschaft) (2003) Abschluss der HRK Jahresversammlung in Dresden: Das Thema 'Frauen in der Wissenschaft' ist Chefsache, Pressemitteilung, May 6.

Kavka, M., & Wiedmer, C. (2001) The glass ceiling in German speaking Switzerland: Structural barriers to women's academic advancement. In C. Wiedmer (Ed.), *Sound changes: An international survey of women's career strategies in higher education* (pp. 35–43). University of Zuerich: Universelle 4.

Kirchhoff, H-G. (1993) Die Vorgänger der Universität Dortmund. In: Uni Report, Berichte aus der Forschung der Universität Dortmund. Heft 18 (Winter):48–57.

Krimmer, H., Stallmann, F., Behr, M., & Zimmer, A. (2003) Karrierewege von ProfessorInnen an Hochschulen in Deutschland, Universität Münster.

Metz-Göckel, S., & Roloff, C. (2002) Genderkompetenz als Schlüsselqualifikation. In: Journal Hochschuldidaktik 13. Jg., Nr. 1, Hochschuldidaktisches Zentrum Universität Dortmund, 7–10.

Metz-Göckel, S., Roloff, C., & Sattari, S. (2003) Gendertrainings zur Entwicklung von Genderkompetenz. Eine Herausforderung für die Leitungspersonen. In: Journal Hochschuldidaktik 14. Jg., Nr. 1, Hochschuldidaktisches Zentrum Universität Dortmund, 13–16.

Minks, K-H. (2000) Studienmotivation und Studienbarrieren. In HIS Kurzinformation Ausgabe 8, Hochschulinformations-System, Hannover.

Morley, L. (1999) *Organizing feminisms: The micropolitics of the Academy*. Basingstoke: Macmillan.

Osborn, M., Rees, T., Bosch, M., Hermann, C., Hilden, J., McLaren, A., Palomba, R., Peltonen, L., Vela, C., Weis, D., Wold, A., & Wennerås, C. (2000) *Promoting excellence through mainstreaming gender equality*. A report from the ETAN Network on Women and Science. Luxembourg: Office for Official Publications of the European Communities.

Pellert, A. (1999) Die Universität als Organisation. Die Kunst, Experten zu managen. Wien, Köln, Graz.

Reininghaus, W. (1993) Der lange Weg zur Universität Dortmund. Ihre Vorgeschichte von 1900 bis 1968. In: Uni Report, Berichte aus der Forschung der Universität Dortmund. Heft 18, Winter, 43–47.

Roloff, C. (Ed.) (1998) Reformpotential an Hochschulen – Frauen als Akteurinnen in Hochschulreformprozessen. Berlin.

Roloff, C., & Evertz, B. (1992) Ingenieurin – keine) lebbare Zukunft. Vorurteile im Umfeld von Gymnasiastinnen an der Schwelle der Leistungskurswahl, Weinheim.

Roloff, C., & Selent, P. (Eds.) 2003: Hochschulreform und Gender Mainstreaming. Geschlechtergerechtigkeit als Querschnittaufgabe. Bielefeld.

Scott, P. (1999) Higher education and social change: Rising expectations of and new opportunities for universities. In J-H. Olbertz, & P. Pasternack, (Eds.), *Profilbildung – Standards – Selbststeuerung. Ein Dialog zwischen Hochschulforschung und Reformpraxis* (pp. 15–25). Weinheim.

Universität Dortmund (2002a) Zahlen, Daten, Fakten 2002. Statistisches Jahrbuch der Universität Dortmund. Dortmund.

——— (2002b) Studierendenstatistik Wintersemester 2002/03. Dez. 2, Dortmund.

VolkswagenStiftung (1998) Leistungsfähigkeit durch Eigenverantwortung – Hochschulen auf dem Weg zu neuen Strukturen, Hannover.

Wasgien, K. (2002) Karriereplanung für Wissenschaft und Beruf in der Raumplanung. In: C. Roloff, (Ed.): Personalentwicklung, Geschlechtergerechtigkeit und Qualitätsmanagement an der Hochschule, Bielefeld, 183–193.

Weiler, H. N. (2002) Wissen, Herrschaft und Kultur – Die internationale Politik der Wissensproduktion und die Zukunft der Hochschulen, Festrede anlässlich der Internationalen Konferenz 'Rethinking University. Ergebnisse der Internationalen Frauenuniversität 'Technik und Kultur' (ifu 2000) im internationalen Vergleich – Impulse für die Hochschule der Zukunft'. Berlin. http://www.vifu.de/ifu-today/ifu-doku/2festreden/2weiler-frametext.html. Retrieved 24 August 2006.

Wildt, J. (2002) Das HDZ im Neugliederungsprozess der Universität Dortmund. In: Journal Hochschuldidaktik 13. Jg., Nr. 2, Hochschuldidaktisches Zentrum Universität Dortmund, 43–46.

Wissenschaftsrat (1998) Empfehlungen zur Chancengleichheit von Frauen in Wissenschaft und Forschung. Köln.

Zimmermann, K. (2000) Spiele mit der Macht in der Wissenschaft. Passfähigkeit und Geschlecht als Kriterien für Berufungen. Berlin.

Chapter Five

Gender Equity and Higher Education Reform in Austria

Ada Pellert and Michaela Gindl

Since the 1970s, the Austrian universities have slowly but steadily become 'feminized'.[1] During the 1970s, Austrian universities saw an immense expansion in terms of both facilities and personnel. Greater options for participation increased the plurality of scientific approaches and modernization of the *research landscape*, and democratization of participation for assistants and students moved to the centre of higher education policy. In this context, although providing more access for women was not an explicit political goal of reform, Austria has successfully increased women's participation numerically across social backgrounds, and the widening participation of women in the tertiary sector has led to a substantial increase of female participation at the universities as well. For example, the rate of women increased among the first-year students from 30% in the academic year 1970/1971 to 53% in the academic year 2002/2003.

A review of the ten-year history of promotion of women in science and research in the state-run higher education system of Austria shows that women have increased their participation in tertiary education and that the representation of women in science and research has improved. The legal and programmatic measures as well as scholarships offered by the Ministry for Education, Science, and Culture have led both to an improved gender ratio, even in higher positions, and to an awareness about the situation of women in science and research. The expected outcomes, however, have fallen short of those necessary to bring about gender equality as a result of unfavourable economic conditions, a bureaucratic system, and traditional organizational cultures. A more detailed analysis of progress towards gender equality, however, shows that the results are mixed and continued change is necessary. Although women still dominate in certain less prestigious disciplines, such as the humanities, both the *leaky pipeline* and the *glass ceiling* persist in Austrian universities.

In order to derive holistic strategies to promote women in science and research in Austria, agents of higher education policy must consider the broader cultural context in which it is embedded:

1. The Austrian higher education system is changing, adopting a new steering model comprised of (1) managerialism, deregulation, and competition; (2) institutional budgetary autonomy as well as personal and organizational

autonomy; and (3) a new steering instrument of goal/output agreements, reports, indicator-based budgets, and university boards.

2. The employment system at universities is stagnant. In the 1970s, when the system expanded, there was a lack of qualified women; now, many qualified women are available for work, but the jobs are not.

3. The Austrian culture is conservative. The general consensus is that women should have a good education, but they are not expected to study beyond the first degree. Childcare policies create expectations for women to do considerable family work while still engaging in the labour market.

4. The integration of Austria into the European Union has helped to reduce gender inequality. EU polices call for Austria to compare its equity performance with other European countries – and Austria compares unfavourably (EC, 2003; Pechar & Pellert, 2004). In addition, the European integration of gender equality emphasizes the 'economic argument'. To achieve the Lisbon Goals, the European Union needs more researchers, and a large pool of highly qualified female researchers is available.[2]

Austria's conservative cultural and social traditions strongly influence gender discourses and attitudes towards female participation in the labour market and familial task sharing.[3] This has an important consequence: women are not explicitly and broadly supported or empowered to advance in the workforce. By European standards, Austria has low participation and graduation rates in higher education for both men and women. For example, in the year 2001, only 12% of the population over 15 years held a tertiary education degree (Wroblewski et al., 2005). A comparison by Organization for Economic and Cooperative Development (OECD, 2003) ranked Austria twenty-sixth among 30 countries.

Background: Higher Education Policy and Reforms

Until the late 1960s, Austrian universities followed the Humboldtian model of organization. Universities were state-owned and government-run agencies, and academics were civil servants appointed by the Minister of Education, Science, and Culture. As long as universities remained small elite institutions, this heavy dependency on the state rarely had negative consequences for academics. Top civil servants and members of the academic oligarchy informally made many of the important decisions within the universities. Academic freedom was regarded primarily as an individual right given only to full professors, those at the top of the academic hierarchy. Within the traditional chair system (*Ordinarienuniversität*), each chair holder was personally responsible for his academic domain, and other academics in that domain were, in some way, personally dependent on the professor.

The expansion of universities in the 1970s irreversibly ended this traditional concept of the Humboldtian university. The first reform cycle opened up the ivory tower by widening participation for students from social backgrounds whose access to higher education formerly had been blocked. The reform also added new fields of study, especially in the social sciences and humanities, that had been denied academic 'respectability'. Furthermore, new forms of decision making were established that more evenly distributed academic authority among the various groups within the university, extending to professors without chair, assistants, and students.

The process of opening and democratizing culminated in the University Organisation Act (UOG) of 1975 (Universitätsorganisationsgesetz 1975). In legal terms, this act marked the end of the old regime of the chair holders (*Ordinarienuniversität*) and the beginning of a much more complex and formalized system of academic decision making, which included the middle ranks of academics (*Mittelbau*, including assistants and assistant professors, or *außerordentliche Professoren/Professorinnen*) and students. Because power was now shared by a greater number of academic *estates*, this new type of academic organization was labelled *group university* (*Gruppenuniversität*) (Neave & Rhoades, 1987), and it was supposed that, within those groups, the interests and beliefs of all members were quite homogeneous. The new act attempted to create a just and balanced kind of equality by means of formal legal procedures. In order to consider the interests of every group now involved, these legal procedures became extremely complicated and made the university one of the most complex institutions of Austrian society (Welan, 1995).

The debate concerning this organizational reform was extremely controversial. The government was the driving force behind UOG 1975 with support coming from *Mittelbau* and students and the majority of professors actively opposing the reform. However, the implementation of the UOG 1975 neither caused the collapse of Austrian universities, as some conservative critics predicted, nor did it lead to a more rational and transparent decision-making process. At the institutional level, *monocratic organs*, such as rectors and deans, remained weak, having little authority except to execute the decisions of the respective collegial body made up of senate, faculty, and institute committees. A strong monocratic organ existed only at the level of the basic unit (*Institut*) with the chair holder (i.e., professor).

Whereas at the beginning in the 1980s, the strong paternalistic tradition in Austrian politics was being undermined, by the end of that decade, greater university autonomy was demanded by student numbers that had continued to grow far beyond the forecasted levels. However, due to fiscal constraints, public expenditures for universities could not keep pace with the growth of student numbers. Only minimal additional income came from private sources because Austrian universities were not allowed to charge fees, and third party funding was low. These circumstances required greater organizational efficiency in the form of entrepreneurial reform strategies.

Influencing the interpretation of the new *university autonomy* were differing concepts of *individual autonomy* and *institutional autonomy*. In the Humboldtian tradition, autonomy was synonymous with academic freedom of the individual academic, or the full professor. Many professors saw this kind of autonomy endangered both by state intervention and by the academic codetermination of the students and *Mittelbau*. From the professorial perspective, 'autonomy' became a buzzword for restoration of the 'old regime' of the *Ordinarienuniversität*.

Embracing the notion of autonomy as *institutional autonomy*, on the other hand, meant that universities were now self-governing enterprises with respect to academic, financial, and administrative affairs. Many academics and students claimed that Austrian universities were capable of assuming this responsibility. However, politicians and state bureaucrats as well as a minority of academics seriously doubted that the existing decision-making structures were adequate for the new tasks. They argued that increased institutional autonomy should be accompanied by the development of professional management (Bast, 1991; Höllinger, 1992).

Under the pressure of opposition by academics and students, a revised draft for a new organizational act, *a White Paper* was published in December 1992. It outlined a traditional chair structure consisting of a multitude of small institutes, many of them with only one professor, that remained basically unchanged. A review process prompted the passage of a new act, UOG 1993, by Parliament in October 1993. Like its predecessor, the UOG 1975, it was one of the most divisive and contested legal acts in Austria. Nevertheless, between 1993 and 1997, 12 universities implemented UOG 1993.

The intent of this act was to improve the efficiency of the universities with the provision of greater institutional autonomy to foster organizational creativity and innovation in a competitive market. However, adverse conditions limited reform. Financing was driven by neither performance nor enrolment, financial autonomy remained low, and budget cuts allowed few financial incentives. The civil service laws coupled with the Austrian bureaucracy's paternalistic traditions and fear of losing control allowed only a modest increase in personal autonomy. The Ministry of Education, Science, and Culture used its formal authority to try to bring about reform but faced much resistance. Nonetheless, as women's participation in Austrian universities increased, initiatives were necessary to incorporate gender equality measures into the reform process.

Managerialism: The Current Situation in Higher Education

As a result of more recent reforms, namely the University Act 2002 (Universitätsgesetz, 2002),[4] Austrian universities are undergoing far-reaching changes associated with managerialism, governance, and autonomy. Since 2004, each university has received a general budget and is expected to function like a private employer of staff. The internal university decision-making structures have also been significantly modified (Pellert, 2003) as universities have assumed authority for areas formally under the jurisdiction of the Ministry for Education, Science, and Culture. Consequently, instruments for advancing gender equality, such as performance contracts, and assessments of women's opportunities in teaching and research have been brought 'home' to the institution. In addition, universities are guided by legal regulations for equality, institutes for affirmative action, incentive programmes (prizes and financial rewards), and expectations for accountability. The UOG 2002 has also called for implementation of additional oversight and monitoring mechanisms that integrate a gender dimension.

Austrian universities are at the beginning of their managerial revolution. Administrative posts, such as rectorships, have been strengthened and new management posts have been created. The new managerialism presents an important opportunity to incorporate gender equality. Austrian universities must develop new organizational attitudes and processes associated with communities, teams, and projects in order for them to function as cohesive organizations instead of loosely coupled multiple individualized decision-making entities. Only with such a shift and an increase in accountability will there likely be an acknowledgement that organizations are gendered, and their processes and structures can create gender inequalities and equalities at the same time.

Core Problems for Women in Science and Research in Austria[5]

Status of Women

With the expansion of the educational system, more young women are gaining the general qualification for entering the higher education.[6] The concentration of women in the areas of business, economics, and secondary education in schools influences women's choices of study in universities. Female students predominate for first degrees in the humanities, social and economic sciences, and in veterinarian/human medicine but are under-represented in the disciplines of technology. For example, the rate of women among first-year students in the academic year 2001/2002 (Wroblewski et al., 2006) ranged from a vast majority of 86% in veterinary medicine and 77% in the humanities, to a majority of 67% in medicine, 63.5% in the natural sciences, 60.5% in law, and 52.7% in the social and economic sciences, with under-representation at 30.9% in technology.

Leaky Pipeline and Glass Ceiling as Part of the University Culture

As figure 5.1 shows, women have indeed caught up in terms of access to the university system; between 1990/1901 and 2002/2003, they constituted the majority of first-year students, master's students, and graduates. Nevertheless, women less frequently begin a doctoral thesis (Statistik Austria, 2004) and have a higher dropout rate than that of their male colleagues.

Few women are full professors. The probability of a woman becoming a university professor is considerably lower than it is for a male academic. In 2001, women's representation among those in habilitation was only 19.2%.[7] This indicates that change is coming slowly at the senior ranks where over a ten-year period women increased their representation to only 8% of the full professors at the scientific universities.[8] Moreover, a comparison of Austrian data with other EU nations shows that Austria has the lowest representation of female professors in natural sciences, engineering, and

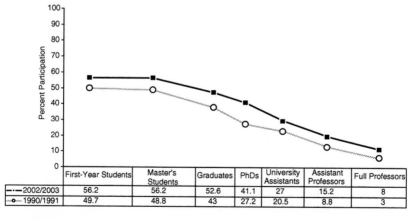

Figure 5.1 Representation of Women among Students and Academic Staff in Austrian Scientific Universities

Source: Statistik Austria (2004) *Hochschulstatistik (Higher Education statistics)*. Vienna: Verlag Österreich GmbH.

the social sciences. Only Belgium has a lower rate of female professors in the humanities, and Austria is in the midfield in medicine (European Commission, 2003).

Austrian universities' rigid career scheme with the required habilitation inhibits the career advancement of women. The habilitation, which scientists complete at the average age of 40, continues to be a prerequisite for a university career and must be completed within ten years. This professional obligation coincides with approximately the same time as women's age of childbearing and rearing. Thus, women are often faced with the burden of having to balance or to choose between meeting important personal (family) and professional obligations or opportunities. Moreover, women tend not to be promoted and supported to the extent that their male colleagues are while completing their habilitation theses. The pivotal phenomenon of *homosocial reproduction* (Kanter, 1977), or *male homosociability* (Witz & Savage, 1992), which suggests that men can and commonly do seek satisfaction for most of their needs from other men, is a highly relevant concept for understanding the persistence of the gender order in academia. Furthermore, Austria's conservative cultural and social traditions strongly influence gender discourses and attitudes that to do not support or empower the participation of women in the labour market and familial task sharing. Until such traditions become less consequential, accompanying adverse career consequences will exist for women and universities seeking the best scientific and research talent.

Austrian university cultures and career structures perpetuate a glass ceiling. Women students are accepted as recipients of university services, but the producers of these services, university scholars, continue principally to be men. Female students, regardless of their disciplines, find few female role models among the professoriate. In contrast, administrative staff members are overwhelmingly female except at the highest ranks. Despite the increasing number of female academic professionals, without strong proactive measures to achieve gender equality, a natural transformation from a male-dominated organization to a gender-balanced one will take at least several decades.

Measures to Advancement of Women

With the University Organization Acts, beginning in 1975 and culminating in 2002, gender mainstreaming has begun to take hold. Contributing to changes towards achieving gender equality are federal legislation; university policies and oversight; programmes, scholarships, and awards; national reports; gender-mainstreaming tools; and collaboration with business and industry.

Legislative Measures

During the 1990s, the Ministry of Education, Science, and Culture and the universities initiated several measures to promote equal opportunity. Legal procedures were implemented in 1990 to reach a balanced ratio between the number of male and female employees in both the ministry and universities. This goal was supported by implementation of affirmative measures, a ban on gender discrimination, a qualification-oriented quota system for admission to the federal service, and the appointment of persons and institutional units responsible for equal treatment matters.

The mid-1990s brought an increased effort to coordinate policy strategies. The *White Paper for the Promotion of Women in Science* (*Weißbuch zur Förderung von Frauen in der Wissenschaft*) (see Bundesministerium fürllissenschaft und Verhehr,

1999), for example, is a key programmatic document. Developed in 1999 by the Ministry of Science in cooperation with female experts from the university and non-university sectors, the *White Paper* contains measures and recommendations, some that already have been partially implemented, to increase the support, financial and otherwise, and to promote women as well as to improve the general conditions of science, research, and art. To reduce hidden and indirect discrimination, the *White Paper* considers preferential treatment, or positive discrimination, of disadvantaged women as indispensable.

The *White Paper* followed the Federal Government Equal Opportunities Act that since 1993 has provided protection from discrimination as well as regulations intended to advance women. Most importantly, it established a 40% target quota of women in all employment groups within federal agencies. This 40% target quota of women was integrated into the University Act 2002 with three salient measures:[9] (1) the equal treatment of women and men is considered a guiding principle of university policy; (2) each university must enact an affirmative action plan; and (3) each university must have an organizational unit to coordinate equal treatment and promotion of women and gender studies.

University Policies and Legal Regulations

Charged with counteracting gender-based discrimination at the university level, the Working Committee on Equal Treatment (Arbeitskreis für Gleichbehandlungsfragen) is at the core of the legal regulations of Austrian universities. Retaining its same basic structure since 1990, the Working Committee is entitled to participate in all employment-related procedures. For example, if sexual discrimination is presumed, the Working Committee has the right to raise an objection, in which case the respective employment procedure is interrupted as long as the responsible authorities deciding on the employment comply with the committee's objection. If the employment authority does not satisfactorily answer to the committee's objection, the University Act 2002 stipulates that the Working Committee has the authority to file a complaint with the Federal Ministry for Education, Science, and Culture, which gives an internal university arbitration commission the final say. That same act also calls for new measures, such as outputs, evaluation, and indicators, for which the gender dimension is to be integrated.

Programmes, Scholarships, and Awards to Promote Women

Several programmes, scholarships, and awards are in place to support women in research. In 1992, The Charlotte Bühler Fellowships for Habilitation[10] and the Hertha Firnberg Programme[11] were established to provide 12–36 months of financial support for women who are beginning their scientific careers, who have taken a childcare break, or who are completing the habilitation stage. In addition, the Austrian Program for Advanced Research and Technology (APART)[12] supports highly qualified young female and male scientists for three years to obtain further qualifications in a renowned research centre in Austria or abroad. Since 1997, in direct response to gender mainstreaming, the Gabriele Possaner Award has been awarded biannually for scientific efforts fostering gender democracy.[13]

The Ministry of Education, Science, and Culture and the European Social Fund are also sponsoring projects to support women gaining qualifications in science and research within and outside of the university. These include childcare (UNIKID)[14] through inexpensive, flexible, walk-in childcare facilities on or near campus with hours tailored to the special demands of teaching and research jobs. Moreover, Coordination Centres for Women's Studies and Gender Research in Universities are operating at six universities to improve the infrastructure for university agendas relating to women, including women's studies and gender research.[15]

Individual universities further assist women negotiating academic careers. The Mentoring Pilot Project for women writing dissertations and habilitation theses began at the University of Vienna in 2000–2003 to facilitate women's access to formal and informal networks and to support them in their transition to university work life.[16] Ten men and women mentors have advised 41 mentees at important stages of scientific qualification. Similarly, the Program for Correcting the Underrepresentation of Women includes both students and scientific staff at three universities in Graz. It targets improvements for women in the areas of education (training), personal development, organizational development, and compatibility of work and family. In 2004, this programme was integrated into university operations with a subsequent project, Potential II.

National Reports, Monitoring, and Rating

Several national activities monitor the integration of gender equity into university policy. The Minister of Education, Science, and Culture's *Women's Report 2002* to the federal chancellor provides information about the status of implementation of equal opportunities and the advancement of women.[17] Likewise, the Equal Opportunities Working Party annually reports its activities to the university council and the rectorate. In addition, since 2003, the Women's Political Advisory Board has advised the minister of Education, Science, and Culture on improvements and recommendations necessary to carry out regulations concerning gender-based discrimination and the advancement of women. The board has addressed the development and integration of measures to advance women into the governing instruments of the University Act of 2002, evaluation and quality assurance, higher education policy, sensitization measures, publicity and public relations, and ways to strengthen the legal implementation framework.[18]

Gender-Mainstreaming Policies and Tools

Following the European Union gender-mainstreaming approach, the Austrian Federal Ministry for Education, Science, and Culture has begun incorporating gender mainstreaming into its approaches to promoting women and equality policies. A pilot research project at the Federal Ministry of Education, Science, and Culture is designed to promote women's participation on research projects, strengthen research by, on, and for women, and create awareness of gender-specific topics in research and teaching. This project analyses funding procedures and the integration of gender criteria in current research programmes and selection procedures and has contributed to an increase of up to 50% women among project leaders, especially in extra-university research. Also, guidelines for science and research events are designed to enhance the visibility of female researchers and gender-specific research results by increasing the number of women as keynote speakers, moderators, and chairs and by intensifying gender-specific topics in seminars, workshops, and research venues. These projects at the ministerial level set an important example of promoting gender equity and improving women's status and participation in the universities.

Initiatives to Promote Women in Industrial Research and Business

Many programmes and measures target the cooperation and the knowledge transfer between science/research and industry. All state-agency-initiated or funded programmes and measures are to be gender mainstreamed. Because women are greatly under-represented in the occupational segments of intensive research and technology, especially in management positions, such initiatives as FEMtech, or Women in Research and Technology, have been designed specifically to promote women by improving access to the profession and career opportunities. FEMtech is an initiative to promote women by funding the development and the implementation of measures to improve equal opportunities within the fFORTE framework.[19]

The Impulse Project

Researchers for the Economy targets university graduates from all technical disciplines and employees of Austrian enterprises employing up to 500 persons. The goals of the Impulse Project are (1) to improve the transfer of knowledge from Austrian universities and enterprises; (2) to increase the number of Austrian enterprises focussing on research and development; (3) to promote young researchers by helping them to acquire key economic competency skills; (4) to increase the proportion of women in research and development; and (5) to create additional research positions in Austria for researchers who are working abroad.[20]

To promote entrepreneurship, the University Graduate Start-Up Enterprises (UNIUN) programme allows university graduates to acquire the necessary skills for entrepreneurship by offering qualification modules and coaching. The goal is to raise awareness among university graduates of entrepreneurship as a career alternative. Fifty percent of the places are reserved for women, and some seminars are offered exclusively to women to help them tackle women-specific challenges in entrepreneurship.[21]

Challenges

Although the aforementioned programmes, initiatives, scholarships, and awards assist women in their academic careers in tangible ways, their impact is limited to the number of women they are able to serve. For changes in gender equity to be sweeping, laws and policies governing gender mainstreaming must be embraced equally by both the state and university policy makers. Austria is making gains in this area. However, it lags behind its counterparts in the European Union, so considerably more work is required to realize the benefits of gender mainstreaming in higher education.

Conclusion

The conservative cultural and social context of Austria and the deeply held tradition of individuality in the Humboldtian university have caused Austria to start further behind some EU nation-states in incorporating gender mainstreaming. There is hardly another sector in Austria, however, where the gender ratio has changed as significantly as it has at the university level owing to the unintended but substantial increase in women's participation with the expansion of the tertiary sector. Although women have outnumbered men entering university study programmes since the early 1990s, a closer look indicates that subtle exclusion mechanisms have had lasting effects upon women's attainment of equality in the university system. Leading positions remain male-dominated, and fewer female employees work at the higher rungs of the career ladder.

Nevertheless, the timing and substantial changes legislated by the University Act 2002 have made gender equality one of several strategic changes experienced within higher education. The legal provisions of the University Act 2002 will shape the strategies of equality change if a significant proportion of university members realize that the improved integration of women is integral to university reform. The recent reform measures have begun to change institutional perceptions. For example, universities are called to view gender equality not only as a legal mandate but as an institutional and innovative strategy as well. In this sense, universities are called upon to take ownership of affirmative action rather than to treat it as an intrusion.

Gender mainstreaming must be fully merged into policies and practices so that top university leaders continue to be held accountable for their institutional outcomes and to personally hold others accountable for reform. Their leadership can be a catalyst for cultural change by actively supporting the recruitment and mentoring of women in scientific careers. Moreover, because women are latecomers in the university system and have often been socialized differently from men, they bring experiences and perceptions of university work that tend to differ from the status quo. Thus, women's experiences and perceptions may be of great value to universities as they attempt to innovate, especially when the old perceptions, attitudes, and experiences are not suited to cope with new challenges. These possibilities can best become realities when more universities recognize that success in increasing the representation of women at all levels is an important condition for meeting Austria's needs.

Notes

1. In 2004, the population of Austria was 8, 171, 244. At that time, Austria had 12 scientific universities and 7 universities of arts. As a result of the implementation of University Act 2004, the number of universities increased to 21.
2. The Council of the European Union agreed in Barcelona in 2002 on objectives to support the achievement of the Lisbon Goals (2000). The Lisbon Goals aim at the reorganization of the European Union until 2010 into the 'most competitive and dynamic knowledge-based economic area of the world who is capable to reach continuing growth, full employment, and broader und coherence'.
3. As in many other European countries, marriage rates are declining and the rates of cohabitations are increasing. Currently, 43 of 100 legal marriages will culminate in divorce in Austria. Sixteen percent of the Austrian families are single parents; most of them single mothers. See http://www.statistik.at.
4. University Act 2002, http://www.bmbwk.gv.at/start.asp?bereich=7&OID=4327&l1=1101&l2=1108&l3=4256. Accessed 22 August 2006.
5. The following section is based on the research carried out during the project *Evaluation of Measures for the Promotion of Women in Science and Research in Austria* (Wroblewski et al., 2005).

6. Usually, a general qualification for university entrance (*Matura*) is achieved after passing the final exam of a comprehensive secondary school (*Allgemeinbildende Höhere Schule or Gymnasium*) or a school providing vocational education (*Berufsbildende Höhere Schule*).
7. Habilitation is a qualification step consisting of an advanced scientific publication (elaborating on perennial research) and a final hearing in order to be formally allowed to apply for a professorship. Although now formally abolished, habilitation is still the main prerequisite of becoming a professor.
8. The combined rate of female professors at the scientific universities and universities of arts reached 11.6% in 2003 (Statistik Austria, 2004) due to greater female representation in music and the arts. The Austrian University system differentiates between scientific universities (social sciences, humanities, law, medicine, engineering, natural sciences, etc.) and the universities of arts (universities for applied and visual arts and for music).
9. http://www.bmbwk.gv.at/medienpool/8019/8019_ug02_engl.pdf.
10. http://www.fwf.ac.at/de/projects/buehler.html.
11. http://www.fwf.ac.at/de/projects/firnberg.html.
12. http://www.oeaw.ac.at/stipref/info/1_stipendien/apart/11_apart-stipendien.html and http://www.oeaw.ac.at/stipref/n_info/1_stipendien/apart_extra/apart_extra.html.
13. http://www.bmbwk.gv.at/forschung/frauen/foerderung/poss_fp_ausschr_2003.xml.
14. The offices are supported by the UNIKID, a Web-based information and exchange system for members of the university community who have children. For details, visit http://www.unikid.at.
15. e.g., http://www.gendup.sbg.ac.at.
16. http://www.univie.ac.at/frauenfoerderung.
17. http://www.bmbwk.gv.at/forschung/frauen/fber.xml.
18. http://www.bmbwk.gv.at/universitaeten/kontakte/Frauenpolitischer_Beirat9901.xml.
19. http://www.femtech.at/index.php?id=133.
20. www.fwf.ac.at/de/projects/impuls.html.
21. http://www.uniun.at/.

References

Bast, G. (1990) Ordinarienuniversität, Gruppenuniversität – und weiter? In *BMWF: Universitäts-Management.* Wien: Federal Ministry for Science and Research (Bundesministerium für Wissenschaft und Forschung).

Bundesministerium für Wissenschaft und Verkehr (1999) *White paper for the promotion of women in science* (*Weißbuch zur Förderung von Frauen in der Wissenschaft*). Wien: Federal Ministry for Education and Traffic (Bundesministerium für Wissenschaft und Verkehr).

European Commission (2003) *She figures: Women and science.* Retrieved from http:// europa.eu.int/comm/research/science-society/pdf/she_figures_2003.pdf. Accessed 22 August 2006.

Höllinger, S. (1992) *Universität ohne Heiligenschein. Aus dem 19. ins 21. Jahrhundert.* Vienna: Passagen Verlag.

Kanter, R. M. (1977) *Men and women of the corporation.* Cambridge: Basic Books.

Neave, G., & Rhoades, G. (1987) The academic estate in Western Europe. In B.C. Clark (Ed.), *The academic profession: National, disciplinary and institutional settings* (pp. 211–270). Berkeley: University of California Press.

OECD (Organization for Economic and Cooperative Development) (2003) *Education at a glance: OECD Indicators 2003.* Paris: OECD Publishing.

Pechar, H., & Pellert, A. (2004) Austrian universities under pressure from Bologna. *European journal of education, 39*(3): 317–330.

Pellert, A. (2003) *Das UG 02 und seine Auswirkungen auf Personalentwicklung und Frauenförderung.* BUKO (Hochschulpolitische Informationen der Bundeskonferenz des wissenschaftlichen und künstlerischen Personals) 03/I-4. Vienna, pp. 28–31.

Statistik Austria (2004) *Hochschulstatistik (Higher education statistics)*. Vienna: Verlag Österreich GmbH.

Universitätsgesetz (2002) http://www.bmbwk.gv.at/start.asp?bereich=7&OID=4327&!1= 1101=1108&13=4256. Retrieved 22 August 2006.

Welan, M. (1995) The new university organisation or the third organisational reform since 1945. In A. Pellert & W. Manfried (Eds.), *The formed anarchy: The challenge of the university organisation* (pp. 113–124). Vienna: WUV-Universitätsverlag.

Witz, A., & Savage, M. (Eds.) (1992) *Gender and bureaucracy*. Oxford: Blackwell.

Wroblewski, A., Gindl, M., Leitner, A., Pellert, A., Woitech, B., Lassnigg, L., & Polt, W. (2006) *Evaluation of measures for the promotion of women in science and research in Austria*. Project report. Vienna: Federal Ministry for Education, Science and Culture (Bundesministerium für Bildung, Wissenschaft und Kultur).

CHAPTER SIX

UNIVERSITY ADAPTATION AND GENDER EQUALITY: A CASE STUDY OF THE VIENNA UNIVERSITY OF ECONOMICS AND BUSINESS ADMINISTRATION

Barbara Sporn

In 2002, the Austrian Board of Ministers integrated gender mainstreaming into its national policies (as noted by Pellert and Grindl in chapter 5 of this book). The adaptation of Austrian universities to gender mainstreaming cannot, however, be adequately understood by tracing the implementation of a single policy or institutional adaptation to a single external force because the integration of gender mainstreaming converged with the University Act 2002 (Universitätsgesetz, 2002), which granted full autonomy to higher education institutions and generated considerable change in internal decision-making structures.

In order to analyse how a national policy is translated into an institutional strategy, this chapter focusses on a single case study of one higher education institution, the Vienna University of Economics and Business Administration (in German, Wirtschaftsuniversität Wien, or WU). The major questions for this chapter are as follows:

- How have gender-mainstreaming policies been translated into institutional realities?
- How has the representation of women changed within the institution?
- What forces account for the changes?

Before addressing these questions, let us briefly review some of the most relevant literature on the topic of adaptation to understand the complexity of universities responding to multiple challenges. Then we will move on to introduce the methodology used to develop the case study.

Theoretical Background and Methodology

The concept of adaptation has drawn from different theories of resource dependence, political economy, natural selection, contingency approaches, open system, institutional isomorphism, and so forth (Gumport & Sporn, 1999; Sporn, 1999). To analyse issues in higher education, it is important to keep in mind that universities are very much embedded in and vulnerable to their environments. This idea was developed early on by scholars such as Victor Baldridge (Baldridge et al., 1977), Karl Weick (1976), and Burton Clark (1983). They remind us not to view institutions of higher education as isolated entities but as organizations with blurred boundaries and strong ties to their institutional environments. One might even argue that it is exactly this characteristic of universities and colleges that has made them one of the oldest organizations in the world.

Starting with this environmental vulnerability, theories of adaptation have primarily used contingency and institutional approaches to address the issue of success or failure of adaptation (Meyer & Rowan, 1992; Meyer, Scott, & Deal, 1992; Scott, 1992). Hence, empirical evidence has shown that universities either imitate each other when it comes to environmental pressure, or they need some crisis or external threat to incite the process of change in the first place (DiMaggio & Powell, 1983; Hackman, 1985; Tolbert, 1985). Research in the areas of creating entrepreneurial universities and adaptive university structures seems most relevant for this chapter.

Burton Clark, a renowned sociologist and higher education expert, has focussed much of his latest work to organizational transformation inside universities, especially European institutions (1998) and most recently universities worldwide (2004). Revisiting his 'factors' of entrepreneurial universities reveals the comprehensive nature of his work on university transformation: a strengthened steering core, an extended developmental periphery, an entrepreneurial culture, a discretionary funding base, and a stimulated heartland (2004, p. 6).

Clark's writing is intriguing because he draws helpful conclusions from very few cases (March, Sproull, & Tamuz, 1991). In his understanding, a *strengthened steering core* implies a model of leadership and administration that is able to manage the institution effectively with modern management tools and at the same time find an alignment with core academic values. An *extended developmental periphery* responds to the needs of many universities and colleges to cross the boundaries of institutions in order to create new entrepreneurial activities, such as technology transfer units. The *entrepreneurial culture* suggests the notion of a value system that rewards individual initiative and stresses the will to change. The *discretionary funding base* forms the foundation for creating entrepreneurial institutions. Through these funds, new initiatives can be financed without being too dependent on one sponsor. In a sense, this independence makes institutions more agile and flexible. Finally, Clark presents the *stimulated heartland*. Academic departments provide core activities in teaching and research – this is the heartland. Once a university is able to create an invigorated atmosphere where traditional values are merged with new administrative capacities and outreach mentality, the university can thrive.

Clark's work has been well received by many scholars of higher education whose interest focusses on critical questions of transformation and sustainability of entrepreneurial universities (Shattock, 2000; Slaughter & Leslie, 1997). However, nowhere in his work does Clark talk about questions of access or gender equality. Still one can assume that with a growing need and pressure from the outside world, universities will begin to change in this direction as well. For example, the European policy of gender mainstreaming is already being received by many institutions of higher education. Most likely, the policy will create a demand-response imbalance and in that way trigger a change process. In this sense, Clark's work can be helpful in understanding what makes universities change and what it takes to start them moving in the right direction.

Clark (2004) has continued his work to include other institutions of higher education from around the world. Again, he uses case studies to depict the many pathways of transformation. It is interesting to note that institutional autonomy and entrepreneurial activity seem to dominate much of the discourse. The state-market dichotomy is resolved by including the institution itself as a very important player. This aspect will also be used for the case study of Vienna University of Economics and Business Administration.

Based on six case studies, a second empirical work by Sporn (1999) analysed adaptive universities structures comparing three European and three U.S. universities. The results show six major factors that influence adaptation to changing socio-economic environments: committed leadership, shared governance, professional management, clear mission, differentiated structure, and entrepreneurial culture. Change happens due to either a crisis or a realization of opportunity by the institution.

- *Committed leadership* refers to the notion that most policies and strategies will be implemented successfully only if the institutional leaders are firmly convinced of their need and dedicate the necessary resources to implement them.
- *Shared governance* emphasizes the importance of faculty involvement during periods of change and adaptation. As Clark (1998) pointed out, the 'heartland' refers to academics being as convinced of institutional transformation as administrators are.
- *Professional management* implements decisions made by leaders and faculty alike. Experienced professionals move the institution forward in the adaptation process.
- In order to focus on the institution, it is necessary to develop a *clear vision and mission* for the institution and orient it in the direction of the aspired change.
- *Differentiated structure* responds to environmental pressures coming from many different directions and enables the institution to respond flexibly to different stakeholders.
- The *entrepreneurial culture* stresses the importance of values and norms that expand activities beyond teaching and research and help both the institution and the individual.

For this chapter, the use of these two pieces of research is critical. Factors most relevant for the interest in equality and change issues will be used to analyse their implementation at the Vienna University of Economics and Business Administration: committed leadership, differentiated structure, professional management, clear mission and goals, and discretionary funding. Shared governance and entrepreneurial culture seem to be less important for the question at stake in this chapter.

Case study research has often been used to capture more in-depth evidence for change processes and outcomes, to illustrate and enrich a theory, and to contribute to the development of new knowledge (Yin, 1994). Accordingly, this chapter is based on a single case study of one institution of higher education in Austria. Conclusions are drawn mainly from policy documents, conversations with university members, personal experiences, secondary data, and statistical information. Generalizations from this single case can develop only slowly, yet informative 'stories' still assist in theory development as Clark (2004) comments on the value of casework to study university change:

> The reality of university change comes in very detailed items – in complicated governance structures, multiplying streams of income, a changing array of base units that stake out different academic territories, a developing set of contradictory beliefs. Without some footing in the intermingled details of inescapable features, analysis readily slips into soggy unanalyzed abstractions, easily contested conclusions appropriate for detached theorizing and commencement-day speeches. The truth is in the details, the details of university infrastructure and the accretion of small changes that cumulatively lead to major change. Specifying change in specific sites is what gives credence to any induced generalizations. (p. 6)

This chapter focusses on details of gender equality and university change at one large and specialized university. Gender mainstreaming, as a policy imperative (and as described by Pellert and Gindl in chapter 5 of this book), forms the basis for understanding the trigger for change not only at the Austrian legislative level but also at the institutional level of many Austrian universities. The following section provides one closer look at the Vienna University of Economics and Business Administration.

The University Background

The Vienna University of Economics and Business Administration (WU) is the second largest university in Austria. It is noteworthy that WU is a specialized institution and still has a large number of students. As most recent statistics show (Statistisches Taschenbuch, 2004), WU enrolled 20,134 students in the winter semester of 2003 followed by the comprehensive University of Graz (19,741 students) and University of Innsbruck (19,363 students) yet far fewer than the largest higher education institution, the University of Vienna (58,758 students). Based upon its student enrolment, WU is the largest business and economics university in Europe.

WU enrolment accounts for 10.5% of all Austrian students, and about 20.8% of WU's enrolments are international students. Most students study either business administration or commerce. The university also offers master's degree programme in economics, business education, and a baccalaureate in information systems.

Regarding female representation in different groups, WU shows a standard picture: 47.5% of all newly enrolled students are women, and 49% women are graduates of one year. Female graduates from PhD studies amount to 33%. At the level of assistant professors, 39.5% are women, and at full professor, 7.8% are female. In administration, 77.6% are women.

WU is mostly a publicly financed institution. In 2004, WU's budget amounted to about 67 million Euros. This includes for the first time the tuition of WU students of approximately 10 million Euros. The state allocates more than 95% of the budget in a lump sum, and the university is relatively free to shift resources between personnel and other categories. More than two-thirds of the budget, however, is spent on salaries.

Staff at WU includes faculty and administration as well as a large number of adjunct professors. In 2004, the university employed 400 full-time equivalent faculty members. Of those, 78 were full professors, 60 were associate professors, and 362 were assistant professors. Some 323 persons worked in the administrative area. Adjunct professors who teach only one or two courses per year account for 600 persons.

WU is a public university committed to educating a large proportion of the Austrian population. Whereas research is an integral part of the university's mission, continuing education and other outreach activities are becoming increasingly important for WU.

The Institutional Autonomy and Planning Shift within a Competitive Market

Since the early 1990s, Austrian higher education system has been changing substantially. Through required budget reforms, revised notions of public management, and the overall trends within the European Union (especially the Bologna Declaration), the Austrian government initiated a change in its policy for all publicly administrated units, including higher education.

In the summer of 2002, Parliament approved a new University Act that culminated the legislative reform process. Earlier, the introduction of (moderate) tuition and the establishment of vocational colleges (*Fachhochschulen*) as well as private universities created a competitive and differentiated market for higher education.

Although the Austrian system has been moving towards competition and markets in the tertiary educational sector, one crucial aspect has been sacred – open access. In responding to a 2005 EU court decision that international and national students must be treated equally for admissions, Austria has had to limit the number of student openings through entrance examinations or selection processes during the course of study in eight high demand areas including medicine, pharmacy, psychology, and biology. *Fachhochschulen*, on the contrary, can select their students, a procedure that has been viewed as a distorted form of competition in Austria. For example, a dynamic developed where students' first preference for enrolment was at the lower-ranked *Fachhochschulen*, and only if they were rejected would they study at universities.

The new University Act 2002 has several important features, such as institutional autonomy, performance contracts and measurement, global budgets, and revised leaner organizational and governance structures (described by Pellert and Gindl in chapter 5 of this book). The most relevant for this case study of WU are changes that had to be implemented by January 1, 2004, in the areas of internal governance and implementation of a Working Group for Equal Opportunity (Arbeitskreise für Gleichbehandlung), which has been equipped with a considerable amount of power and influence over the university decisions.

Most importantly, the new law has granted full institutional autonomy. WU formerly functioned as a ministry subsidiary; now it is an independent legal entity operating with a governing board (*Universitätsrat*). Boards have been formed for each institution. Half of the board members are appointed by the ministry and half by the institution. Board members must come from outside the respective university and should not work in the Ministry of Education, Science, and Culture in Austria. The board of WU consists of five members – four men and one woman.

The board appoints the rector, approves the budget, and comments on all strategic initiatives of the institutions. The rector has a team of vice-rectors in charge of different key functional areas of the university (finance, infrastructure, research and teaching, IT, development, etc.). The power of this leadership team (*Rektorat*) increased after the reform. The *Rektorat*'s responsibilities range from organization and strategy to employment and finances. This body is also directly accountable to the board and is responsible for implementing strategies of gender equality at the institution.

The senate has decreased in size and power with the University Act 2002. Previously, it had full representation of all professors and the authority to decide on all issues, including budget and personnel. Like other Austrian universities, senates now have between 12 and 24 members representing the different disciplinary areas. Full professors form the half of the votes, and students occupy 25% of the seats. The remaining 25% are shared by associate and assistant professors as well as administrators. A member of the equal opportunity working group is always present at senate meetings. The senate's main responsibilities include deciding on university by-laws (*Satzung*), announcing and recommending three candidates for the rector's position, dealing with curricular issues and academic programmes, and independently deciding to discontinue existing studies or create new programmes as needed. The *Rektorat*, however, approves financing for programmes, so a close working relationship between the *Rektorat* and senate creates the most efficient climate in which to manage change among the Austrian universities.

One additional important feature of the University Act 2002 concerns global budgets and performance contracts. Departing from past practices, the Ministry of Education, Science, and Culture decided to grant universities 'global budgets' as lump sums to be spent freely depending on specific institutional needs and strategies. Traditional categories of personnel, literature, and material have been abolished, which has helped institutions become more flexible. At the same time, measurements for accountability have been created, such as a required yearly performance report as well as the introduction of performance contracts and performance funding.

These changes indicate that the power has shifted from the state to the institution and institutional leadership. In addition, governance and management have become much leaner and more concentrated in a couple of important groups, mainly the *Rektorat*, the senate, and the university board. This comprehensive restructuring through the University Act 2002 put Austria ahead of higher education reform in Europe (Titscher & Höllinger, 2003, 2004). For example, before the legislation, Austria had a more traditional model of higher education with strong organization at the state level and powerful chaired positions at the institution. With the new legislation, the component of leadership and strategy of university management have been empowered with all the necessary tools for flexibility (e.g., global budgets and autonomy). Compared to Germany, Switzerland, many of the Central European countries, and Southern Europe, this change can be considered quite innovative.

In order to implement the University Act 2002, WU had to develop a strategy (*Entwicklungsplan*) that defines a distinctive institutional profile and future directions. This document forms the basis for performance contracts with the Ministry of Education, Science, and Culture. Beginning in 2007, 20% of the public budget will be assigned based on the performance goals. These contracts will be critical instruments in promoting policies important to the ministry. One of those priorities is to provide equal opportunities for women. The ministry has already communicated clear goals for increasing the number of women in all functions at the university. Hence, WU has had to define clear goals of equality. In this sense, 'imposed' policies of equality by the ministry are turned into institutional strategies of affirmative action in order to be successful in resource allocation. The following section of this chapter focusses on this aspect.

Gender Equality and Affirmative Action at Wirtschaftsuniversität Wien

In order to describe gender equality and affirmative action at WU, figure 6.1 shows how the participation of women has changed over a ten-year period (1993–2003). WU has shown some notable improvements. In 1993, 41% of those who studied at WU were women. In 2003, the percentage increased by more than 6% to 47.5%. At the level of graduates, 40% of all graduating students at WU were woman compared to 49% in 2003. Female graduates from PhD studies changed from 23% in 1993 to 33% in 2003.

At the level of academic staff, WU showed similar improvements. In 1996, the university had 2.7% women as full professors, 4.8% as associate professors, and 29% as assistant professors. By 2003, those numbers had increased to 7.8% as full professors, 15.5% as associate professors, and 39.5% as assistant professors.

The following section gives a more detailed picture of comparative data. Unfortunately, through many changes in reporting standards, data from a longer-term perspective are hard to retrieve. Hence, the focus will lie on the last five years, i.e., 1999–2003.

Austrian legislation concerning equality for women requires the university to publish yearly reports on their gender activities and to report to the senate or a subcommittee about the implementation of affirmative action measures at the respective universities. According to the Equal Opportunity Law of 1993, universities need to develop strategies to reach a 40% representation of women in administrative and academic positions. On top of that, special policies have to be implemented to support women who look for an academic career (*Frauenbericht, Gleichbehandlungsgesetz*).

The yearly report has a specific format covering the following areas: employment in different categories, visiting professors, termination of employment, career paths, specific academic courses, support activities, and research collaboration. Because the affirmative action goal is that 40% of the staff should be women, the following subgoals have been defined:

- If one category has 0% women, then the percentage needs to be increased to 5%.
- If the representation of women lies below 10%, then the percentage needs to be doubled.
- If the representation of women lies above 10%, the percentage needs to be increased by 20%.

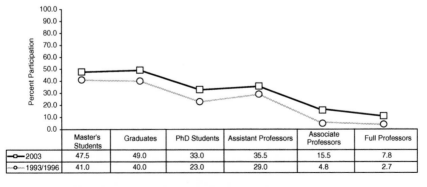

	Master's Students	Graduates	PhD Students	Assistant Professors	Associate Professors	Full Professors
2003	47.5	49.0	33.0	35.5	15.5	7.8
1993/1996	41.0	40.0	23.0	29.0	4.8	2.7

Figure 6.1 Representation of Women among Students and Academic Staff at the Vienna University of Economics and Business Administration

Source: Internal statistics from the Vienna University of Economics and Business Administration.

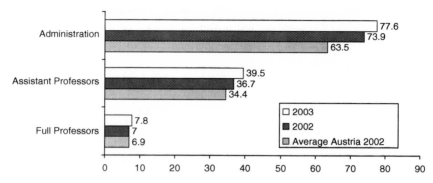

Figure 6.2 Representation of WU Women within Different Staff Categories, 2002–2003
Source: Internal statistics from the Vienna University of Economics and Business Administration.

In 2002, for the first time, representation of women at WU was higher than the Austrian average of 28%. As is shown in figure 6.2, WU improved women representation among full professors (+11%), assistant professor (+8%), and administration (+5%). Overall, 35% of all academic staff members were women.

The distribution among the different WU faculties gives a diverse picture for the representation of women. In 2003, the largest Faculty of Business Administration had the fewest women at 27.8% whereas the Faculty of Social and Formal Sciences and Humanities showed the highest representation of women at 43.6%. The Faculty of Law had good representation of women at the assistant professor level (43.2%), but there were no women at the level of full professor in 2003. The Faculty of Economics came closest to the WU average of 35% with 33.3% women.

Compared to the overall policy of reaching a representation of 40% women for all public offices, WU reached that goal in only one area in 2003: 39.5% of assistant professors were women. Associate female professors were 15.5%, which was also above the Austrian average of 14.4%. However, at the level of full professors, much work still needs to be done. Only 7.6% of that rank were women (Austrian average is 6.9%).

At the level of administration, WU is also above average when it comes to representation of women: 77.6% of all administrators are women (Austrian average 63.5%). Nevertheless, women holding leadership positions is also rare at WU. Only 6% of heads of departments or institutes are women (Austrian average 5.4%). In contrast, heads of administrative units are at a level of 32% women (Austrian average 24.3%). WU had one female vice-rector. The low representation of women is much greater in the academic realm than it is in the administrative area.

After this overview of recent trends at WU, it is necessary to turn to the most important policies for gender equality. With the new University Act 2002, all institutions are required to observe an affirmative action plan. Accordingly, WU approved an Affirmative Action Plan (*Frauenförderungsplan*) as part of its by-laws in 2004. The following describes the major parts of this plan.

WU's Major Policies for Gender Equality: The Affirmative Action Plan

Women at WU predominate in academic and administrative positions at lower levels, such as assistant professor and service units. A higher number of female professors work in the area of language and communication studies, economics, and sociology. WU's affirmative action plan focusses on the role of women in society and acknowledges the need to treat men and women equally. This plan corresponds with WU's policy of equal opportunity in issues of personnel/staff, research and teaching, and, perhaps most importantly, the allocation of resources. Persons in leadership positions are responsible for implementing this general policy.

Affirmative action at WU includes the preparation of students as potential faculty members. The plan calls for specific role models to be offered to students in order to make an academic career more attractive and for research and teaching to be organized for and completed equally by men and women. WU wants to provide equal conditions to men and women for research, teaching, and lifelong learning as well as personal development.

Consequently, special attention is given to financial incentives. The plan specifies that activities that lead to legal and personal equality are to be rewarded financially. Accordingly, the distribution of budgets for institutes and departments takes representation of women into consideration. In addition, funding for research and teaching recognizes the advancement in equal rights and the position of women at WU. For example, individual departments receive 5% of their annual budgets based on the number of women working at each respective academic unit and 5% based on research and teaching output.

After these more general principles, the plan defines specific goals that need to be respected under all circumstances:

- Equal opportunity – women are equal partners on all hierarchical levels. Access to every position should be open at all times.
- Gender mainstreaming – the principles of gender mainstreaming are observed in all decisions made at WU.
- Affirmative action for women at WU – the work of women (ranging from female students to full professors) should be especially supported. Enhancing research productivity increases the number of assistant professors, research projects, and promotions of women in general.
- Abolishment of under-representation – WU is committed to address under-representation of women in all positions and hierarchical levels.
- Avoidance of discrimination – WU is also committed to avoid all discrimination of students or employees at the university.
- Workspace – the working environment for all employees at WU must permit the combination of work and life as well as the dignity of the person. This includes preventive measures against sexual and other forms of harassment of women at WU.
- Information – internal information and communication regarding equality for women and men is seen as an integral part for implementing any type of affirmative action policy.
- Infrastructure – securing an adequate infrastructure guarantees the realization of equality and affirmative action for women at WU. For example, complaints may be filed with the Working Group for Equal Opportunity, and assistance for the resolution of conflicts is provided by special councils.

As this plan shows, WU developed an elaborate set of goals that are intended to be addressed over the next couple of years. To meet these goals, they must be integrated into the performance contracts to be implemented in 2006. WU already defined under-representation as the representation of women at any hierarchical level under 40%. The university wants to reach this goal within a long-term perspective. More specifically, its policies address information, research, and teaching as well as infrastructure, organization, and governance.

The information policy includes the use of gender-neutral language, the use of a separate site for all gender-relevant information on the university website, the integration of gender issues in all public relations of the university, and the information regarding all relevant legal regulations that could be useful to the WU community. The major offices, such as the Working Group for Equal Opportunity and the contact persons, must be easily identified on the web. This information policy also includes the obligation to collect continuous data on women's representation and salary levels within the university (e.g., faculty, administration, students, adjuncts, visitors).

In the area of research, WU's plan to establish a distinct research agenda has led to the creation of a chair for Gender and Diversity in Organization within the Faculty of Business Administration using state funds. The Ministry of Education, Science, and Culture funded this proposal because it fit with the overall gender-mainstreaming policy in higher education, and the addition of the chair added to the profile of WU. As the data earlier in this chapter showed, women have the lowest representation in the Business Faculty.

Apart from a professorship for gender studies, WU's affirmative action plan specifies that gender-specific research is as valuable for promotion eligibility as any other area of research. Promotions under the plan also include new hires and promotions to the tenure position. Gender issues include all topics that specifically focus on the historical and recent social role of women as well as those that address the relationship between men and women. Gender-sensitive research is also considered favourable in any decision on resource allocation. An even distribution of monies is considered in all research-support activities at WU under the affirmative action plan.

In the area of teaching and academic programmes, gender-specific courses and lectures are integral part of WU. For example, the offer of semester-long series exploring women's issues was established more than ten years ago and has become a well-regarded tradition at WU. The aforementioned professor for Gender and Diversity in Organizations is responsible for developing all relevant curricula. Apart from that, other academic programmes should ideally include gender-specific courses as well at both the compulsory and elective levels of course offerings. In order to guarantee this inclusion, the Working Group for Equal Opportunity has the right to comment on the development of any new curriculum.

Personnel issues and organizational development must also address gender to increase the percentage of women at the university. Observing gender mainstreaming, WU has implemented instruments to support research by women, female junior faculty, and continuing education and qualification. In addition, hiring according to international affirmative action standards plays a very important role in favouring women among candidates who are equally qualified. For example, job announcements specifically encourage women to apply – standard practice at many international universities – which indicates a proactive search for women. These strategies and activities are enhanced at WU by naming a member of the Working Group to every search and promotion committee to ensure that a sufficient number of applications are received for every position.

WU also promotes mentoring in order to support equal opportunities for women. For instance, heads of departments and institutes are asked to observe a mentoring function. Their responsibilities include systematic training in aspects of professional academics, such as organizational and social introductions and career planning. Mentoring is also offered in the form of continuing education for women, requiring sufficient resources to be assigned to this area. For all offers of employment as academic staff, women have preferred access until the 40% female representation is reached. Junior female faculty are not only encouraged to pursue an academic career but are also given special attention. Nevertheless, the success of such policies lies primarily in the hands of full professors as department chairs because the university leadership provides only incentives, such as budget allocations, to increase awareness and to motivate departments to promote women.

From a governance perspective, all decisions on promotion and tenure necessitate consultation with the Working Group for Equal Opportunities. Furthermore, all committees should have female members. Based on the principles of gender mainstreaming, the Working Group for Equal Opportunities has the right to be part of all committees that deal with personnel issues and to veto any decision.

In addition to promotion and hiring, working conditions create special concerns for women. Work hours that account for family obligations, childcare, and kindergarten, as well as actions against sexual harassment must be installed in order for jobs to be attractive to women in the first place. Even though paid leave before and after birth is a standard policy, enough time must be reserved for a proper re-entry into work. WU has taken three significant steps to meet these needs. First, the university sponsors a kindergarten as a childcare facility and regularly evaluates it. Quite popular in the university community, this facility is used mostly by young female professors who rely on it as an asset allowing them to continue their academic careers. Second, WU provides a special leave programme for women who aspire to a tenured position. Such women may take up to one year's paid leave from teaching to concentrate exclusively on their research. Nearly ten women have already profited from this programme and have been promoted to the level of associate professor. Third, to provide protection against sexual harassment, the university offers a hotline and an office to which women may submit their complaints and receive appropriate help and advice. All department heads and other leaders are obliged to watch for and ensure that no sexual harassment occurs within the university. The Working Group for Equal Opportunities also steps in when incidents occur by reporting them to university leadership and taking other necessary actions to resolve the issue.

The structural arrangements for equal opportunity and women rights are prerequisite to long-term changes at each university. The rights and agenda of the Working Group for Equal Opportunities are defined by the Equal Opportunity Plan for Women (Frauenförderungsplan). This group can call for legal counsel should any form of discrimination occur at the university. The Working Group also runs an office that gives administrative support for all activities on equality, especially legal and personnel advice. In addition to the efforts of the Working Group, WU is building a strong network with other offices at Austrian universities in order to learn and exchange experiences. Additionally, contact persons (Kontaktfrauen) are installed for advising and counselling. Primarily, these advisers are women already working for the university who volunteer for the positions. Two contact persons working for WU are women who have been with the university for a number of years; one as an assistant in the office of the Working Group for Equal Opportunities representing administrative staff and the other as associate professor representing academic staff.

For the above initiatives in gender equity to succeed, instruments must exist that govern budget and resource allocation, reward systems, and incentives. WU's budget allocation process takes gender mainstreaming into consideration. As mentioned earlier, part of the budget (5%) is allocated to institutes and departments according to the share of women on the staff of the respective unit. This has been a very contested but effective instrument to foster discussion and implement incentives to support women. The argument critical of this allocation is that hiring and promotion should be based on qualifications rather than gender; however, this argument obscures the notion of promoting based on qualification and gender simultaneously, a neglected practice that has facilitated the need for policies of gender equity in the first place. The university leadership has persisted in keeping this allocation in place for several years. As a next step, it will give even more attention to the number of doctorates and promotions to tenure (Habilitation) by women. A yearly report of this indicator will be required for the performance contract with the ministry.

Reporting systems ensure that equality of women is well documented. The plan includes regulations for reporting numbers of women in departments and institutes as well as the university as a whole. This reporting system differentiates between research and teaching and the amount spent in each category. Each year the report describes how far the university has come in implementing the policies described above. The 40% rule is always kept in sight as a goal for the near future. Personnel and organizational development have to be constantly revised in order to institutionalize the principles of gender mainstreaming. All reports need to be publicly available either on the Web or in printed form. The Working Group for Equal Opportunities receives all relevant copies for their records.

Critical Review of Current Strategies

The university's plan for affirmative action shows that WU has developed a comprehensive set of policies to reduce gender inequality for women at the university. Even though not all of the policies have been successfully implemented, those that are in place have proven to be effective overall. In this last section, strategies will be reviewed for their relative effectiveness. The chapter closes with a presentation of some of the critical factors that emerged from this case study.

Returning to Sporn's (1999) theoretical frame, five factors influence adaptation to changing environments: committed leadership, a differentiated structure, professional management, clear mission as well as goals, and discretionary funding. The policy for equal opportunities for women changes the environment for universities. It is important to understand how the university adapts and which influences are positive or negative.

First, it is critical to note that the Austrian Ministry mandated gender mainstreaming in universities in the first place. With the new legal framework of the University Act 2002, the situation changed. As this new steering instrument evolves, it has been interpreted less as a legal requirement and more as an idiosyncratic policy of affirmative action at the university. For example, WU has been required to promote women for many years, but only with the passage of University Act 2002 did the leadership of the senate and *Rektorat* decide to rewrite the affirmative action plan and include it in the university by-laws. Consequently, university members tend to perceive the policy as an obligation shaped more by internal rather than external forces. In reality, the trigger for change came from the outside, that is, the Ministry of Education, Science, and Culture, and the university responded by defining the change as an opportunity. This response was consistent with Sporn's (1999) research on change occurring either in the event of crisis or as an opportunity for change. For example, WU saw the opportunity to obtain more funding from the ministry to finance a new chair in Gender and Diversity in Organizations, a move that would create a more distinct profile for WU in the future even if the decision to fund the chair were contested in the short run.

Second, the WU policy raised the consciousness among the university personnel regarding gender equity. With the plan in place and the many small steps taken towards equality, many members of the institution began to pay attention to the issues of women. The implementation of new university initiatives with consequences, such as professorship in times of constrained resources, became easier. It should not be underestimated how important it is to understand thoroughly the many perspectives of university members in order to implement strategies successfully. As the case of WU shows, awareness is critical when it comes to affirmative action and women's equality. The university has been successful by gradually implementing a full set of programmes, incentives, and policies. The budget allocation procedure, the new chair position, and the paid-leave programme are examples from an array of large and small triggers, which, taken together, change the perception of the university members.

Third, an improved women-friendly infrastructure supports women tremendously in negotiating their careers. WU has successfully defined these policies, which have materialized into such entities as the offices for mentoring and harassment, the special research support and leave programmes, and the childcare facilities. Together, these administrative units form an environment that is supportive and helpful for women who want or need to combine family and work.

Prerequisites to successful equality programmes are imposed strategy, new culture, and supportive infrastructure. Professional management (as described in our theoretical framework) is also a very important factor and is found in WU's Office for Equal Opportunity for Women as well as in the representation of women on all committees and decision-making bodies. WU provides the high level of professionalism necessary to move gender equity forward by having persons in charge of counselling, committee work, and personnel issues who are trained in gender issues by the Ministry of Special Programs. This training guarantees the type of service necessary to counsel women in questions of discrimination and sexual harassment and to advise department chairs and members of the *Rektorat*.

To adapt to these new environmental conditions, the university uses a differentiated structure by establishing the new professorship for gender studies along with the Working Group for Equal Opportunities. Because WU has more than one structural arrangement designated responsible for women issues, both the academic and the administrative sides of the university are involved in achieving the same goals of gender equity.

Because funding always matters, discretionary funding used to support activities for women is constantly improving the status of women at the university. Incentives work best if the budgeting process is tied to elements of the affirmative action plan.

WU's indicator-based budget allocation system, which is sensitive to women's representation, has made a great difference. Although the amount is not great (500–1,000 Euros), the effect of the allocation is powerful in that department heads are made aware of the policy despite their level of criticism for it. In contrast, the paid-leave programme for female academics demonstrates a tangible measure of gender equality.

Visions and goals matter as much as funding, and both have been well communicated at WU. Together with a committed leadership represented mainly by the *Rektorat*, the institution is encouraged to focus on gender equality and to put it on the strategic agenda. For example, even though the *Rektorat* has one female member out of five, the leadership decided to include affirmative action in its by-laws, thereby reinforcing the goals of gender equity.

Although many positive developments can be reported about WU, there are of course impediments to gender equality. At WU (and probably at many other Austrian universities), the culture advocating equality for women is weak. In times of budget crisis and associated constraints, the faculty is often the first to criticize investments in 'fringe' subjects such as gender equality. For example, because it came at a time of financial restrictions, when the proposal was made for the new chair in gender studies, the faculty was split in their support for it. The leadership insisted on the position's importance to profile development and gender mainstreaming, convinced key opinion leaders of it, and funding was granted. Similar discussions among faculty emerge readily when resource allocation or strategic decisions are at stake. Without the commitment of the leadership team, the university's focus on gender equality would soon be at risk.

This resistance leads to another phenomenon, that is, slow, incremental change. As the above example demonstrates, many small steps must be taken to lead to noticeable change. Many projects and instruments, small and large, over some years are needed to keep gender equality on the agenda. Patience, persistence, and commitment on the part of institutional leadership are imperative to sustain the momentum.

As much as leadership is important at the central level, it is as important to have like-minded leadership at the decentralized level of departments, institutes, and administrative units. Unfortunately, the commitment to gender equality at this level is often missing or lacking the sense of importance that is necessary to implement real changes in policy. In times of financial constraints, priorities are governed by apparent necessities, such as raising more funds for traditional programmes or hiring available persons rather than conducting large-scale expensive searches. Thus, the gender issue can easily lose consideration. Consequently, owing to the nature of decision making at this level, it often requires more effort and discussion to convince this level of leadership that gender equality is also a necessity. Success in this area at WU is found in the influence of the rector whose research in social policy and founding membership in the Working Group for Equal Opportunity fosters an understanding and belief system that favours equality of men and women.

Finally, institutionalizing strategies and practices to achieve gender equality in the time of crisis, change, and transformation is another problematic area at WU. It seems that in the university at large, little attention is being paid to 'new' topics, such as gender equality. It is a problem requiring more communication among faculty and administration about the direction of the institution, especially in terms of gender equality's role in contributing to the institution's competitive advantage.

Conclusion

Gender equality has emerged in Austria's higher education strategy. The developments as described in this chapter show that with a general public policy and with concrete institutional plans, such as the one at WU, Austrian universities are improving the situation of women in their institutions. Many obstacles remain, however, and change is mostly incremental, but the commitment of legislation and leadership are in place for success. Now, the success of equality of women depends on women's and men's sensitivity and willingness for change at the institutional level. University managers must have the courage to argue, discuss, and convince other disbelievers of the benefits of women's rights. It is a task that is often contested and difficult. These managers need the strength that their convictions and actions are right for the institution and, hence, society. Key to success at this level is the relationship among the rector and his or her team, the faculty, and administrative units. Sustainable success is possible only if the leadership can promote and convince the university community of the efficacy of gender equality at its institution. The additional critical factor for success is the active involvement of immediate supervisors, that is, department chairs. They are the individuals responsible for hiring, supporting, mentoring, and counselling women for academic careers and shaping a culture in which male academics are receptive to gender equality. Now and in the immediate future, there is hope that with a new generation of professors, university managers, and administrators, a culture more inclusive of women will emerge. Perhaps then implementing policies and instruments for gender equality will be met with less resistance, and universities will benefit by the full inclusion of the majority of its students and a representative promotion of women academics.

References

Baldridge, J. V., Curtis, D. V., Ecker, G. P., & Riley, G. L. (1977) Alternative models of governance in higher education. In G. L. Riley & J. V. Baldridge (Eds.), *Governing academic organizations* (pp. 2–25). Berkeley, CA: McCutchan.

Clark, B. R. (1983) *The higher education system: Academic organization in cross-national perspective*. Berkeley, CA: University of California Press.

——— (1998) *Creating entrepreneurial universities: Organizational pathways of transformation*. Oxford: Pergamon.

——— (2004) *Sustaining change in universities: Continuities in case studies and concepts*. Berkshire, UK: Open University Press.

DiMaggio, P. J., & Powell, W. W. (1983) The iron cage revisited: Institutional isomorphism and collective rationality in organizational fields. *American sociological review, 48*: 147–160.

Gumport, P. J., & Sporn, B. (1999) Institutional adaptation: Demands for management reform and university administration. In J. Smart (Ed.), *Higher education: Handbook of theory and research* (pp. 103–145). New York: Agathon.

Hackman, J. (1985) Power and centrality in the allocation of resources in colleges and universities. *Administrative science quarterly, 30*:61–77.

March, J. G., Sproull, L. S., & Tamuz, M. (1991) Learning from samples of one or fewer. *Organization science, 2*(1):1–13.

Meyer, J. W., & Rowan, B. (1992) The structure of educational organizations. In J. W. Meyer & W. R. Scott (Eds.), *Organizational environments: Ritual and rationality* (pp. 71–98). London: Sage.

Meyer, J. W., Scott, W. R., & Deal, T. E. (1992) Institutional and technical sources of organizational structure of educational organizations. In J. W. Meyer & W. R. Scott (Eds.), *Organizational environments: Ritual and rationality* (pp. 45–67). London: Sage.

Scott, W. R. (1992) The organization of environments: Network, cultural, and historical elements. In J. W. Meyer & W. R. Scott (Eds.), *Organizational environments: Ritual and rationality* (pp. 155–175). London: Sage.

Shattock, M. (2000) Strategic management in European universities in an age of increasing institutional self reliance. *Tertiary Education and Management*, 6(2):93–104.

Slaughter, S., & Leslie, L. L. (1997) *Academic capitalism: Politics, policies, and the entrepreneurial university*. Baltimore: Johns Hopkins University Press.

Sporn, B. (1999) *Adaptive university structures: An analysis of adaptation to socioeconomic environments of US and European universities*. London: Jessica Kingsley.

Statistiches Taschenbuch (2004) *Vienna: Bundesministerium fur Bildung*. Wissenschaft und kultur.

Titscher, S., & Höllinger, S. (Eds.) (2003). *Hochschulreform in Europa – konkret*. Opladen: Leske+Budrich.

——— (Eds.) (2004) *Die österreichische Universitätsreform: Zur Implementierung des Universitätsgesetzes 2002*. Wien: Wiener Universitätsverlag.

Tolbert, P. S. (1985) Institutional environments and resource dependence: Sources of administrative structure in institutions of higher education. *Administrative science quarterly, 30*: 1–13.

Universitätsgasetz (2002) (University Act of 2002) No. 120/2002/9 August 2002. http:www.bmbwk.gv.at/medienpool/8019/8019_ug02_eng.pdf#search=%22University %20Act%202002%22%22. Retrieved 22 August 2006.

Weick, K. E. (1976) Educational organizations as loosely coupled systems. *Administrative science quarterly, 21*:1–19.

Yin, R. K. (1994) *Case study research: Design and methods* (2nd ed.). London: Sage.

CHAPTER SEVEN

WOMEN IN UNIVERSITIES IN FINLAND: RELATIVE ADVANCES AND CONTINUING CONTRADITIONS

Liisa Husu

Finland is a small, sparsely populated country of 5.2 million people with long traditions of promoting gender equality and higher education for women. The country has received high rankings in overall gender equality by international comparisons (e.g., UNDP, 1995, 2004; World Economic Forum, 2005). With 36% of the female population aged 25–64 having tertiary education, the country ranked highest among the European Union countries in 2002 (Eurostat, 2003). Finland is also one of the leading countries in research and development in both relative intensity and investment, and it is at the forefront globally in information and communication technology (Statistics Finland, 2005; UNDP, 2001). Furthermore, Finnish society is characterized by women's full-time employment in a still gender-segregated labour market, women's long-term and active political participation, as well as governmental commitment to gender equality (e.g., Statistics Finland, 2001; Husu & Niemelä, 1993).

The Finnish university system dates back to 1640. Currently, the country has a higher education system consisting of 20 universities and 29 relatively new polytechnics that were created in the 1990s. This chapter focusses on the universities. The Finnish university network covers the entire country from the capital Helsinki to the University of Lapland on the Arctic Circle. It consists of ten multifaculty universities, three universities of technology, three schools of economics and business administration, and four art academies. All universities are state-funded but exert autonomy over academic matters. The level of core funding is guaranteed by law (MinEdu, 2004a, 2004b).

The expansion of female participation in higher education has been described by some education sociologists (Kivinen & Rinne, 1995, p. 103) as 'women taking over the university institution'. Views framing the feminization of the student pool as problematic have increasingly been heard both in the public discussion and from the top of the university hierarchy (Raivio, 2002; *Helsingin Sanomat*, 2003). The Finnish context thus provides an interesting setting in which to explore women and university change.

Students and Degrees: Women in the Majority

Finnish women have entered higher education earlier and in larger numbers than have women in other Nordic countries. In 1908, some 21.4% of all students were women at the University of Helsinki (the only university in the country at that time). This same level of attendance was not reached in neighbouring Norway and Denmark until 25 years later (Ståhle, 1996). In the early 1950s, the proportion of women among the undergraduate students had reached a third and in the mid-1960s nearly half (SVT, 1981).

Women's share of university degrees has grown at all levels. Since 1987, women have been in a majority of those obtaining master's degrees as well as in the majority among recipients of all types of university degrees since the mid-1990s. Women have shown a growing interest in obtaining higher academic degrees as well: in the early 1980s, women's share of PhDs was 22%, but it increased rapidly to nearly 40% by the end of the 1990s and was approaching 50% in 2004 (MinEdu, 1982; SVT, 1998; KOTA database) (see figure 7.1).

The 1990s were a period of growth in higher education in general and in PhD production in particular. The proportion of women among students also grew in all fields, except medicine and dentistry, which have traditionally had high female representation. The expansion is evidenced by the growth rates of degrees in the 1990s. From 1990 to 1999, the number of master's degrees awarded to women grew by 41% (11,856 in 1999), and the number of doctoral degrees grew by 138% (1,165 in 1999) (Statistics Finland, 1999). In 2003, 12, 411 master's degrees were awarded, 60% of which were granted to women, and 1,257 doctoral degrees, 46.5% of which were awarded to women (KOTA Database). The proportion of women among doctoral degree recipients is currently among the highest in the original EU member states (EU-15); however, several new EU member states from Central and Eastern Europe have somewhat higher proportions (EC, 2003) (see figure 7.1).

In 2004, the largest numbers of women were found in technology (22%), humanities (16%), and natural sciences (15%) (MinEdu, 2005). Despite the expansion of higher education, entry to universities has remained highly competitive. Students are selected mainly through entrance tests, and approximately one-third of applicants receive entry. Women are a majority of the applicants for higher education, but male applicants' success rate is clearly higher. For example, in 2003, 63% of all university applicants were women and 37% were men. Of those admitted, 57% were women.

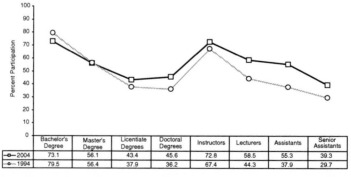

	Bachelor's Degree	Master's Degree	Licentiate Degrees	Doctoral Degrees	Instructors	Lecturers	Assistants	Senior Assistants
2004	73.1	56.1	43.4	45.6	72.8	58.5	55.3	39.3
1994	79.5	56.4	37.9	36.2	67.4	44.3	37.9	29.7

Figure 7.1   Representation of Women among Students and Academic Staff in Finnish Universities

Source: KOTA Database. National statistical online database updated annually on universites and higher education.

Nearly every other male applicant was admitted (48%), but only 38% of females were admitted (KOTA Database). One explanation for this disparity is gender segregation in fields of study: fields popular among men have much higher acceptance rates than do those programmes popular among women. In 1996, natural sciences and technology, fields most favoured by male applicants, accepted nearly half of their applicants. Several fields popular among women had considerably lower acceptance rates. Among these, for example, were veterinary medicine (accepting 7.4% of applicants), psychology (7.4%), education (15.2%), and medicine (15.8%). In all these fields, over 60% of the applicants were women (SVT, 1998, pp. 56–57). In 2004, the picture was very much the same: the acceptance rates were highest in male-dominated technology and in the nearly gender-balanced field of natural sciences (with acceptance rates around 50% and 40% respectively), but it was under 20% in medicine and education sciences, both favoured by women, and under 10% in very female-dominated disciplines of veterinary medicine and psychology (MinEdu, 2003a; KOTA Database).

Since the mid-1970s, some shifts have occurred in the gender segregation by fields of study. From 1975 to 1995, male-dominated fields were feminized somewhat by their student populations, and the number of fields with a balanced gender composition (i.e., 41–60%) increased. For example, natural sciences, agriculture, forestry, and law were still male-dominated in 1975 but became gender-balanced by 1995. Furthermore, earlier female-dominated fields became even more feminized numerically, and the number of female-dominated fields increased, the most dramatic example being veterinary medicine that was a balanced field in the mid-1970s but is currently predominantly studied by women. (SVT, 1998, pp. 89–91). In the beginning of the twenty-first century, the only male-dominated field of study was technology, which was also the field with largest numbers of students. Currently, only a fifth of technology students are women (KOTA Database).

Though somewhat unorganized prior to the mid-1990s, research training became more systematized in the latter half of the 1990s owing to the creation of a graduate school system at national level (MinEdu, 2000). Consequently, the number of PhDs increased dramatically and more than doubled in the 1990s. During the same period, the proportion of women among new PhDs increased from 23% to 43%, or in absolute numbers, from 155 to 523. By 2004, the fields of medicine, natural science, and technology produced 58% of all PhDs. Two fields producing the highest numbers of female PhDs in 2004 were medicine and natural sciences, accounting for 43% of all female PhDs that year, whereas every other male PhD received his doctoral degree in technology or natural sciences (SVT, 1998; KOTA Database).

Faculty

By 1980, Finland had more women at all academic staff levels than other Nordic countries (Denmark, Iceland, Norway, and Sweden) (Luukkonen-Gronow, 1983), and Nordic data from the mid-1990s (Ståhle, 1996) showed that this was still the case. In the mid-1990s, Finland had higher levels of female representation in all major disciplinary fields (humanities, social sciences, natural sciences, etc.) in professorships as well as in other academic posts (pp. 98–106).

However, among faculty, the same gendered patterns are found in Finland as they are elsewhere: the higher the position, the fewer women (see figure 7.1).[1] The proportion of women among the professoriate has reached one-fifth in the beginning of the twenty-first century but appears to have stagnated at that level. In 2003, professors comprised 28% of the teaching personnel in Finnish universities, senior assistants 8%, assistants 17%, lecturers 28%, and full-time untenured teachers (*päätoimiset tuntiopettajat*) 17% (KOTA Database).

In a comparison of the 25 EU countries, Finland, Portugal, and Latvia are the only countries where the current proportion of women among full professors is over 20% (EC, 2003). In Finland, the highest proportions of female professors are found in humanities (31%), social sciences (23%), and medicine and health sciences (21%). In natural sciences and technology, only 8% of professors are women, and their share did not change between 1990 and 2002. The age profiles for female and male professors do not show significant differences (Kurki, 2003) (see figure 7.1).

Are women taking over the universities? I would argue that this view is highly exaggerated. Despite the increase in women among higher degree holders, women are still in the minority among professors, and the number of women attaining professor-ships has grown very slowly, from 6.3% in 1983 to 11.3% in 1993 to 22% in 2004 (KOTA Database; MinEdu, 1998). Women are in the majority of faculty only at the lower levels in the academic hierarchy. Although the proportion of women in the pro-fessoriate increased slowly beginning in the early 1980s, the figures in the early 1990s showed a standstill, and there was a drop in women's recruitment to the professoriate in fields with large female recruitment potential, such as the humanities and social sciences. Among lower level posts, the advancement of women also stagnated in the mid-1990s (Academy of Finland, 1997). The abolishment of the category of associate professor in 1998 explains the sudden jump of 5% in one year in the proportion of women among full professors, from 13% in 1997 to 18.4% in 1998. In the first five years of the twenty-first century, the proportion of women in the professoriate has increased only by 1.9%, from 20.1% in 2000 to 22% in 2004. The proportion of women among professors is at the same level as the proportion of women among PhD recipients nearly 20 years ago.

Policy Influence: Professors by Invitation

One explanation that may contribute to the slow recruitment of women into the pro-fessoriate despite feminization of the recruitment pool is the practice of appointing pro-fessors by invitation. All universities in Finland are public organizations and professors are civil servants. Until 1998, professors were appointed by the president of the Republic. The appointment procedure for professors was regulated by specific legisla-tion. Traditionally the appointment process has been more transparent than in many other countries: positions are filled by open competition, and the information on the list of applicants, the evaluations of the merits of the applicants by external referees, and the recommendations of the appointment committee are public documents and are available to all interested parties.

In the early 1990s, however, the use of invitation procedure to fill a professorship was made possible by the Act on the Appointment of Professors and Associate Professors in Universities (Act 856/1991). The act stated that a professorship can be filled by invitation in three cases: first, if a person with very high merits can thus be appointed; second, if filling the position quickly is especially important in order to organize teaching, research, or artistic activity in the field; or third, if the appointment is made for a fixed term. Furthermore, the act stated that only a person who is undoubtedly competent for the position can be invited to a professorship and that referee statements on the competence and merits of the invited person shall be requested.

The increased use of the invitation procedure towards the end of the 1990s has been suggested as a major contributor to the gender imbalance in professorial appointments and to the slow increase in appointments of women into the professoriate (Husu, 1997, 2000, 2001; Academy of Finland, 1998). Initially, invitation was used in only a few cases overall in the early 1990s, and at first, only men were invited to professorships (Academy of Finland, 1997). However, in the mid-1990s, the invitation procedure gradually became more commonly used so that, by 1997, 55% of all professorial appointments in the country were made by invitation. The increased use of the invitation procedure in appointments eventually caught the attention of the Parliament. When discussing the draft of the proposed new university legislation in 1997, the Parliament stated that the invitation procedure was intended to be an exceptional method of appointment and that using the invitation procedure to the considerable extent it was being used could not be justified because it prevented other competent persons from applying for professorships. Furthermore, the Parliament stated that limiting the use of the invitation procedure served the interests of justice. Even though no comprehensive statistical analysis has been made on the use of invitation procedure by gender, discipline, type of post, and type of university, what scarce statistical information exists suggests that the invitation procedure has favoured men (Husu, 2000, 2001; MinEdu, unpublished statistics).

Even though gender equality was not used as an argument in the discussion, the Parliament strengthened the law to stipulate that the invitation procedure could be used only when a very distinguished and undoubtedly competent person was interested in the position. Needing to fill the post rapidly because of the impending need to organize teaching or research was removed by the new act (Act 648/1997). In addition to giving stricter rules on the use of the invitation, the category of associate professor, which was less male-dominated than the full professor category, was abolished, and all associate professors were upgraded to full professors.

Did the situation change with the new Act on Professorial Appointments? Even after the new appointment legislation was passed, the invitation procedure continued to be used in over half of the appointments for a long time. The appointments made after the new act continued to show the same trend: women had better chances in open competition.

What is noteworthy is that at the end of 1990s, the proportion of women appointed *to* the professoriate (13.7%) was lower than the proportion of women *in* the professoriate, which was 18.4% in 1998 and 17.9% in 1999. No systematic data are currently available on appointment age by gender, but traditionally women have been appointed to professorships at an older age than men are, creating the effect of shortening their 'time in service'. Consequently, this development did not promise rapid changes towards better gender balance in the professoriate in the coming years.

The universities enjoy autonomy in academic matters, such as individual professorial appointments and contents of research and teaching, and the role of the Parliament is to set broad legislation and budgetary frames. Thus, the stricter formulation of the grounds for using invitation was an important signal to universities where over half of the professorial appointments in the country were in fact closed from open competition. However, judging by their actual appointment behaviour, the universities were rather slow to respond to the signal that the Parliament had sent.

As a result, the outcomes of the invitation procedure favouring men attracted some national media attention and generated discussion in internal university magazines. In response, several universities addressed in their equality plans the importance of monitoring the invitation procedure from a gender perspective (e.g., the University of Helsinki Gender Equality Plan 2001–2003 and the University of Tampere Gender Equality Plan 2000–2002). The issue also received some international attention. The European Technology Assessment Network (ETAN) Report (Osborn et al., 2000) took up the invitation issue, citing a Finnish Policy Report by the Academy of Finland (1997),[2] and the United Nations Committee on Elimination of Discrimination against Women (CEDAW) (2001) expressed a view that the Finnish invitation procedure for professorial appointments may conflict with gender equality principles.[3]

By 2000, the figures finally showed a decline in the use of the invitation procedure. Between February 2000 and February 2001, clearly a lower proportion, only 35% (184) of the professorial appointments were made by invitation versus more than half in previous years, and the difference between the proportion of women among the invited and those appointed in open competition had also decreased significantly (20% women among the invited and 22.7% women among those appointed in open competition) (MinEdu, unpublished statistics). It should be noted, however, that despite such improvements, gender equality is hardly evident in a 20%:80% ratio of women to men appointees.

High Research Intensity

Currently, Finland is one of the world's top funders of research in relation to the gross national product of the country, and all Finnish universities engage in research and teaching. The proportion of external research funding of universities grew very rapidly in the 1990s, from a third to half of all research expenses in the period 1991–2000, which allowed an increase in the number of fixed-term researchers in universities (Hakala et al., 2003). In 2003, external research funding consisted of funding from the National Research Councils (19% of the total external funding), from the Finnish National Technology Agency (TEKES) (12%), Finnish corporate funding (14%), other Finnish funding (40% ministries, foundations etc.), EU funding (11%), and other foreign funding (4%) (MinEdu, 2004b).

In 1996, the Finnish government adopted a programme to raise the level of R&D funding from 2.35% of GDP in 1995 to 2.9% by the end of 1999. This increase was intended to promote the 'functioning of the national innovation system for the benefit of the economy, employment, and business sectors'. This programme and the strong investment by the private sector in R&D helped to raise the R&D share of the GDP to 2.9% in 1998, increasing since then to 3.5% in 2002 – in 2002 the EU-15 average was under 2% and the United States figured 2.7%. However, this development did not signify a dramatic increase in the funding of academic research because the increase was distributed unevenly among research sectors. For universities, the increase was slight during the 1990s whereas the state research institutes and sector research experienced a decline in funding. Of the total R&D investment, the private sector currently funds the greatest share: almost 70% in the first years of the twenty-first century. Half of the private sector research funds have been used in electro technology, which during the 1990s was nearly exclusively in the electro technological industry itself (Statistics Finland, 1999, 2001, 2005).

From a gender perspective, it should be stressed that the new investment in R&D was thus made largely in the field of technology, the most male-dominated disciplinary field in which women earned only 19% of doctorates in 2004 (KOTA Database). As a result of their significant under-representation in technology, women have benefited less from the new opportunities offered by increased investments in R&D than men have.

In general, the public sector R&D, which has enjoyed fewer new investments, employs proportionally more women than does the private sector R&D. Women form one-third of the total R&D personnel in Finland and 30% among R&D personnel with at least a tertiary level degree. In universities and public sector research, nearly half of the R&D personnel are women whereas in the private sector research women number only one-fifth (Statistics Finland, 2005).

Interventions Promoting Gender Equality in Academia

There has been a surprising lack of evaluation and research on Finnish equality policies in general (see, however, Holli, 2003) both in the fields of higher education and in science specifically. The first national level report addressing the position of women in academia was published as early as 1964 by the Finnish Cultural Foundation (Tuohinto, 1964). It was not a policy-oriented report, however, but rather a descriptive one. Issues of gender inequality in academia were introduced comprehensively to the Finnish university and science policy agenda starting from the early 1980s. In 1980, the Finnish government adopted the first National Action Plan to promote gender equality, focussing on the years spanning 1980–1985. The plan for the latter half of the UN Decade of Women noted, among a number of other issues, the need to monitor obstacles that academic women encounter.

Since then, clear fluctuations can be observed in the weight given to the issue of gender equality in mainstream science and university/higher education policy. Periods of high activity and visibility have been followed by those during which gender issues have been pushed aside or defined as a problem that will soon be solved by the steadily rising numbers of female students, especially graduates with higher degrees (Husu, 1999, 2001). However, systematic policy analysis of these fluctuations has not been conducted yet. Having observed and participated in this field for nearly 25 years in various positions,[4] I would suggest that, in a small country like Finland, the role of a few key gatekeepers and policy makers in science and university policy is pivotal to understanding these fluctuations. According to my observations, even though the national gender equality machinery and women's studies/feminist academics' lobby continually try to keep the issue of gender (in)equality in academia on the agenda, major interventions in the field have usually taken place only when they are clearly backed by highly positioned and influential gatekeepers, most often particular ministers of Education and research directors or general directors of the National Research Council system (i.e., the Academy of Finland). Interestingly, it is difficult to find a simple common denominator to describe these gatekeepers because among them are influential women and men from the political left and right.

The main actors promoting gender equality in academia and scientific research since the early 1980s have been, on one hand, the central educational and science policy authorities and, on the other hand, the national gender equality machinery. The central educational and science policy authorities are the Ministry of Education and the Academy of Finland,[5] which is the Finnish National Research Council having a key national role in forming science policy and allocating funding for academic research. The national gender equality machinery currently consists of three units in the Ministry of Social Affairs and Health: the Council for Equality between Women and Men, the Equality Ombudsman's Office, and the Equality Unit. The oldest of these, the Council for Equality between Women and Men, was founded in 1972 and is a parliamentary advisory committee with a permanent secretariat. Its charge is to monitor and promote gender equality in all areas of society and to promote both research and its utilization in promotion of gender equality. The Equality Ombudsman's function and office were established in 1986 to monitor the new Gender Equality Act and to promote gender equality more generally. As a result of restructuring of the field, a governmental gender equality unit was established in the Ministry of Social Affairs and Health in 2001.[6]

Cooperation among these key actors in higher education, science policy, and gender equality policy has contributed significantly to the promotion of gender equality in universities. It is my personal experience that this cooperation has been very much facilitated by the small country setting where 'everybody knows everybody'. The interventions and measures applied can be divided into monitoring and promoting gender equality in academia, especially promoting women researchers' and university teachers' careers, gender equality promotion in universities more generally, as well as promoting women's studies and gender research.

Beginning in the early 1980s, the Academy of Finland allocated funding to women's studies for research projects, national coordination, and networking. The Academy of Finland research director at that time Dr. Elisabeth Helander was a key figure and gatekeeper in this development. Helander was one of the few highly positioned and influential women in Finnish science policy in the 1980s and was keen to promote gender issues (Husu, 2005a). In 1981, the Academy of Finland and the Council for Equality between Women and Men created a full-time post of a national coordinator of women's studies in the Secretariat of the Council for Equality. The Council's Subcommittee on Research was founded in 1981 to support the activities of the coordinator and the Council in this area, and it has been active since. Serving as chairs of the subcommittee have been members of the Council for Equality who are politicians (usually female and male MPs, and other politicians); the expert membership appointed to the subcommittee were academics and gender scholars from different disciplines from all over the country as well as representatives of the Ministry of Education, Academy of Finland, Statistics Finland, and sector research institutes. Initially, the Academy Research Director Dr. Elisabeth Helander was also one of the expert members in the subcommittee.

The main activities of the national coordinator and the Subcommittee on Research have been to promote women's studies and gender research, to facilitate contacts between researchers in this field and their contacts to administrators and policy makers, and to monitor and promote gender equality in academia and gender research through conferences, publicity, lobbying efforts, and advisory and information services, including a national quarterly newsletter on women's studies published since 1981. With the restructuring of the national equality machinery in 2001, the role of the national coordinator was discontinued despite protests from the women's studies community. In 2003, however, the future organization of women's studies coordination and information services in Finland was taken up at a highest political level, namely in Prime Minister Matti Vanhanen's Government's Program (2003), and later in the Equality Plan of the government of Finland for 2004–2007. In the summer 2005, however, this effort had not yet led to concrete solutions regarding national coordination activities. The Equality Plan of the Finnish government promised (1) that responsible ministries of Education, Social Affairs, and Health would investigate alternatives for arranging information and documenting activities on gender equality on a permanent basis; (2) that the Ministry of Education would develop coordination of women's studies with the universities to inform and strengthen the position of women's studies as part of university level research; (3) that the Ministry of Education would appoint a working group to develop professional research careers in general and to promote both women's research careers and equality in research careers. Following the Governmental Equality Plan, the Ministry of Social Affairs ordered a report on information and documentation related to gender equality in 2004. The report (Grönroos, 2005) recommends that the current Minna web portal (www.minna.fi, a national Web portal on gender equality and women's studies, funded by Ministry of Social Affairs but only for a fixed term) should be maintained and developed, making a general national information service on women's studies, studies on men, and gender equality available to a large range of users in Finland and abroad, and mainstreaming general sources of information regarding the promotion of gender and equality in the production and development of mainstream sources of information in Finland. Whether the proposals are going to be implemented is not known yet.

Currently, the Ministry of Education funds a national university network of women's studies, the HILMA network, which is an endeavour of eight universities to promote cooperation mainly in women's studies teaching (see http://www. helsinki.fi/hilma/). An important and well-informed gatekeeper in these recent efforts has been the minister of Education (2003–2005) Ms. Tuula Haatainen who is Social Democratic MP,[7] a longtime member and chair of the Council for Equality.

National Policy Reports Promoting Women in Academia and Research

The first high level national policy report on women in academia dates from early 1980s. In most other EU countries, except Sweden, the issue was taken up at the ministry level considerably later (Osban et al., 2000). In 1981, the Minister of Education, Kaarina Suonio, a Social Democrat interested in gender equality issues, appointed the first national level committee to monitor women's status in academia (MinEdu, 1982, 1986). The Ministry of Education Committee argued, 'Harsh and obvious gender-related discrimination in the scientific community is apparently rare. This may be so because, to start with, the competition for posts is relatively closely controlled and the criticism [evaluation] is public' (MinEdu, 1982, p. 24). This statement was made five years before gender discrimination was legally prohibited in Finland by the Equality Act of 1986.

The Ministry of Education Committee consisted of high profile female academics, mainly professors who could lend expertise on gender issues. Included on the committee was the internationally recognized science studies expert Veronica Stolte-Heiskanen, and Elina Haavio-Mannila, one of the pioneers of Finnish studies on women and gender equality, chaired the committee.

Many members had personal experience combining successful academic careers with motherhood. Problems with arrangements for childcare had been a central concern in the 1970s and 1980s among academic women. The childcare problem was to be solved largely in the 1990s by general development of generous childcare policies in Finland, which substantially improved the possibilities of all working and studying parents to combine work, study, and family (Ministry of Social Affairs and Health, 1999, 2005a). Thus, universities have not had to respond independently to the childcare problem. For postgraduate students pursuing doctorates in the new graduate schools created in the mid-1990s, having children had no significant delaying effect on the duration of doctoral studies – either for men or women (MinEdu, 2000). On the much-debated 'family as an obstacle' issue, the 1982 Committee acknowledged that children and family can slow down women's scientific career, but according to empirical studies, they also seemed to have positive influences on both men's and women's scientific productivity. The key conclusion of the committee was that in a scientific career 'the double burden of women did not seem to be the worst obstacle, but their weaker and unequal position in the scientific community' was.

The 1982 Committee also took up the still contested issue of age and suggested that age as a criterion should not be used in recruitment and fund allocation. Officially, age is not used as a recruitment criterion, but unofficially it appears to play a role. In my qualitative study on discrimination experiences of academic women (Husu, 2001, 2005b) several informants described how their age had been used against them in recruitment or evaluation. In the current Finnish science policy, supporting young researchers into a professional research career is strongly stressed, but it is questioned whether this goal is incompatible with the goal of recruiting more women into research, considering that women have traditionally been somewhat older than men in all career stages. Discussions on 'academic age' versus 'biological age' have not yet been very vocal in the Finnish academic setting.

The Ministry of Education's 1982 Committee made several proposals to promote the advancement of women in the scientific community and to reduce inequalities. Proposals that have been realized to a large extent include the following: the increase of women's representation in scientific decision-making bodies and in allocating grants; the development of postgraduate supervision; the promotion and inclusion of women's studies in university curricula; the recommendation to fund research on women; accounting for childcare costs in grants for study and research abroad; compensation for parental leave by an equally long extension of the term in fixed-time teaching and research posts; and gathering more statistics on gender in higher education research.[8]

The most radical 1982 proposal was made on positive discrimination in student and postgraduate recruitment as well as in recruiting for research posts, especially in fields with very few women. Adopted from Norway, the idea of positive discrimination was suggested in its moderate form, only to be applied when a decision was to be made between equally qualified male and female candidates. This proposal did not receive much support in the scientific community, even from academic women. The Equality Act of 1986 enables the use of positive action such as positive discrimination in appointments, if the action is part of an equality plan of the organization. Some universities have included the possibility of positive discrimination in their equality plans, but to my knowledge, positive discrimination or quotas in favour of women in appointments have not been used in Finnish university appointments.

The Role of Gender Equality Policies

National gender equality policies have been influencing gender equality in academia through the efforts of the Council for Equality, its Subcommittee of Research, and the National Coordination of Women's Studies. When the Finnish 'gender equality machinery' was strengthened in 1986 with the Equality Act to prevent discrimination based on sex and to promote equality between men and women in society, it also included a paragraph directing educational institutions to ensure that research and instructional materials promote gender equality.

A position of Equality Ombudsman was created to supervise observance of the act and give guidelines for promoting gender equality. In 1990, the Equality Ombudsman issued *Guidelines on Promoting Gender Equality in Universities*. These guidelines were discussed and developed in cooperation with the Council for Equality's Subcommittee for Research and the national coordinator for Women's Studies. An important part of this developmental work were the site visits the Equality Ombudsman and the national coordinator conducted in the late 1980s in most universities to discuss the new equality legislation with the rectors and heads of administration. These guidelines were later included in the Equality Plan of the Ministry of Education (Husu, 2004).

The Equality Act made overt discrimination in academia more visible because academic women could file formal discrimination complaints in reference to the Equality Act. For example, between January 1991 and May 1997, 33 complaints were filed to the Equality Ombudsman from various universities.[9] Some of them have proceeded to court and some universities have paid compensation to the plaintiff, but, thus far, no systematic analyses of these complaints and their outcomes have been made.

In 1995, the Equality Act was amended, and gender quotas were introduced. According to the revised act, minimum percentages of both women and men in government committees, advisory boards, and other corresponding bodies should be 40% unless special reasons exist to act to the contrary. This reform has also affected the composition of the most important funding gatekeepers of academic research, the Academy of Finland and its four National Research Councils, the Academy Board, and the National Council of Science and Technology, the composition of which has become gender-balanced. Another amendment to the Equality Act in 1995 concerned equality planning. All employers with a staff of at least 30 should include measures to promote gender equality in the workplace in the annual personnel and training plan or equivalent. However, until the passage of an amendment in Equality Act 2005, no legal sanctions existed for non-compliance.

The Equality Act was amended in 2005 (Act 232/2005). It also harmonized the Finnish legislation with the EU legislation on gender equality in work settings. Most important changes included a clearer definition of direct and indirect discrimination, defining sexual and gender harassment as discrimination, making gender equality planning obligatory, and including educational institutions (but not schools) under the scope of equality legislation. Harassment and discrimination of both students and staff in educational institutions became sanctioned, and compensation could be paid to the victims of discrimination in educational settings. Earlier, the act concerned only staff in educational institutions. Gender equality planning in workplaces became obligatory, supervised by Equality Ombudsman, and a fine was set for non-compliance. Detailed guidelines on equality planning were also introduced. The plan called for report on placement of women and men in different job categories and a report on work tasks and salaries by gender, including the gender pay gap, measures adopted to promote gender equality and equal pay, and an evaluation of the realization of earlier measures.

In educational institutions, the Gender Equality Act called for reports on the state of gender equality in the institution, detailing problems and measures promoting gender equality, paying special attention to gender equality in student recruitment, teaching arrangements, student evaluations, and measures to prevent and stop sexual harassment.

The 2005 amendment of the Equality Act was much needed in order to facilitate gender equality promotion in many organizations, and the extension to educational institutions including students was long overdue. However, the university sector has, in fact, been more active in introducing equality planning than have many other sectors in society, such as municipalities, public administration, and business (Husu, 2004; Ahponen & Paasikoski, 2003). Since the beginning of the late 1990s, gender equality has been on the agenda in most universities, in some universities much earlier, with regard to some kind of infrastructure and policy documents. The equality agendas are typically rather long (cf. Cockburn, 1989; Kirton & Greene, 2000), increasingly adopting mainstreaming as a main background strategy, including measures related to student recruitment, studies, teaching, career advancement, recruitment, decision making, sexual harassment, and pay. Lately, the agenda has broadened to include diversity policy in the spirit of the anti-discrimination law from 2004. By the latter half of 1990s, most universities had formed gender equality committees. Although equality committees usually do not have executive power or ombudsman functions, they act more with regard to agenda setting, planning, and information functions. Most universities either have accepted equality plans or have included equality issues among other plans, such as personnel development plans. In addition, guidelines for the prevention of sexual harassment have been issued in several universities (Mankkinen, 1999); gender equality surveys have also been conducted in several universities: University of Helsinki (Mankkinen, 1995), University of Turku (Voutilainen, 1996; Keskinen and Vallenius, 2003), University of Kuopio (Sinkkonen, 1997), University of Joensuu (Varjus, 1997), Helsinki School of Economics (Rahunen, 1999), &Arign;bo Akademi University (Välinoro & Siimes, 1998), University of Tampere (Pasanen, 2003), and University of Lapland (Naskali, 2004). Since 1995, the Equality Committees of Universities have organized an annual national conference, and they also have a national discussion and information email list.

Finland has also played a key role in initiating European cooperation among universities regarding gender equality. The first European conference on gender equality in higher education was convened by the University of Helsinki in 1998 (Fogelberg et al., 1999), and it led to both a series of regular conferences in Europe (Zürich, Switzerland, 2000; Genova, Italy, 2003; Oxford, UK, 2005) and a European Network of Gender Equality in Higher Education, which functions between the conferences through an email discussion list moderated by the University of Helsinki with over 380 members from over 30 countries.

The Academy of Finland has become actively engaged in equality planning as well. In the 1990s, the only national level report on academic women's careers was the Academy of Finland Working Group Report (1997, in English 1998). The Academy of Finland adopted its first Gender Equality Action Plan in 2000 and substantially updated it in 2005. The plan consolidated and articulated the academy's policy on equality and set up new concrete measures to promote gender equality throughout the academy's research funding and management. Based on the principle of main-streaming, the Academy Plan of 2000 set up a target of 40% of the minority gender for appointments and advocated the principle of positive discrimination, which prefers the minority group candidate in cases where two candidates are equally mer-ited. It also established a key principle that maternity, paternity, and parental leave should not shorten a funding period. In addition, it allocated 20% higher grants for study or working abroad for recipients with dependent children, and it established a new, short-term 'spin-off' funding for young researchers, female researchers, and researchers who return from parental leave (Academy of Finland, 2000). The plan was very well received by the scientific community (Academy of Finland, 2000). In 2005, an update of the Equality Plan broadened the agenda towards diversity issues following the Non-Discrimination Act (21/2004), which forbade discrimination based on age, ethnic, or national origin, language, religion, nationality, conviction, opinion, health, disability, sexual orientation, or other person-based grounds. The plan enabled positive discrimination in allocating research funding in a situation where two applicants were considered equally scientifically competent (Academy of Finland, 2005).

Further Activities Promoting Women's Studies

Women's studies developed rapidly during the 1980s and 1990s, but as a new inter-disciplinary field, it has suffered chronically from inadequate resources. In 1995, the Council for Equality and the National Association of Women's Studies in Finland (SUNS) jointly launched a national action plan called Women's Studies 2000 (Naistutkimus, 2000, 1996). About the same time, women's studies resources were strengthened considerably when the Ministry of Education created eight professor-ships in women's studies for five years. Beyond that period universities were expected to finance those professorships themselves. A key gatekeeper to make this major inter-vention possible was the Minister of Education Olli Pekka-Heinonen from the National Coalition (Conservative Party) (Heinonen, 1999). In 1998, in addition to the university chairs in women's studies, the Academy of Finland created a five-year rotating research professorship in interdisciplinary women's studies and gender equal-ity research: the Minna Canth Professorship, named after a pioneer of women's rights, author Minna Canth. Beginning in 2007, on Minna Canth's birthday, March 19 will be officially celebrated as 'Minna Canth's day', or the day of gender equality. Canth is the first woman in Finland to receive an official flag-raising day in the calendar.

Conclusion

Important societal changes in Finland since the 1980s positively affecting gender equality in academia include the introduction of equality legislation (Equality Act of 1986, amended 1992, 1995, 1997, and 2005) and improved childcare and parental leave provisions. These changes have obviously improved gender equality and condi-tions of women more generally in the Finnish society. Have been accompanied by changes in family and work experiences.

Important changes in academia include the intensification and expansion of doctoral education, increased competition for positions and funding, increased internationalization of research, and increased managerialism (see, e.g., Hakala et al., 2003). Gender-related changes in Finnish academia include the rapid growth and institutionalization of women's studies in universities (see, e.g., Husu & Bergman, 1993; Academy of Finland, 2002), the introduction of gender equality and anti-harassment planning in universities, and gender quotas in the composition of the National Research Councils of the Academy of Finland. The gender balance in academia has somewhat improved in all degree and job categories. The proportion of women in the recruitment pool has continuously increased, and the most dramatic change has occurred in doctoral education; women obtain currently nearly half of PhDs, and in many fields over half. Individual women have been appointed to all top positions in Finnish universities and science, except in the position of general director of the Academy of Finland. However, it was only recently, in 2003, when the first Finnish academic woman, Medical Professor Pirjo Mäkelä, received the honorary title of academician for outstanding academic achievement, awarded only to 12 living academics at the time.[10]

Although increased managerialism, accountability, and quality management have been introduced to the Finnish system, women continue to be under-represented in the highest managerial posts. The first female university rector in a multifaculty university was appointed in 1992 in the University of Jyväskylä and the first female chancellor as late as 2000 in the University of Turku. Of all rectors and vice-rectors in Finnish universities, 20% were women in 2000 (Pulkkinen, 2000). No national statistical information has been gathered on the gender division of administrative directors or deans (heads of faculties). For example, the largest and oldest of universities, the University of Helsinki, appointed its first female dean in 1992, and she remained the only female dean for several years. In 2005, only 2 out of 11 deans were women.

Despite the relatively high proportion of women in Finnish academia, relatively high overall gender equality, and the relatively early mass enrolment of women in Finnish higher education and research, the structures and culture of Finnish academia have remained gendered. The same structural features characterize academic position of women in Finland as they do elsewhere: male-led hierarchies that seem relatively resistant to change, women more frequently holding lower-rank positions, and gender segregation in choice of study field. The divergent views of academic women and men in several surveys suggest that women do not share the illusion that gender equality has been realized whereas, for men, the situation concerning gender equality appears to be unproblematic (Rahunen, 1999; Voutilainen, 1996). In a survey of all academic staff of the largest business university, Helsinki School of Economics, young academics – both male and female – assessed gender equality in their school as fairly well realized (75% and 70% respectively) whereas, among staff employed in the university for 11–20 years, 82% of men but only 48% of women saw gender equality as well realized, and none of the women used the alternative 'very well' (Rahunen, 1999, pp. 55–56).

The small country setting where academic circles are also small and 'everybody knows everybody' creates both opportunities and limitations for the promotion of gender equality in academia. At the national and systemic level, gender equality promotion in academia clearly has been facilitated by close cooperation, informal contacts, and networks among major stakeholders of higher education/science policy and equality policy. However, at the level of the individual, a small country setting can be problematic, as indicated by the fear of many academic women being labelled as persona non grata in their disciplines or in the larger national context if they dare to challenge discriminatory practices.

The rapid growth in female recruitment potential and the rapid increase in the size and funding of the R&D sector have not led to radical improvements in the status of academic women. First, owing to the increase of resources mainly in fields such as technology wherein women continue to be significantly under-represented as students and academics, entry into technological studies is remarkably easier than is entry into several female-dominated fields. Second, as the number of women in the recruitment pool to higher academic posts increased in the 1990s, appointment procedures became more closed, especially with the appointment of professors by invitation. The diminished use of the appointment by invitation is a promising development not only in general terms of fairness and transparency but also in terms of gender equality. The influence of activities of gender equality committees and research highlighting the gendered consequences of this seemingly neutral procedure or gender-sensitive media reporting should not be underestimated in raising the invitation issue on the agenda.

During the 1980s and the 1990s, gender awareness has been increasing in the Finnish academy in the forms of women's studies programmes, the introduction and implementation of policies of gender equality and anti-sexual harassment, and the establishment of equality committees in universities. Gender discrimination also has become more visible because it can be legally challenged. Challenging gender discrimination through a legal process is very rare though in part because in the small Finnish scientific community female academics fear being labelled as troublemakers in questioning appointments and decisions they see as discriminatory.

Despite relatively advanced gender equality in many respects, several contradictions and problems nevertheless remain. In as much as women have increased their presence as producers and disseminators of knowledge, academic women in the late 1990s have reported similar kind of experiences of hidden discrimination as they did according to research conducted in the early 1980s (Husu, 2001, 2005b). Gender discrimination has been forbidden by law, and gender equality is promoted by equality plans, but as several researchers, such as Paula Caplan (1993), Nijole Benokraitis (1997), and Joe Feagin (Benokraitis & Feagin, 1995), have pointed out, sanctioning anti-discrimination by law does not mean that it will vanish; rather, discrimination assumes more subtle forms that are more difficult to address. Even though harsh gender discrimination appears to be relatively rare, multiple forms of hidden discrimination continue. Women continue to report invisibility as colleagues in relationship to their male colleagues, lack of encouragement and support, and relative isolation. Although reports of these kinds of experiences seldom reach the public arena, some encouraging recent examples reveal and politicize women's exclusion and marginalization in mainstream fora (e.g., Kaartinen & Korhonen, 2001).

In my 2001 study on sexism, support, and survival in academia, academic women described discrimination that they had experienced in appointments, in allocation of such resources as space and computer facilities, in formal and informal division of labour in their settings, in informal collegial interaction, and in career support. The most striking difference over time has been the framing of sexuality in the context of unequal treatment as a private versus public issue. Sexual harassment policies were adopted in universities beginning the mid-1990s, and they have been problematizing sexual relations in the university context and sensitizing students and staff to the phenomenon that was hardly recognized and seldom named in the early 1980s (Varsa, 1993). Illustrating this is the Ministry of Education 1982 Committee Report on the obstacles to women's research careers wherein sexuality was discussed only in a footnote in the context of women's 'internalized role models' as one basis of exclusion. It was suggested that women dare not try to enter informal male networks because their behaviour could be seen as 'unfeminine or odd' (p. 25). The experiences of informants that would currently be framed as sexual harassment were also hidden in a footnote.[11] The data on sexual harassment elicited in my 2001 study demonstrate not only the seriousness of sexual harassment in academic contexts but also how easily the phenomenon remains covert even after organizational interventions.

How do academic women envision themselves changing universities into more women-friendly institutions? In Finland, the currently high and rising participation rates of women in higher education and postgraduate education has created a widely shared view that reaching gender equality in academia will be only a matter of time. Academic women whom I interviewed for my 2001 study did not share this view, however. They were not convinced that generational shifts would automatically lead to a more gender-equal university; some even saw signs of a rising new macho generation. None of the interviewees framed the 'feminization' of universities and higher education as a threat. Instead, some successful academic women mentioned how their success seemed to be experienced as a threat by some male colleagues.

How women perceive and envision the future of universities is obviously affected by their visions and assessment of their own futures inside the system. Even if most of the informants in my 2001 study could be characterized as ambitious and motivated researchers, many found it very difficult to answer when asked in the interview how they assessed their professional situation in five or ten years' time. This appraisal was especially difficult for those in fixed-term positions, a group to which a majority of mid-career academics in Finland belong. I would not interpret this hesitation and insecurity as lack of motivation or inadequate career planning but rather as a rather realistic inability to evaluate future opportunities in the light of both the research revealing the slow advancement of women in academic hierarchies in Finland and the scarce support that these women had received in their research careers.

Despite women forming a majority among students and rising proportions of women in the recruitment pool to academic positions, universities are still gendered organizations (Acker, 1992; Mills & Tancred, 1992) characterized by official and unofficial gendered division of labour, gendered symbols, gendered forms of interaction, and gendered perceptions of one's own place and future in the organization. Envisioning one's own future and career opportunities in this kind of a contradictory setting is difficult. On the other hand, academic women act as important agents of change in universities. For example, a majority of the participants of my 2001 study indicated that they had intervened in one way or another when encountering various forms of gender discrimination (Husu, 2001, pp. 179–225; 2005b). These interventions, however small they may be, contribute to identifying hidden discriminatory practices, thus making it easier for others to challenge them in the future.

Academic women in my 2001 study valued highly gender equality interventions and policies developed in Finnish universities since the early 1990s. Keeping gender equality on the official university agenda was considered as important as radical inter-ventions, such as gender quotas. Many participants stressed continuity: they thought that gender equality issues should be kept constantly on the university agenda in a variety of forms and should be given even more visibility. They strongly trusted infor-mation and enlightenment. Many academic women believe that in order to make changes happen, the problems should be made public.

These informants were not activists of gender equality or science policy; rather, they were 'rank and file' researchers in different phases of their career paths. The gender equality activists, or members of gender equality committees and networks, would probably envision matters quite differently. These kind of 'change agents' of universities – a group into which I count myself as well – have a much more critical view on the impact of information and enlightenment activities in making change happen. Even if gender equality has been taken up on the university agenda generally, targets and goals seem to turn into practices only slowly, and many kinds of passive resistance can be observed (see, e.g., UNESCO/CEPES 2000; especially Bagilhole, 2000; Müller, 2000; MIT, 1999). Universities are highly resistant to change, as the late science studies scholar Veronica Stolte-Heiskanen has amply remarked (1991, p. 7). Working for gen-der equality in universities can indeed be characterized as 'hard work in the academy' (Fogelberg et al., 1999). In addition to implementing specific gender-marked interven-tions, gender impact analysis must be applied to more general trends, such as the increase of fixed-term contracts and external funding, and their unintended gender consequences should be explored. A strategy of mainstreaming has been increasingly adopted as a framework in Finland for work on gender equality both in the national gender equality policy (Ministry of Social Affairs, 2005b) as well as in universities and other academic organizations. It is, however, a challenging and demanding strategy to implement (EC, 2001), especially in such large and complex organizations as universi-ties, and it is far too early to evaluate how successfully it is going to be implemented in the Finnish academic setting.

Notes

1. The system of academic posts in Finnish universities includes five main categories, which need some clarification for the non-Finnish reader: *Professor* – Highest-ranking member of the academic staff, including fixed-term professorships and rotating professorships; required qualifications are a high scholarly or artistic competence, teaching skills, and the necessary familiarity with the subject area. *Lecturer* – a teacher next in rank to an associate professor (the category of associate professor was abolished completely in 1998 by the new University Law); required qualifications are a licentiate or doctoral degree, good teaching skills, and the necessary familiarity with the practice of the subject area. *Senior assistant* – a fixed-term office for which the required qualifications are a licentiate or a doctoral degree, good teaching skills, and the necessary familiarity with the practice of the subject area. *Assistant* – an academic whose task is to practice independent scholarly research and/or postgraduate studies in a fixed-term office for which a higher academic degree is required. *Untenured full-time teachers and part-time teachers*. In addition to the aforementioned cate-gories, a growing number of full-time researchers with fixed-term contracts also belong to the academic staff of universities. They are funded from various external funding sources, such as the National Research Councils, private foundations and industry, and ministries as well as from the research funds of the respective universities. Reforms of the structure of academic positions have recently been taking place in some universities concerning the mid-categories, and a more comprehensive reform is being discussed. The Council of

University Rectors (FCUR), consisting of all university rectors, has made a proposal in 2004 on a national reform of the position structure and appointment procedures (see http://www.rectors-council.helsinki.fi/), but the issue has not proceeded further yet. [English translations of the terms and their clarifications are taken from the University Glossary (1998), compiled by the Ministry of Education, the Rectors' Council, and the Prime Minister's Office.]

2. Osborn et al.'s (2000) ETAN Report describes 'policy points' on quality and fairness in scientific professions include 'end of use of patronage to fill posts and jobs tailored to fit particular candidates' (p. 31), and the report states that 'good male scientists have nothing to fear from transparent, fair and effective recruitment and promotion practices' (p. 30).

3. Among its principal areas of concern and recommendation to Finland, the CEDAW Committee stated, 'The Committee is concerned about the low presence of women in high-ranking positions in many areas, particularly in academia, where women's presence has been constantly declining as one moves up the academic ladder. The Committee is concerned that the current system of hiring professors by invitation instead of open competition places women at a disadvantage'.

4. For a discussion on the 'multiple agent perspective' of the author, including work as the National Coordinator of Women's Studies and Senior Advisor in the national gender equality machinery during 1981–1996, see Husu (2001).

5. On the Academy of Finland, see http://www.aka.fi > English.

6. The Council for Equality secretariat was first located in the Prime Minister's Office (1972–1986). Since 1986, the secretariat has been located in the Ministry of Social Affairs and Health, which has also housed the other bodies in the Finnish gender equality machinery: the Equality Ombudsman's Office and the Gender Equality Unit. See http://www.stm.fi/Resource.phx/eng/subjt/gendr/index.htx

7. Finland has a multiparty system. The national governments are usually multiparty Coalitions formed by one or several of the largest four parties in the Parliament and additionally by one or few of the small parties. The four largest parties are from right to left: National Coalition Party (the conservative party), the Center Party (former Agrarian Union), the Social Democratic Party, and the Left-Wing Alliance. The small parties that have participated in recent Government coalitions include the Greens, the Swedish People's Party, and the Christian Democrats. After the Parliamentary Elections 2003, the Center Party had 55 MPs out of the total 200, Social Democrats 53, National Coalition 40, Left Alliance 19, Greens 14, Swedish People's Party 9, and the True Finns 3. The Finnish government of Prime Minister Matti Vanhanen was formed in 2003 as a coalition of Center Party, Social Democrats, and Swedish People's Party (on the Finnish party system, see Soikkanen, n.d., and on the history, role and activities of the Parliament, see http://www.eduskunta.fi/ > in English).

8. Development of gender-sensitive statistics on higher education and research has been more advanced in Finland than in many other European countries. National higher education statistics have included sex as a variable since 1966–1967. The Ministry of Education national statistics database on universities, the KOTA database, is searchable online free of charge (http://www.csc.fi/Kota/Kota.html) and from 1988–1989 onwards, includes gender as one variable for students, degrees, and academic positions. Unfortunately, it does not include statistics combining position and discipline by gender. In addition, statistics on applicants and appointments to academic positions by gender are not gathered systematically on a national basis.

9. Records of the Equality Ombudsman's Office.

10. On the Academy of Finland's proposal, the president of the Republic bestows the honorary title of academician on Finnish and foreign scientists and scholars as a mark of recognition for their outstanding academic merit. The title can be held by no more than 12 Finnish scientists and scholars at a time.

11. This footnote stated, 'These fears are as such not ungrounded. Unofficial interaction can create situations, which lead to attempts at sexual approaches. The letter data the

Working Group received had indications that refusal of sexual interaction can lead to the woman becoming under pressure or becoming a target of discrimination' (MinEdu, 1982, p. 25).

References

Academy of Finland (1997) *Naisten tutkijanuran edistäminen. Suomen Akatemian asettaman työryhmän muistio.* Suomen Akatemian julkaisuja 13, 1997. Available also in English:
––––––– (1998) *Women in academia. Report of the working group appointed by the Academy of Finland.* Helsinki: Academy of Finland.
––––––– (2000) *Suomen Akatemian tasa-arvosuunnitelma vuosille 2001–2003 [The Academy of Finland gender equality action plan for 2001–2003].* Helsinki: Academy of Finland.
––––––– (2002) *Women's studies and gender research in Finland.* Evaluation Report. Helsinki: Publications of the Academy of Finland 8.
––––––– (2005) *Suomen Akatemian tasa-arvosuunnitelma vuosille 2005–2007 [The Academy of Finland gender equality action plan for 2005–2007].* Helsinki: Academy of Finland.
Acker, J. (1992) Gendering organizational theory. In A. J. Mills and P. Tancred (Eds.), *Gendering organizational analysis* (pp. 248–260). Newbury Park: Sage.
Ahponen, S., & Paasikoski, A. (2003) *Suunnitelmista tekoihin. Tasa-arvovaltuutetun selvitys tasa-arvosuunnittelusta työpaikoilla* [From plans to deeds: Report of the Gender Equality Ombudsman on gender equality planning in workplaces]. Tasa-arvovaltuutetun toimisto, Sosiaali-ja terveysministeriö, Tasa-arvojulkaisuja 2003:1 [Helsinki: The Office of the Gender Equality Ombudsman, Ministry of Social Affairs and Health, Equality Publications].
Bagilhole, B. (2000) Too little too late? An assessment of national initiatives for women academics in the British university system. *Higher education in Europe, 25*(2):139–145.
Benokraitis, N. V. (1997) *Subtle sexism: Current practice and prospects for change.* Thousand Oaks: Sage.
Benokraitis, N. V., & Feagin, J. R. (1995) *Modern sexism: Blatant, subtle and covert discrimination* (2nd ed.). Englewood Cliffs, NJ: Prentice Hall.
Cockburn, C. (1989) Equal opportunities, the short and long agenda. *Industrial relations journal, 20*(3):213–225.
EC (European Commission) (2003) *She figures 2003: Women and science statistics and indicators.* Luxembourg: Office for Official Publications of the European Communities.
Eurostat (2003) Women in the EU, 8 March 2003: International Women's Day. *Eurostat News Release*, March 5.
Fogelberg, P., Hearn, J., Husu, L., & Mankkinen, T. (Eds.) (1999) *Hard work in the academy: Research and interventions on gender inequalities in higher education.* Helsinki: Helsinki University Press.
Grönroos, M. (2005) *Tasa-arvon tietopalvelu Suomeen. Informaatio – ja dokumentaatio toiminnan selvityshenkilön raportti* [Gender equality information services in Finland: A report on information and documentation]. Sosiaali – ja terveysministeriön työryhmämuistioita 2005:13. [Working Group Memorandums of the Ministry of Social Affairs and Health]. Helsinki.
Hakala, J., Kaukonen, E., Nieminen, M., & Ylijoki, O-H. (2003) *Yliopisto. Tieteen kehdosta projektimyllyksi* [University: From a cradle of science into a project mill]. Helsinki: Gaudeamus.
Heinonen, O-P. (1999) Promotion of gender equality in higher education and research: The role of the Ministry of Education. In P. Fogelberg, J. Hearn, L. Husu, & T. Mankkinen (Eds.), *Hard work in the academy: Research and interventions on gender inequalities in higher education* (pp. 20–24). Helsinki: Helsinki University Press.
Holli, A. (2003) *Discourse and politics for gender equality in late twentieth century Finland.* Acta politica, no. 23. Helsinki: Department of Political Science, University of Helsinki.
Helsingin Sanomat (2003) Tutkijat pelkäävät naisten vyöryä avainpaikoille. Naisvaara [Researchers afraid of women's landslide to key positions. Woman danger]. November 16.

Husu, L. (1997) Kutsu käy, mutta kenelle. Professorinimitykset ja sukupuoli vuonna 1996 [Who is invited? Professorial appointments and gender in 1996]. *Naistutkimus – Kvinnoforskning, 10*(3):33–35.

———— (1999) Gender equality in academia: Contradictions and interventions. In P. Fogelberg, J. Hearn, L. Husu, & T. Mankkinen (Eds.), *Hard work in the academy: Research and interventions on gender inequalities in higher education* (pp. 25–35). Helsinki: Helsinki University Press.

———— (2000) Gender discrimination in the promised land of gender equality. *Higher education in Europe, 25*(2):221–228.

———— (2001) *Sexism, support and survival in academia: Academic women and hidden discrimination in Finland.* Social psychological studies 6. Helsinki: University of Helsinki, Department of Social Psychology.

———— (2004) Naisystävällisempään yliopistoon? Tiedenaiset ja muutoksen visiot [Towards a more woman friendly university? Academic women and visions of change]. *Naistutkimus – Kvinnoforskning 17*(1):4–21.

———— (2005a) Suomen Akatemia ja naistutkimuksen nousu [The Academy of Finland and rise of women's studies]. In M. Pohls (Ed.), *Suomen Akatemian historia II: Yhteiskunta ja tutkimus* [The history of the Academy of Finland II: Society and research]. Helsinki: SKS.

———— (2005b) Women's work-related and family-related discrimination and support in academia. In M. Segal & V. Demos (Eds.), *Gender realities: Local and global.* Advances of gender research 9 (pp. 161–199). Amsterdam: Elsevier.

Husu, L., & Bergman, S. (1993) Women's studies in Finland. In M. Van der Steen & T. Levin (Eds.), *European Women's Studies Guide* (pp. 60–63). Utrecht: WISE.

Husu, L., & Niemelä, P. (1993) Finland. In L. L. Adler (Ed.), *International handbook of gender roles* (pp. 59–76). Westport, CT: Greenwood Press.

Kaartinen, M., & Korhonen, A. (2001) Miesten tiede! Politiikka, sukupuoli ja historian tiedeyhteisö [Men's science! Politics, gender and the scientific community in the history discipline]. *Tieteessä tapahtuu, 19*(1):57–63.

Keskinen, S., & Vallenius, J. (Eds.) (2003) *Tasa-arvo Turun yliopistossa* [Gender equality in University of Turku]. Turun yliopisto, Rehtorinviraston julkaisusarja [Turku: University of Turku, Publication Series of the Rector's Office], no. 1.

Kirton, G., & Greene, A. (2000) *The dynamics of managing diversity: A critical approach.* Oxford: Butterworth Heinemann.

Kivinen, O., & Rinne, R. (1995) Korkeakoululaitoksen kastijako [The caste division of higher education]. *Janus, 2*:97–116.

KOTA Database. National statistical online database updated annually on universities and higher education. Retrieved 24 August 2006 from http://kotaplus.csc.fi.7777/ online/Etusiv.do?Ing=en.

Kurki, H. (2003) Sukupuoli tutkimusjärjestelmässä [Gender in the research system]. In T. Oksanen, A. Lehvo, & A. Nuutinen (Eds.), *Suomen tieteen tila ja taso Katsaus tutkimustoimintaan ja tutkimuksen vaikutuksiin 2000-luvun alussa. [The state and level of research in Finland: Review on research activities and impact of research in the beginning of 2000]* (pp. 136–149). Helsinki: Suomen Akatemian julkaisuja 9 [Publications of the Academy of Finland].

Luukkonen-Gronow, T. (1983) Naistutkija, perhe ja työ [The female researcher, family and work]. *Sosiologia, 20*(1):23–32.

Mankkinen, T. (1995) *Akateemista nuorallatanssia. Sukupuolinen häirintä ja ahdistelu Helsingin yliopistossa [Sexual harassment in the University of Helsinki].* Helsinki: Yliopistopaino.

———— (1999) Walking the academic tightrope: Sexual harassment at the University of Helsinki. In P. Fogelberg, J. Hearn, L. Husu, & T. Mankkinen (Eds.), *Hard work in the academy: Research and interventions on gender inequalities in higher education* (pp. 219–221). Helsinki: Helsinki University Press.

MIT (Massachusetts Institute of Technology) (1999) A study on the status of women faculty in science at MIT. *The MIT faculty newsletter, 11*(4). Retrieved 22 August 2006 from http://web.mit.edu/fnl/women/Fnlwomen.htm.

Mills, A. J., & Tancred, P. (Eds.) (1992) *Gendering organizational analysis*. Newbury Park: Sage.

MinEdu (Ministry of Education, Finland) (1982) Naisten tutkijanuran ongelmat ja esteet. Opetusministeriön asettaman työryhmän mietintö [The problems and obstacles of women's research career: Report of a committee appointed by the Ministry of Education]. Komiteamietintö, report no. 33 [Official Committee Report].

——— (1998) Taulukoita KOTA-tietokannasta [Tables from the KOTA database]. Koulutus – ja tiedepolitiikan osaston julkaisusarja 56 [Helsinki: Publication series of the Ministry of Education Department of Education and Science Policy].

——— (2000) *The graduate school system in Finland: Survey of functioning, results and efficiency by 2000*. Helsinki: Ministry of Education, Department of Education and Science Policy.

——— (2004a) *Finnish universities 2003*. Retrieved 24 August 2006 from http://www.minedu.fi/julkaisut/2004/yhopistot_universiteten_2003?lang=en&extra_locale=en.

——— (2004b) *Research in Finland*. Retrieved from http://www.minedu.fi/julkaisut/Research_in_Finland/Research_in_Finland.pdf.

——— (2005) *Universities 2004. Annual Report*. Ministry of Education Publications 2005:13. Retrieved 24 August 2006 from http://www.minedu.fi/OPM/ sulkaisut/2005/yliopistot2004_vuosikertumus?lang=en&extra_locale=en.

Ministry of Social Affairs and Health (1999) *Finnish family policy*. Helsinki: Ministry of Social Affairs and Health.

——— (2005a) *Family policy and services*. Retrieved from http://www.stm.fi/Resource. phx/eng/subjt/famil/index.htx.

——— (2005b) *Hallituksen tasa-arvo-ohjelma 2004–2007 [Gender equality program of the Government of Finland 2004–2007]*. Helsinki: Sosiaali – ja terveysministeriön julkaisuja [Publications of the Ministry of Social Affairs and Health].

Müller, U (2000) Gender equality programmes in German institutions of higher education: The North Rhine-Westphalia case. *Higher education in Europe, 25*(2): 155–161.

Naistutkimus 2000 (1996) 'Naistutkimuksen valtakunnallinen kehittämissuunnitelma. Suomen Naistutkimuksen Seura, Tasa-arvoasiain neuvottelukunta' [National action plan on developing women's studies, by the Finnish Women's Studies Association and Council for Equality between Women and Men]. Sosiaali – ja terveysministeriö, Tasa-arvoasiain neuvottelukunta, Naistutkimusraportteja, report no. 2 [Helsinki: Ministry of Social Affairs and Health, Council for Equality, Women's Studies Reports].

Naskali, P. (2004) Eihän meillä ole mitään ongelmia? Henkilökunnan ja opiskelijoiden kokemuksia tasa-arvon ja yhdenvertaisuuden toteutumisesta Lapin yliopistossa [On experiences of gender equality in University of Lapland]. Lapin yliopiston hallinnon julkaisuja 43. University of Lapland: University Administration Publications.

Osborn, M., Rees, T., Bosch, M., Hermann, C., Hilden, J., McLaren, A., Palomba, R., Peltonen, L., Vela, C., Weis, D., Wold, A., & Wennerås, C. (2000) *Science policies in the European Union: Promoting excellence through mainstreaming gender equality. A report from the ETAN Network on Women and Science*. Brussels: European Commission, Research Directorate-General.

SVT (Official Statistics of Finland) (1981) *Korkeakoulut 1970–1979 [Higher education 1970–1979]*. XXXVII: 9. Helsinki: Statistics Finland.

——— (1998) *Koulutus Suomessa [Education in Finland]*. Helsinki: Statistics Finland.

Pasanen (2003) *Sitä ei voi enää nimittää pelkäksi vitsailuksi. Selvitys sukupuolisesta häirinnästä ja ahdistelusta Tampereen yliopistossa* [You cannot call it only joking anymore: A report on sexual harassment in the University of Tampere]. Tampereen yliopisto tänään ja huomenna, Yliopiston sisäisiä kehittämisehdotuksia, muistioita ja raportteja 61. [Tampere: University of Tampere today and tomorrow. Internal development proposals, memoranda and reports from the University of Tampere].

Pulkkinen, P. (Ed.) (2000) Naiset ja miehet vallankahvassa. Päätöksentekoindikaattoreita eri hallinnon aloilta ja organisaatioista [Women and men in positions of power: Decision making indicators from different branches of administration and organizations]. *Tilastokeskus: Sukupuolten tasa-arvo* 2000: 003 [Statistics Finland: Gender Statistics]

Rahunen, P. (1999) 'Tasa-arvon toteutuminen Helsingin kauppakorkeakoulussa' [Gender equality in the Helsinki School of Economics]. Unpublished master's thesis, Department of Management, University of Helsinki, Helsinki, Finland.

Raivio, K. (2002) Muuttuuko yliopisto tyttökouluksi? [Is the university turning to a girls' school? Editorial of the University of Helsinki magazine]. *Yliopisto, 50*(16).

Sinkkonen, M. (1997) *Tasa-arvo Kuopion yliopistossa [Gender equality in the University of Kuopio].* Kuopio: Kuopion yliopiston julkaisuja F [Kuopio University Publications].

Soikkanen, T. (n.d.) Structure and development of political parties. Retrieved from http://virtual.finland.fi/Politics_society/ >.

Statistics Finland (1999) *Education in Finland. Statistics and indicators.* Helsinki: Statistics Finland.

――― (2001) Women and Men in Finland 2001. In *Statistics Finland: Gender statistics* 2001:02. Helsinki: Statistics Finland.

Statistics Finland (2005) *Tiede ja teknologia 2004, 5 [Science, technology and research].* Helsinki: Statistics Finland.

Stolte-Heiskanen, V. (1991) Introduction. In V. Stolte-Heiskanen, V. Acar, F. Acar, N. Ananieva, & D. Gaudart in collaboration with R. Fürst-Dilič (Eds.), *Women in science: Token women or gender equality?* (pp. 1–8). Oxford: Berg.

Ståhle, B. (1996) *Universitetet och forskarna – från stagnation till förnyelse. Universitetsforskare, forskarurbildning och forskarrekrytering i Norden.* Köpenhamn: Nordiska Ministerrådet.

The Government Programme of Prime Minister Matti Vanhanen's Government (2003).

Tuohinto, A. (1964) *Suomalainen nainen ja tieteellinen työ. Painettuihin lähteisiin pohjautuva selvitys* [The Finnish woman and scientific work. A report based on printed source material]. Helsinki: Suomen Kulttuurirahasto.

CEDAW (United Nations Committee on Elimination of Discrimination Against Women) (2001) *Concluding Observations of the Committee on the Elimination of Discrimination against Women: Finland.* Consideration of reports of States parties, 3rd and 4th periodic reports, January 24, 2001.

UNDP (United Nations Development Programme) (1995) *Gender and human development.* UNDP Human Development Report 1995. Retrieved 25 August 2006 from http://hdr.undp.org/reports/global/1995/en/.

――― (2001) Making new technologies work for human development. *UNDP Human Development Report 2001.* Retrieved 25 August 2006 from http://hdr.undp.org/reports/global/2001/en/.

――― (2004) Cultural liberty in today's diverse world. *UNDP Human Development Report 2004.* Retrieved 25 August 2006 from http://hdr.undp.org/reports/global/2004/.

UNESCO/CEPES (United Nations Educational, Scientific and Cultural Organization\ European Centre for Higher Education[Centre Européen d¥Enseignement Supérieur]) (2000) A special issue on academe and gender: What has and has not changed? *Higher education in Europe, 25*(2), L. Husu and L. Morley (Eds.).

Välinoro, J., & Siimes, M. (1998) *Jämställdhet vid Åbo Akademi. En kartläggning om jäm-ställdhet bland de anställda vid ÅA. Rapport* [Gender equality in the Abo Academy university. Report of a survey on gender equality among the employees in the Abo Academy]. Åbo: Åbo Akademi.

Varjus, T. (1997) *Pihlajanmarjoja ja tiiliseiniä akateemisessa maailmassa. Katsaus tasa-arvoon Joensuun yliopistossa* [A review on gender equality in the University of Joensuu]. Joensuun yliopiston yhteiskuntapolitiikan ja filosofian laitos, Yhteiskuntapolitiikan tutkimuksia 6 [Joensuu: University of Joensuu, Studies from the Department of social policy and philosophy].

Varsa, H. (1993) *Sukupuolinen häirintä ja ahdistelu työelämässä: näkymättömälle nimi* [Sexual harassment in working life: Naming the invisible]. Sosiaali – ja terveysministeriö, Tasa-arvojulkaisuja, sarja A, Tutkimuksia 1 [Helsinki: Ministry of Social Affairs and Health, Equality Publications, series A, Research Reports].

Voutilainen, J. (1996) *Naisten akateemiseen uraan vaikuttavista tekijöistä Turun yliopistossa* [On factors influencing women's academic career in the University of Turku]. Turun yliopiston hallintoviraston julkaisuja 1. [Turku: University of Turku, Publications of the administration office].

World Economic Forum (2005) *Women's empowerment: Measuring the global gender gap.* Cologny/Geneva: World Economic Forum.

References to Legislation

Act 232/2005 on Changing the Act on Equality Between Women and Men.
Act 609/1986 on Equality between Women and Men: Amendments in 1992, 1995, 1997, 2001.
Act 648/1997 on Changing the Act on Appointment of Professors and Associate Professors.
Act 856/1991 on Appointment of Professors and Assistant Professors in Universities.

CHAPTER EIGHT

PROMOTION OF GENDER EQUALITY IN THE UNIVERSITY OF HELSINKI

Liisa Husu and Terhi Saarikoski

The University of Helsinki is the oldest and largest university in Finland. Its precursor institution, The Royal Academy of Turku, was established in 1640 in the city of Turku as a Swedish university when Finland was part of Sweden. In 1809, Finland became an autonomous Grand Duchy of Imperial Russia as a result of the Swedish-Russian War of 1808–1809, and the Royal Academy of Turku was renamed the Imperial Academy of Turku. The Russian emperor transferred the university from Turku to Helsinki in 1828 and renamed it the Imperial Alexander University in Finland. After Finland became an independent state in 1917, the name of the university was changed to University of Helsinki in 1919 (University of Helsinki, n.d.a).

Until 1909, the University of Helsinki was the only university level institution in Finland and, until 1919, the only multifaculty university in the country. It is currently one of the largest universities in the Nordic countries in terms of the number of students and the range of disciplines. It has four major campuses in Helsinki and various units in at least 20 other locations in Finland from the southern coast to Lapland within the Arctic Circle. The university is bilingual (Finnish and Swedish, the official languages of the country), and tuition is increasingly offered in English.

The faculty is the basic administrative unit in Finnish universities, usually consisting of several departments in one broad field of study. The University of Helsinki consists of 11 faculties: theology, law, medicine, arts, science, education, social sciences, agriculture and forestry, veterinary medicine, biosciences, and pharmacy. In addition, the university hosts several independent research institutes, often interdisciplinary in their orientation, in, for example, Russian and East European studies (Alexander Institute), economic research (Helsinki Center of Economic Research), information technology (Helsinki Institute of Information Technology), genome research (Finnish Genome Center), biotechnology (Institute of Biotechnology), neuroscience (Neuroscience Center), and social sciences and humanities (Helsinki Collegium for Advanced Studies).

In the University Strategic Plan for 2004–2006, there is a strong emphasis on developing research, researcher training, and research-based teaching (University of Helsinki, 2003). The Strategic Plan identifies the vision of the university as follows: 'University of Helsinki will establish its position among the best

European multi-disciplinary universities. The level of its research and degrees are relied upon, and especially interdisciplinary research and research-based teaching are flourishing there' (p. 5). Helsinki participates currently in over half of the nationally selected Centres of Excellence in research, hosts 24 national level graduate schools, and participates in 55 national graduate schools coordinated by other universities. The university is a member of the League of European Research Universities (LERU), a network of leading European research universities. The university is actively engaged in international cooperation around research and teaching, having 80 cooperation agreements with universities throughout the world and participating actively in Nordic Nordplus Cooperation, European Union SOCRATES Cooperation, and EU Framework Programmes.

Universities in Finland are publicly funded, and their activities are regulated by national university legislation, but they have a high level of autonomy in academic matters and internal management guaranteed by the constitution. Both the highest officials and decision-making bodies are elected internally from among the university staff and students, and the key decision-making bodies have representation of professors, academic and non-academic staff, and students. In the University of Helsinki, the highest university management consists of the rector, vice-rectors, and the university senate (the highest university board, called the Consistorium). In addition, the University of Helsinki has a chancellor, whose task is to promote sciences generally, to act as a figurehead for the university, to supervise the activities of the university, and to serve as the formal appointing authority in highest academic appointments, including hearing of appeals in application matters. The rector is the head of the university and is responsible for the management of the university. He or she is elected for a five-year period from among the candidates that have been put forward by the university community.[1] The rector is elected by the Electoral College consisting of professors, researchers and teachers, non-academic staff, and students. The chancellor is appointed for five years by the president of Finland after the Electoral College has put forward three candidates for consideration for the position.[2]

The university level strategies and guidelines have to be approved by the university senate. In addition to the rector, who acts as a chairperson, the senate currently has 14 members: five professors, two other teachers, two representatives of staff, four students, and one external member. At the faculty level, the decision-making body is the faculty council, chaired by the dean, and at the departmental level, the department-leading group, chaired by the head of the department. The faculty and departmental level have a high level of autonomy in academic matters. The university senate, the faculty councils, and the department-leading groups are all elected for a three-year period. The faculties play a central role in the appointment of academic staff, in awarding higher degrees, and in many other academic matters. The faculty council is the principal decision-making body at the faculty level concerned with research and teaching. The dean is the head of the faculty and chairperson of the faculty council and is responsible for general management in the faculty. The dean is elected by the faculty council members for a fixed-term period. Recently, most faculties have begun electing vice-deans to handle research, teaching, and outreach issues.

The position of dean is important because they traditionally have formed the recruitment pool for the rectorate. The rector appoints the vice-rectors from among the professoriate after consulting with the university community. According to the

University of Helsinki Regulations, 'In electing the rector and vice-rectors, it should be aimed for that different disciplinary fields and campuses be represented as evenly as possible and that gender equality be promoted' (University of Helsinki, 2003). The highest management of the University of Helsinki has been very male-dominated until very recently, but currently two out of four vice-rectors are women. The first woman vice-rector was Theology Professor Raija Sollamo, and she was appointed in 1998. Earlier, she was also the first female dean, appointed in 1992, in the Faculty of Theology. Of the 11 faculties, only 2 other faculties have ever had a female dean: Humanities and Education. In 2005, only 2 of the 11 deans were women, but several women have recently been appointed as vice-deans. The university has never had a woman rector or chancellor.

Of the 38,500 degree students at the University of Helsinki, 63% are women. In 2004 4,177 degrees were taken, 395 of which were doctorates. Since 2001, women have comprised over half of the doctoral degree recipients, accounting for 56% in 2004. The total number of staff, including administrative, technical, and academic staff is 7,500, of which 4,635 (62%) are researchers or teachers. Of academic staff, 7% are professors, and 20% are researchers funded mainly by external funds. The proportion of women among full professors was 25% in 2004, which is somewhat higher than the national average (see figure 8.1).

Multiple Roles and Their Implications

Systematic research has yet to be conducted on gender equality policies in Finnish higher education in general and related activities of individual universities, including the University of Helsinki. In this chapter, we draw primarily on official university documents and statistics and on our long-term experiences in the field associated with several roles: student, activist, gender equality adviser at the national and university levels. Additionally, we have also drawn from information obtained from a few other insiders or key players in gender equality promotion, such as previous chairs of the Equality Committee and several persons who have acted as equality advisers or secretaries of the Equality Committee since the mid-1990s.

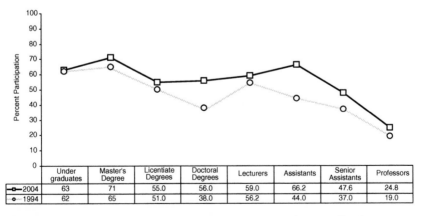

	Under graduates	Master's Degree	Licentiate Degrees	Doctoral Degrees	Lecturers	Assistants	Senior Assistants	Professors
2004	63	71	55.0	56.0	59.0	66.2	47.6	24.8
1994	62	65	51.0	38.0	56.2	44.0	37.0	19.0

Figure 8.1   Representation of Women among Students and Academic Staff at the University of Helsinki

Source: Author's University of Helsinki internal institutional statistics.

Our multiple roles have provided us with useful insider perspectives and privileged access to much tacit knowledge on gender equality developments in the University of Helsinki (see authors' biographical statements). However, these roles also restrict us to some extent; we both have accumulated an extensive amount of relevant confidential knowledge throughout the years that can be disclosed only in very general terms for ethical reasons. We have attempted to maintain a critical perspective of our university setting, yet we recognize that our insider roles in the processes we are describing make the task far from unproblematic.

Introducing Gender Equality in the University Agenda: From Grassroots towards Institutional Incorporation

During the 1990s and until 2005, the issue of gender equality has been brought gradually onto the official agenda of the University of Helsinki, and an infrastructure for gender equality promotion, prevention of discrimination, and related strategies, policies, and practices has been developed. This university was among the first Finnish universities to adopt a gender equality plan and appoint an Equality Committee, and it is currently the only university in Finland with a full-time equality adviser. In 2005, the core of the gender equality infrastructure consisted of the Equality Committee, which represents groups of staff and different faculties and has student representation. Because gender equality is named as a field of responsibility in the division of tasks among the four vice-rectors, one of them chairs the committee. Appointed by the university senate for a three-year term, the committee works closely with the equality adviser and has recently created a network of contact persons in all units in the university in order to better reach the departmental level where many important decisions concerning teaching, research, and appointments are made. The key instruments for promoting gender equality and diversity in the university are the Gender Equality Plan and the Action Plan against Discrimination, drafted by the committee and adopted by the university senate. In addition, guidelines for the prevention and handling of sexual harassment have been issued. The Gender Equality Plans of 2001–2003 and 2004–2006 are based on the principle of gender mainstreaming.

The development of gender equality promotion in the University of Helsinki can be divided roughly into three phases: an *initial phase* (1989–1991), *consolidation phase* (1992–2000), and *gender equality and diversity phase* (2001–present). These are briefly described and discussed in this chapter, and the roles of some key players and influences are explored. We also assess the extent to which formal university level policies and strategies have been actually implemented and practiced at the departmental/unit and faculty levels where many important decisions are made. Furthermore, we not only identify contradictions, tensions, and dynamics of resistance but also highlight some success stories of the Helsinki case. Finally, we discuss future challenges for gender equality promotion.

Initial Phase: Activism and a Reluctant Opening

The introductory phase of gender equality promotion, 1989–1991, was characterized by enthusiasm and activism among many university women and a gradual and somewhat reluctant opening of the University of Helsinki for gender equality as an issue that had relevance for the organization. In the Helsinki case in the late 1980s and early 1990s, initiatives for taking up gender equality issues on the official university agenda did not come from top-down, that is, from university management, but rather from outside and inside the university from bottom-up: from the national gender equality authorities, from some women faculty, and from feminist students' groups. Women faculty active in this initial phase had been involved in the activities of a vibrant and active NGO, the Association of Women Researchers in Helsinki (Helsingin Tutkijanaiset ry.), which was established in 1982 and which brought together several hundred academic women in Helsinki area in regular informal meetings to discuss the position of women academics and women's studies (Nordgren, 1984). Some of the women faculty activists had also been long-term expert members in the National Council for Equality Subcommittee for Research (on the subcommittee, see chapter 7 in this book). Women's studies was rapidly gaining ground at the national level with a national association and scientific journal launched at the end of the 1980s. The first Equality Act had come into force in 1987, and the Equality Ombudsman had given the universities detailed guidelines on how to promote gender equality in 1990 (see chapter 7 in this book).

Nevertheless, the university management in the early 1990s hardly perceived gender inequality as a problem or issue that would concern universities. One of the early gender equality activists, Professor Raija Sollamo, who was later to become the first female dean and vice-rector of the university, describes the views of university management during this initial phase:

> An illusion of gender equality already realized prevailed in the University of Helsinki [in the early 1990s]. The management believed that gender equality had been realized whereas, in other positions, people were sure that it had not. (personal communication, January 11, 2005)

The prevailing gender climate in the university in the initial phase is also illustrated by an episode from the site visit of the Equality Ombudsman at the University of Helsinki in the late 1980s. The Equality Ombudsman together with the national coordinator of Women's Studies conducted site visits in most universities to discuss how the new act was going to affect universities. Liisa Husu, then national coordinator, recalls how the rector greeted them in a friendly manner but hastened to add that the new act would not be relevant for universities because '[w]e make all decisions based on objective scientific criteria' (Husu 2001, pp. ix–x).

Faculty and students who were actively developing women's studies in Helsinki played a key role in pushing the university into action for gender equality in the early 1990s. Women's studies had been developed gradually in the University of Helsinki and elsewhere in Finnish academia during the 1980s. In Helsinki, women's studies and gender research were introduced by a small group of women faculty, scattered throughout different departments, mainly from the Faculties of Arts and Social Sciences. Networking of these women had been facilitated by their engagement in the Association of Women Researchers in Helsinki and membership of the Subcommittee of Research by the National Council for Equality. Many activists came from humanities, among them historian Päivi Setälä, who later became the first women's studies professor in the university. The first women's studies courses in Helsinki were coordinated from the Department of Finnish, the academic home of one early senior women's studies activist, Associate Professor Auli Hakulinen. It is noteworthy that both Setälä and Hakulinen had been long-term members of the National Council for Equality Subcommittee of Research since the early 1980s.

Academic staff who were teaching women's studies submitted a formal motion to the university senate in January 1989 that the university establish a Gender Equality Committee and that the first task of the committee should be to prepare a gender equality plan for the university. The motion was discussed and the decision to establish an ad hoc committee was finally taken in the third meeting in March 1989. The composition of this first Equality Committee was very interesting because many of the members later took important leadership roles, including the current rector of the university, Professor Ilkka Niiniluoto. Like the subsequent standing Gender Equality Committees, the ad hoc committee had both female and male members.[3]

The first activities of the ad hoc Equality Committee included mapping the state of the issue, which resulted in a report of gender equality in the university, the first of its kind, and a motion to the university senate to establish a women's studies institute. After appointing a committee to complete the preparatory work for setting up such an institute, the university senate established a women's studies institute in May 1990: the Christina Institute of Women's Studies, named after Queen Christina of Sweden, who established the university in 1640. Helsinki was the third university in Finland to establish a women's studies institute, after Åbo Akademi University (1986) and University of Tampere (1990).

The motion for the first Gender Equality Plan was presented by the committee late 1990 to the university senate, who after four meetings gave the green light to a Gender Equality Decree, which the chancellor confirmed in late 1990. This decree defined the administration of gender equality promotion in the university. It also defined the set up of the standing Equality Committee, including its composition and responsibilities. The committee was to have ten members: one member from the university senate, three representing teaching and research staff, and one representing the administrative staff. In addition, the Trade Union associations of the university staff were to propose three members, the Student Union two members, and the Christina Institute of Women's Studies one member. The responsibilities of the Equality Committee were to promote and monitor gender equality in the university and to prepare the Gender Equality Plan. The equality adviser was also mentioned in the decree, but it took nearly ten years, until 2000, before the first full-time equality adviser was appointed.

Consolidation Phase: Building an Infrastructure

The consolidation phase, from 1992 to 2005 can be divided into two phases: (1) an initial institutional phase (1992–1994) during which the first standing Equality Committee prepared the initial equality plan, creating a platform for activities and systematically collecting information on gender equality promotion; and (2) the actual consolidation phase (1995–2000) during which extensive equality plans were implemented.

The first standing Equality Committee was appointed in the autumn 1992, and Vice-Rector Paul Fogelberg, professor of geology, was appointed chair. The initial institutional phase included training of the key players, the chair and secretary of the committee, in gender equality promotion by participating in an extensive national training programme on gender equality. The chair and secretary created contacts and exchanged ideas and experiences with gender equality committees and key players in other Finnish and Nordic universities. The main task of the first standing Equality Committee was to prepare an equality plan for the university.

The consolidation phase followed when the first Gender Equality Action Plan 1995–1999 came into force. Since the beginning, the University of Helsinki equality plans have applied a 'long agenda' (Cockburn, 1989; Kirton & Greene, 2000) on gender equality, including a broad range of issues, instead of a short agenda of fulfilling only the minimum requirements of the equality legislation. The first plan covered teaching, research and doctoral training, and issues related to the work environment. The plan included broad guidelines of gender equality promotion and was to be complemented by annual action plans using concrete measures.

One significant initiative during this phase concerned a mentoring programme for staff. The Equality Committee's initiative for such a programme came through contacts with Swedish equality committees. The programme was first piloted in cooperation with both the Personnel Department and the Alumni Association and was considered so successful that mentoring programme became part of the personnel training offered to the university staff for both women and men (Evers, 2000). A second important initiative addressed prevention of sexual harassment and is discussed below in more detail.

Sexual Harassment on the Agenda

An important new issue in the Finnish equality context of the mid-1990s was inspired by contacts with Swedish universities: sexual harassment and how to prevent it in the university environment. At the same time, sexual harassment was for the first time introduced as a concept in Finnish legislation, in the 1995 amendment of the Equality Act. According to the sixth clause of the act, the employer must make sure that no employee shall be subject to sexual harassment in the workplace. Efforts against sexual harassment have since been a part of the gender equality agenda in the University of Helsinki. In this, Helsinki has been a pioneer among Finnish universities. In 1995, the Equality Committee commissioned an extensive empirical study of sexual harassment in the university (Mankkinen, 1995, 1999) among staff and students. Mankkinen's study was path-breaking because it was the first large sexual harassment survey in either a university or large workplace in Finland. Several other universities followed the example, often using the Helsinki study as a model. The study included both qualitative and quantitative approaches to measure the frequency and nature of sexual harassment in the university to suggest possible ways to prevent it. According to the study, 11% of the staff (both academic and non-academic) and 6% of the students had experienced sexual harassment during their time at the university. Of those staff members who had experienced sexual harassment during the past two years, 78% were women; the corresponding figure for students was 70%. Mankkinen (1995) concluded that sexual harassment has a demoralizing effect on the general work atmosphere, lowers job satisfaction, decreases female students' motivation, and prolongs their studies.

As an outcome of the harassment study, guidelines on the prevention of sexual harassment were first issued in 1996 and revised in 2004. Sanctions for harassment are caution, reprimand, or notice of termination, and in physical assault cases, application of the penal code. Activities to prevent sexual harassment and create means of active intervention have been systematized since the mid-1990s, and the university has appointed contact persons responsible for dealing with alleged sexual harassment of both staff and students. Currently, the equality adviser works as the contact person for staff, and the Student Union employs two contact persons for students. To monitor the prevalence of sexual harassment in the university, the equality adviser annually collects statistics on harassment complaints, methods of handling them, and measures taken. The equality adviser arranges training for management of units and contact persons of the Student Union and for officials and student organizations of other Finnish universities on sexual harassment prevention and the handling of alleged harassment cases.

Between 2001 and 2003, the University of Helsinki equality adviser recorded 65 contacts, most of which were related to alleged gender discrimination or sexual harassment. To intervene in a case of alleged harassment, the equality adviser usually cooperates with the head of the unit where alleged harassment has taken place, if this is possible, and generally works together with a team usually comprised of the university lawyer and the occupational health specialist of personnel services. They have found this cooperation to be fruitful, offering wide-ranging expertise. The University of Helsinki equality adviser, Terhi Saarikoski, has found that those cases of alleged harassment reported to her have usually been handled properly in the faculties and other units of the university, but sometimes responsibilities are not clear to the management. They would benefit from support and training to deal with cases of sexual harassment.

It is also sometimes difficult to distinguish discrimination from harassment and bullying (Hearn & Parkin, 2001). Consequently, the University of Helsinki has developed common guidelines for handling inappropriate treatment such as discrimination, harassment, and bullying, not simply those that are identified as gender-related (University of Helsinki, n.d.b). Presenting a challenge for prevention and intervention practices, sometimes the victims of discrimination or harassment do not seem to want any measures taken and may express a desire only to tell somebody what has happened. This reticence is obviously problematic from the perspective of the organization, which is asked to offer only relief and validation for the victim but is not able to address the source of the problem in order to stop the harassing behaviour that may target others. The equality adviser does not proceed in an alleged harassment case if the person alleging harassment does not consent to proceed. The reluctance to proceed is often linked to the vulnerable position of most students and staff. Most students and large groups of academic staff in fixed-term positions are in dependent positions vis-à-vis their teachers, supervisors, and employers, and their reluctance to proceed in harassment cases when they are dependent on the alleged harasser may reflect a realistic fear of potential retaliation. It obviously witnesses a mistrust in the implementation of university's intervention policies and ability to protect the victim and is a challenge to be taken seriously. It should also be stressed that all cases of harassment are not necessarily reported and recorded.

Long-term monitoring of the situations of people who have been involved in harassment cases is now included in the equality plan in order to prevent retaliation by the harasser. However, this kind of monitoring has been complicated by scarce resources, lack of continuity in the equality adviser function, and transparency problems in the settings where harassment has taken place. Retaliation may also be targetted to other members of staff who have tried to intervene in a harassment case, which can be skillfully masked as normal scientific or administrative behaviour. Husu's 2001 study on gender discrimination of academic women, with data from 11 universities, revealed retaliation processes that included harassers' attempts to sabotage and cause professional damage to a person – colleague and even a female boss – who had tried to intervene and stop his sexually harassing behaviour in the setting. Because the occurrence of sexual harassment goes unnoticed by many people in the setting and because formal complaints documenting the harassment are rare, retaliation and sabotage caused by rejection or the intervention by others can appear to others in the setting as 'normal' professional behaviour (Husu, 2001, pp. 252–253).

Gender Equality and Diversity Phase: Broadening Agenda and Tensions

The third ongoing phase of gender equality promotion began in early 2000. During this phase, the gender equality agenda was broadened to cover diversity issues and discrimination on grounds other than gender, such as ethnicity, age, sexuality, nationality, and disability; thus, the composition of the Equality Committee was changed accordingly to include members who had expertise in these areas. This development was prompted partly not only by the development of international, especially European, anti-discrimination legislation but also by a local racist incident against a black student that took place in front of a central university building and for which the university was criticized for being passive in its response. The Equality Committee had heard the complaints of the student in question and discussed potential measures. Professor Thomas Wilhelmsson, the new vice-rector elected in 1998 to be in charge of gender equality issues, was approached and asked to take action. He recalls,

> I thought that the easiest solution would be to broaden the field of the Gender Equality Committee and asked the university lawyer to draft a change for the Gender Equality Decree. He hinted that it would not be so easy, and I soon understood that, as a new vice-rector, I had been quite naïve, thinking that the issue could have been solved so easily. The delegations of supporters of 'traditional' equality issues, when hearing about the ideas, came to see me and expressed their dissatisfaction that their issues would be mixed with these quite different things. The issue was not brought [first] to the university senate, even if a motion had been prepared by the university lawyer, but to the Equality Committee. This resulted, for a good reason, in a broader and more thorough preparation of the issue, which later led to broadening of the scope [of the plan and the committee]. (personal communication, January 11, 2005)

As the quotation indicates, there was some resistance and tension among those engaged in gender equality promotion around broadening the university's equality agenda to diversity issues. One of the central concerns was fear of losing resources from gender equality work, considering that the only specifically designated resource person for gender equality promotion at the time was the part-time equality adviser. The Equality Committee was ready to make a move, however, and prepared a Diversity Plan, which introduced measures by which discrimination on grounds of ethnic origin, religion or belief, disability, age or sexual orientation, or any other corresponding factor can be prevented.

The committee, however, stressed that if the equality agenda was to be broadened, a full-time equality adviser was needed in order to manage the new demands and expanding workload. This argument was successful, and a full-time equality adviser was appointed in the beginning of 2000.

The Gender Equality Decree was revised in 2000. The role of the Equality Committee was strengthened, expanding its agenda from gender equality to include diversity promotion more broadly and making more explicit its link to the highest university management. The committee was to work under the leadership of one vice-rector, who was given responsibility for monitoring and promoting equality in the university.

The university senate accepted the first Diversity Plan in 2001. Anti-discrimination legislation came into force in Finland somewhat later in the beginning of 2004. In 2005, the Equality Committee began to revise the Diversity Plan to make its provisions more concrete and to better address multiple discrimination. The intent of the anti-discrimination practices was to take into account the special problems faced by the people who belong to more than one group vulnerable for discrimination.

Key Players of Gender Equality Promotion in the University of Helsinki: The Equality Committee and the Equality Adviser

The Equality Committee has broad representation of staff and students and is linked to the highest management, but it should be stressed that the committee lacks executive power. It functions more as a university-level agenda-setting, planning, monitoring, advisory, and information body. It develops policies, formulates general operational principles and good practices, and disseminates information about them. The committee works closely with the equality adviser.

However, the Equality Decree allows the Equality Committee to be consulted and to give opinions in alleged discrimination cases. The chancellor of the University of Helsinki, who appoints university professors after receiving proposals from the faculty councils and who investigates appeals by candidates against these proposals, has consulted the Equality Committee in a few cases of alleged discrimination in professorial appointments before making the final appointment decision. Furthermore, in a few cases, an individual who is alleging discrimination in hiring has asked the committee to give a statement regarding her or his case before taking further steps in a complaint.[4] In such cases, however, the committee's recommendations are not binding and are not necessarily followed by the decision makers. One such case involving the committee led finally to a suit brought against the university for gender discrimination, and the university had to pay compensation to a female scholar.[5] The Equality Plan states that the financial compensation in case of breaking the Gender Equality Act must be paid by the department or faculty responsible for the discriminatory decision.

As the first contact person for staff and students for gender equality problems, the equality adviser provides advice, counselling, information, and training in matters relating to equality, develops equality-related activities in the university, and prepares reports on equality. The equality adviser is located administratively in the personnel services, but there has been some ambiguity surrounding the location of the post. The post of the equality adviser has been fixed-term until recently, meaning there has been a lack of continuity in this central function. Several previous equality advisers have characterized the post as highly motivating because of its aim to promote gender equality and diversity and have found rewarding the cases they had managed to solve successfully. On the other hand, the task was considered emotionally challenging and burdensome, and job counselling was seen as much needed support for coping in the task.

The role of the equality adviser may involve in-built tension because of high expectations and his or her actual capability to intervene. Among the staff and students, the expectations on the equality adviser are high partly because the job profile is still slightly vague. On one hand, the equality adviser, as a representative of the university, is expected to be fair and objective, but, simultaneously, he or she must give proper advice and support to employees or students as well as to the management of the university units who are responsible for resolving the cases of alleged discrimination or harassment. Because the department and unit managers and the collective decision-making bodies have the formal authority to decide cases, the task to take measures in alleged discrimination cases or in promoting equality is made more difficult whenever they are reluctant to cooperate. The position of the equality adviser at the University of Helsinki is thus far unique among Finnish universities, which means that there is little possibility of professional support from colleagues with similar responsibilities from other universities. Furthermore, the image of the job may suggest that the equality adviser has more power than she or he actually has.

Incentives to Encourage and Support Gender Equality Initiatives

Promoting gender equality in universities is often experienced as working against the grain or 'hard work in the academy' (Fogelberg et al., 1999). To give recognition and encouragement for these activities, since 1996, the University of Helsinki has annually acknowledged a person, group, or unit that has actively promoted equality or has produced research and information about gender equality in the university. This award, the Maikki Friberg Prize, named after an early gender equality activist and scholar, is given to raise consciousness about equality issues. The amount of the award is 4,200 Euros (2005).

To encourage and support new equality initiatives throughout the university, annual funding of 40,000 Euros has been divided among several projects promoting equality in the university units since 2002. These projects are related to administration, research, or teaching, and any individual, group, or unit within the university may submit proposals and apply for funding. Thus far, the university has financed some 20 equality projects. The purpose of these projects is to produce new knowledge and develop good practices that promote equality and diversity in the university.

The equality project funding has made possible some in-depth studies of particular departments and faculties for the purpose of understanding academic climates and cultures and the overt and covert forms of discrimination as points for bringing about change. Two studies were conducted in especially male-dominated settings: Department of Political Science (Kantola, 2005) and Faculty of Law (Ahtela, 2004). Johanna Kantola's study on gender equality at the Department of Political Science highlighted the gendered structures and gender dynamics of that department. Women comprised over 60% of the department's undergraduate and 40% of the postgraduate students but only 18% of those obtaining PhDs; there were no women teaching staff – all professors and lecturers were men. The study demonstrated that gender awareness among undergraduate students was low and that the department had not provided them with intellectual tools to approach gender issues. In the evaluation of students, gender differences were found in men's favour. In the department, men were three times more likely than women were to get a top grade for their master's theses between 1990 and 2003. Subjective experiences of postgraduate students varied also by gender. Postgraduate male students were fairly satisfied with the supervision they had received in the department whereas female postgraduates were highly dissatisfied. Opportunities to teach as postgraduate students – important experience if one is aiming for an academic career – had been offered to some of the men but not to any women. As a result, many women felt like outsiders at the department.

Evaluating Success of the Equality Plan

The large size of the university with its 11 faculties, several independent institutes, and decentralization into four campuses has complicated the task of monitoring gender equality development in different parts and units. A comprehensive evaluation of the Gender Equality Plan for 2001–2003 was designed and carried out to monitor its development and to better understand the views, actions or lack of them, and gender climate within different faculties. In addition to analysing available statistics, the committee conducted interviews (Tasa-arvotoimikunta, 2004) and found that mainstreaming as a basic policy principle had not functioned as expected. The contents of the Gender Equality Plan were not generally well known in all faculties, and awareness of gender equality problems appeared to be low among many faculty leaders. Many of the measures included in the plan had not materialized. Faculties did not systematically monitor their appointment policies by gender and collect statistics on these. Several key goals, such as the appointment of more women to the professoriate, had not been achieved. Even if the proportion of women had increased among the PhDs, very little change had occurred in the gender balance of the professoriate. The proportion of women in the professoriate seemed to have stagnated at around 20%.

One of the committee's objectives in the gender equality evaluation was to reach the faculty level more comprehensively by gathering information on the views of faculty management, such as deans and administrative heads of faculties, on the promotion of equality. The committee was well aware that the gender dynamics and awareness varied considerably among faculties, but it had proved difficult for the committee to monitor gender equality developments across the faculties. The equality adviser personally interviewed deans and the heads of administration of the 11 faculties about the realization of the plan in general and in their own faculty in particular and about current gender equality problems and priorities for the future within the university and their own faculty. Most faculty leaders expressed a view that a high degree of gender equality had already been achieved in the faculties, even in those with very few or hardly any women in the professoriate. Furthermore, many considered the increasing proportion of women in the undergraduate student pool to be problematic, having negative implications for gender equality. A concern that men may become disadvantaged among students had also been expressed by Rector Raivio in an editorial for the university's internal magazine *Yliopisto* (Raivio, 2002). The evaluation identified a rather low level of awareness of gender equality problems among many faculty managers. The conclusion of the evaluation echoed the description of the gender climate as it was described in the early 1990s: one of the major obstacles appeared to be lack of gender awareness across the university and the belief that gender equality had already been achieved.

The evaluation also concluded that creation of a network of contact persons in the university units was a positive step. However, owing to the diverse formal positions of the contact persons (from head of department to secretary), considerable variation existed in their visibility, initiative, and possibility for monitoring and influencing the decision making in their respective units. Some contact persons at lower level of the hierarchy found it difficult to obtain information about decisions made in their units.

The evaluation contributed to the revision of the Gender Equality Plan. The university senate approved the Gender Equality Plan 2004–2006 in May 2004. The plan focuses, as does the previous one, on mainstreaming gender equality into all university activities. According to the plan, the key areas of activities are committing the university community more strongly to the promotion of equality by incorporating equality issues into the strategic plans of the university, developing and improving gender-sensitive statistics, ensuring the continuation of women's studies, and developing teaching from the perspective of equality.

As a new attempt to reach the important and sometimes challenging faculty level, the Gender Equality Plan 2004–2006 requires the faculties to develop their own equality plans. Response to this has been rather slow. A few faculties started actively preparing such a plan, whereas others have yet to do so. In the summer 2005, only 3 of the 11 faculties, arts, behavioural sciences, and veterinary medicine, were in the process of drafting their equality plans; interestingly, all three were heavily female-dominated by their student pools. Faculties with active gender research and teaching in women's studies tend to have more positive views on promoting equality and often have informal networks, such as students and gender scholars, who push gender equality issues in their fields.

Experiences of Equality Promotion in the University of Helsinki

How is the scene of gender equality promotion experienced by those involved in the Equality Committee or by those who have acted as equality advisers through the 1990s and beyond? It was generally considered important that the Gender Equality Plan of the University of Helsinki have a long agenda and contain many detailed guidelines and policies. Paul Fogelberg, a long-term chair of the committee in the late 1990s highlighted the proactive role of the committee:

> One factor contributing to the success of gender equality promotion has been ... the role that the committee adopted from the very beginning: the committee aims to actively monitor the situation by commissioning different reports and by creating strategies and lines for action. A proactive approach has been predominant, not only a reactive monitoring or a role of the watchdog. (personal communication, May 1, 2005)

Several of the key players remark how some of the policies have been actively followed and some not implemented at all. Those actively involved in gender equality activities consider important the existence of detailed guidelines approved by the highest decision-making body, the university senate, as such. As was also evidenced in the evaluation of the plan, discussed earlier, many earlier key players remarked that the faculties' commitment to or awareness of gender equality issues was sometimes low or lacking, and the faculty management did not always seem fully convinced of the benefits of equality policies. Resistance to equality activities, reluctance, and inaction are sometimes justified by the faculty management pointing to their heavy workloads and lack of time. According to this thinking, gender equality and diversity promotion are low on the priority list and are perceived as burdens or bureaucratic demands creating little more than extra work. These efforts are not seen as a way to transform university into a more inclusive, fair, and excellent organization. This kind of resistance calls for multiple forms of promotion and repeated justification for resources needed to promote equality. The equality adviser currently has no right to attend the faculty council meetings; granting this right would be a step forward according to some former equality advisers.

Even if gender equality is on the official agenda of the university in the beginning of the twenty-first century, the importance of gender equality has not been unanimously accepted throughout the university, as witnessed by those who have been working as equality advisers. Two former equality advisers described various kind of resistance they encountered in the task:

> Both overt and silent resistance came from the representatives of faculty and departmental management. For example, the head of administration of one faculty told the equality adviser directly that he does not consider gender equality significant because it is competence that counts in appointments and that he considers gender equality legislation to be a failure. Another head of department expressed to the equality adviser that quarrels among employees did not concern him; another head of department said that gender equality is impossible to reach in appointments in any case. One member of the faculty council even asserted that promotion of gender equality is a ridiculous waste of university funding. (Marja Nykänen and Johanna Pakkanen, personal communication, October 1, 2005)

The Equality Committee has been chaired by two male vice-rectors, Paul Fogelberg and Thomas Wilhelmsson, and currently by a female vice-rector, Hannele Niemi. Paul Fogelberg, who chaired the Equality Committee from its establishment as a standing committee until his retirement in 1998, was frequently invited to give presentations on promotion of gender equality to other Finnish universities and at times felt as an 'ambassador' of the cause. He stresses the role of watchdog for the committee and its chair in a situation where, he suggests, most of the people in the university relate positively to gender equality in theory but easily forget the issue in everyday decision making:

> Because I was also a member of the senate, I often had to remind others that gender equality principles had been forgotten [in drafts for decisions for the senate]. It very often turned out that it really was about forgetting, even if the fundamental cause for forgetting might have been a hidden attitude. (personal communication, May 1, 2005)

Fogelberg asserted that because of the work of the Equality Committee, the opinions related to gender equality had been gradually changing in the university:

> Gender equality is paid more attention than it was earlier, and gender equality perspectives are taken into account when drafting strategies and plans and when developing the university in general. However, old-fashioned attitudes that have been formed throughout centuries are difficult to change in such a short time. (personal communication, May 1, 2005)

The equality adviser and the chair of the committee/vice-rector are in very different positions in the university hierarchy, and their different structural positions are reflected in their experiences as official spokespersons for gender equality. Until recently, all of the equality advisers have been young women in their late twenties or early thirties on fixed-term contracts. In contrast, those in management positions at the central, faculty, and departmental levels are most often middle-aged men who are well embedded in the official and unofficial networks inside the university. The equality adviser may encounter more outspoken acts of grassroots resistance from those in middle management in faculties and departments than does the vice-rector, a senior (until recently, most often) male colleague at the highest level university management.

Success Stories and Future Challenges

What are the success stories in the Helsinki case? From a structural perspective, it is significant that gender equality has been gradually integrated into highest university management by defining gender equality as an area of responsibility of one of the vice-rectors. In fact, a vice-rector already chaired the first standing Gender Equality Committee, a practice that proved to be very useful and was later confirmed in the Equality Decree. Several key players have considered important the anchoring of gender equality promotion to the highest university management. Furthermore, gender equality has been successfully integrated into the university owing to the creation of an infrastructure for monitoring and promoting gender equality. This infrastructure is comprised of the Equality Committee, Equality Decree, and the permanent position of equality adviser.

From the perspective of building ownership for gender equality promotion within the university organization, it has been crucial that the committees have always had both women and men as members and that several male Equality Committee members have been active. This has, according to Paul Fogelberg 'succeeded in stressing to the university community that realizing gender equality is not only in the interest for women but benefits all' (personal communication, November 9, 2005).

In the University of Helsinki, students are involved in the collegial decision-making bodies at all levels: department, faculty, and senate level. Active involvement of students has also been evident in the Gender Equality Committee since the beginning. Student members frequently have been enthusiastic and hard-working members of the committees. Several equality advisers commented on the positive effect and support they had received in their tasks from students. On the other hand, in a few cases, some student members of the university senate have resisted gender equality initiatives more than representatives of the staff have (P. Fogelberg, personal communication, November 9, 2005).

From a substantive perspective, the University of Helsinki has successfully introduced new issues on the equality agenda in Finnish universities. The University of Helsinki was a pioneer in the country in comprehensively addressing sexual harassment among staff and students as early as the mid-1990s in the form of a large survey (Mankkinen, 1995), and since then the university has been systematically building sexual harassment prevention and monitoring practices. Several other Finnish universities have used the Helsinki policies and practices as a model.

The University of Helsinki has been active and successful in enhancing and consolidating both national and international networking for gender equality promotion in universities. The university began a series of annual national meetings for gender equality committees and, since 2000, has hosted the national email discussion list of equality committees in Finland. The university is also responsible for initiating European cooperation by organizing the first European conference on gender equality in higher education in 1998, resulting in a regular series of conferences of this kind across Europe and launching and moderating a European discussion list on gender equality in higher education, the eq-uni list (Fogelberg et al., 1999; see chapter 7 in this book by Liisa Husu).

One of the strengths of the University of Helsinki's gender equality agenda is that it has been strongly informed by gender research. Here, the University of Helsinki is in a fortunate position because of its strong women's studies and gender research community. From the perspective of knowledge production on gender equality, promotion of women's studies and gender research as part of the gender equality agenda has been successful and fruitful in several ways. First, it has resulted in support for building and securing the infrastructure and continuity for women's studies in the University of Helsinki by the establishment of the Christina Institute of Women's Studies in 1991, which, in 2005, offers a women's studies programme at master and doctoral levels. Second, many scholars in gender studies in law in the Faculty of Law have offered fruitful expertise in gender equality promotion. Gender studies in law covers a wide range of thematic areas on gender-related issues, including equality legislation, anti-discrimination law, and theoretical and historical analyses on law and gender. Its leader, Professor Kevät Nousiainen, was appointed Minna Canth Academy Professor of Women's Studies for 2004–2008 and acts as a permanent adviser for the Equality Committee. The gender equality advisers also stress the importance of research on gender in academia, in working life, and in society more broadly. They also promote gender studies in general, including lesbian, homo, and queer studies, and research on racism.

In general, the University of Helsinki hosts the largest number of gender researchers in Finland (Academy of Finland, 2002), many of whom have been activist scholars and leaders involved in the gender equality promotion. Several equality advisers strongly emphasize the importance of the support of the women's studies community for work on gender equality in the university. High quality and innovative gender research and an extensive women's studies programme serve the university as well as the broader society by providing scholarly gender expertise and by training gender-sensitive future experts in various disciplines.

It must be pointed out, however, that gender researchers do not always feel accepted and welcome in the mainstream departments where most are currently located. The integration of gender scholarship into the mainstream disciplines varies widely, and the degree of integration does not necessarily correlate with the number of gender researchers in a particular setting or with the high quality of their gender research.

In the university, the managers, directors, members of the board, and departmental leading groups in the faculties, the departments, and independent institutes act as important gatekeepers for gender equality promotion. As gatekeepers, they act either as promoters and facilitators or as hinderers and excluders (Husu, 2004). Thus far, equality issues often appear to be given low priority at the faculty level, are frequently dealt with indifference, or evoke passive and sometimes active resistance, but there are also some faculties with a proactive and positive approach to gender equality promotion. It seems that constant lobbying by informal networks of gender-aware staff and active students is needed to push the faculty management to action of equality issues.

The recent reform of the equality legislation, the Equality Act amended in 2005 (232/2005) (see chapter 7 in this book), brings new challenges to universities, not the least of which is monitoring gender equality development with statistics. It has been a continuous challenge to develop the gender equality knowledge base enabling effective monitoring of division of labour, wages, and recruitment by gender. Gender statistics enabling effective monitoring of change are still not gathered and produced to a satisfactory degree even though the demand to develop gender-sensitive university statistics has been central in all gender equality plans and policy documents since the early 1990s.

Thus far, most of those contacting the equality adviser have done so because they encountered problems related to either gender discrimination or sexual harassment. However, since the Anti-Discrimination Act came in to force in 2004, ethnic discrimination complaints have increased. The same development has also been observed nationally by the Ombudsman for Minorities. Annually, the equality adviser is contacted by approximately 30 people, and ethnic discrimination accounts for the second largest group of these contacts after gender discrimination and harassment. Because consciousness of discrimination has increased due to the publicity surrounding the Anti-Discrimination Act and the amendment of the Gender Equality Act, which restricts discrimination of students in educational environments, the number of complaints for alleged discrimination will presumably continue to increase.

In general, the scope of the activities and responsibilities of the Equality Committee and equality adviser have expanded remarkably without a significant increase in resources since the agenda has been broadened to include diversity issues. The field of diversity promotion is complex and demanding and requires broad expertise. The process of monitoring, promoting, disseminating information, and reaching out to different parts of the large university community demands more resources to be effective. Some gender equality activists fear that gender equality promotion and monitoring will become secondary in this development, not denying the importance of broadening the agenda towards diversity issues as such.

Conclusion

The University of Helsinki is a large, heterogeneous organization wherein the gender climate and gender awareness vary greatly across the organization. Women are a majority among students at the master's and doctoral levels, but the change towards a better gender balance in the professoriate has been very slow. Despite gender equality legislation, university-level gender equality strategies, anchoring gender equality with top management, active women's studies community, it is clear that building ownership of gender equality in this kind of an organization is complex and demanding. With its 11 faculties, independent institutes, 4 campuses, and autonomy decentralized to the faculty and departmental levels, a university-wide gender equality plan and guidelines can serve only as a starting point for effective mainstreaming policy. Gender equality is currently included in strategic planning and personnel training at the university level. However, even the incorporation of equality into various policy documents does not easily convert to practice. Gender equality planning and monitoring at the faculty and department levels where many important decisions on academic matters, including recruitment of academic staff, are drafted and made should become an integral part of their general action plans. Until then, mainstreaming of gender equality in all activities and at all organizational levels will be thwarted.[6]

Notes

1. Ten or more persons belonging to the university, such as students or academic or administrative staff, can put forward their candidate for rector's elections. The candidates must hold a doctorate or be appointed to a professorship in some university.
2. Until 1998, the final appointment of professors was by the president of Finland; after that the right to appoint professors was given to universities themselves.
3. The committee included, in addition to the current rector, Professor Ilkka Niiniluoto; Professor Kirsti Rissanen, current permanent secretary of the Ministry of Justice, Professor Simo Knuuttila, an academy professor; and, as student members, two feminist activists from the Helsinki University Student Union, Ilka Kangas and Hille Koskela, who later to become postdoctoral researchers at the university.
4. For a case of a discrimination complaint in a professorial appointment related to nationality, see Hearn, 2003, 2004.
5. The case was briefly as follows: a female applicant approached the Equality Committee, asking the committee to give a statement in a case of appointment to a one-year acting professorial position. A male scholar with a lower degree (licentiate) was proposed for the post ahead of a female scholar who had a doctorate, and, in its statement, the Equality Committee considered this proposal discriminatory. However, the faculty proceeded to appoint the male applicant with a lower qualification, and the female scholar later sued the university in the court for gender discrimination. The court ruled that the university had broken the gender equality legislation and ordered the university to pay compensation to the female scholar (Helsinki magistrate's court, decision no. 3037, 8.10.2003).
6. We thank Paul Fogelberg, Jeff Hearn, Teija Mankkinen, Marja Nykänen, Raija Sollamo, Johanna Pakkanen, and Thomas Wilhelmsson for their useful comments and feedback.

References

Academy of Finland (2002) *Women's studies and gender research in Finland: Evaluation report.* Publications of the Academy of Finland 8/02. Helsinki: Academy of Finland.

Ahtela, K. (2004) *Selvitys sukupuolen merkityksestä oikeustieteen jatko-opinnoissa ja oikeustieteen tohtoreiden urakehityksessä* [*A study of the meaning of gender in graduate studies in law and in the career development of Ph.D.s in law*]. Helsinki: University of Helsinki.

Cockburn, C. (1989) Equal opportunities, the short and long agenda. *Industrial Relations Journal, 20*(3):213–225.

Evers (2000) Mentorointi Helsingin yliopistossa [Mentoring in the University of Helsinki]. In T. Juusela, T. Lillia, & J. Rinne (Eds.), *Mentoroinnin monet kasvot* [*The many faces of mentoring*] (pp. 98–103). Helsinki: Yrityskirjat.

Fogelberg, P., Hearn, J., Husu, L., & Mankkinen, T. (Eds.) (1999) *Hard work in the academy. Research and intervention on gender equality in higher education.* Helsinki: Helsinki University Press.

Hearn, J. (2003) Organization violations in practice: A case study in a university setting. *Culture and Organization, 9*(4):253–273.

———— (2004) Personal resistance through persistence to organizational resistance through distance. In R. Thomas, A. J. Mills, & J. Helms Mills (Eds.), *Identity politics at work: Resisting gender, gendering gesistance* (pp. 40–63). London: Routledge.

Hearn, J., & Parkin, W. (2001) *Gender, sexuality and violence in organizations: The unspoken forces of organization violations.* London: Sage.

Husu, L. (2001) *Sexism, support and survival: Academic women and hidden discrimination in Finland.* Social Psychological Studies 6. Helsinki: University of Helsinki.

———— (2004) Gate-keeping, gender equality and scientific excellence. In *European Commission: Gender and excellence in the making* (pp. 69–76). Luxembourg: Office for Official Publications of the European Communities.

Kantola, J. (2005) *Mykät, kuurot ja kadotetut. Sukupuolten välinen tasa-arvo Helsingin yliopiston valtio-opin laitoksella* [*The deaf, the mute and the lost: Gender equality at the Helsinki University Political Science Department*]. Acta Politica 29. Helsinki: Yliopistopaino.

Kirton, G., & Greene, A-M. (2000) *The dynamics of managing diversity: A critical approach.* Oxford: Butterworth Heinemann.

Mankkinen, T. (1995) *Akateemista nuorallatanssia. Sukupuolinen häirintä ja ahdistelu Helsingin yliopistossa* [*Walking the academic tightrope: Sexual harassment in the University of Helsinki*]. Helsinki: Yliopistopaino.

———— (1999) Walking the academic tightrope: Sexual harassment in the University of Helsinki. In P. Fogelberg, J. Hearn, L. Husu, & T. Mankkinen (Eds.), *Hard work in the academy. Research and intervention on gender equality in higher education* (pp. 219–221). Helsinki: Helsinki University Press.

Nordgren, N. (1984) Organisationer för kvinnliga forskare i Finland [Organisations of female researchers in Finland]. In *Organisering av jämställdhets- /kvinnoforskning i Norden. Rapport från Nordiska Ministerrådets konferens den 8–10 november 1983 på Lejondals slott i Bro, Sverige* [*Organising of gender equality/women's studies in the Nordic Countries. A report of a conference organised in Lejondal castle, Sweden, by the Nordic Council of Ministers, November 8–10, 1983*] (pp. 63–66). Göteborg: Nordiska Ministerrådet.

Raivio, K. (2002) Muuttuuko yliopisto tyttökouluksi? Pääkirjoitus [Is the University turning into a girls' school? Editorial]. *Yliopisto, 16*, 3.

Tasa-arvotoimikunta [Equality Committee] (2004) *Vuosien 2001–2003 toiminnallisen tasa-arvosuunnitelman arviointiraportti* [*Evaluation report of Gender Equality Plan 2001–2003*]. Retrieved November 30, 2005, from the University of Helsinki, Personnel Services Website, http://www.helsinki.fi/tasa-arvo/suomi/TASUARVRAP.pdf.

University of Helsinki (n.d.a) *University of Helsinki – 365 years.* Retrieved November 29, 2005, from the University of Helsinki Website, http://www.helsinki.fi/yliopistonhistoria/english/index.htm.

———— (n.d.b) *Epäasiallisen kohtelun ja häirinnän ehkäiseminen Helsingin yliopistossa* [*Guidelines on how to prevent inappropriate treatment and harassment in the University of Helsinki*]. Retrieved November 28, 2005, from the University of Helsinki Intranet.

———— (2000) *Equality plan 2001–2003.* Helsinki: University of Helsinki.

———— (2003) *Helsingin yliopisto. Strategia 2004–2006. Helsingfors universitet.* [*University of Helsinki. Strategic plan for 2004–2006.*] *Helsingfors universitet. Strategi för perioden 2004–2006.* Helsinki: Yliopistopaino.

———— (2004) *Equality plan 2004–2006.* Retrieved December 28, 2005 from the University of Helsinki, Personnel Services Website, http://www.helsinki.fi/tasa-arvo/english/TASU04–06_EN.pdf.

———— (n.d.) *Policy against discrimination.* Retrieved November 29, 2005, from the University of Helsinki, Personnel Services Website, http://www.helsinki.fi/tasa-arvo/english/discplan.html.

Act 232/2005 on changing the act on equality between women and men.

CHAPTER NINE

GENDER AND U.K. HIGHER EDUCATION: POST-FEMINISM IN A MARKET ECONOMY

Louise Morley

Policy Silences

Gender is a silence in current U.K. higher education policy. Economics, rather than sociology, is the driving disciplinary force in education policy. In a market economy, individuals, rather than social groups, are the unit of analysis. Where structures of inequality are included, such as enhancing the participation of working-class students in higher education (HEFCE, 2001), education policy addresses a theory of disadvantage rather than a theory of privilege. The emphasis is on lifting the barrier to let in more members of excluded communities rather than on debating the nature of the barrier itself. There is little policy attention as to how the modalities of higher education reproduce social class or gender privilege or how higher education can play a role in creating a more inclusive society.

Gender equality in U.K. higher education is fraught with contradictions for women. It offers opportunities for the acquisition of social and cultural capital, mobility and economic independence, pleasure and intellectual fulfillment while simultaneously reflecting and reproducing gendered divisions of labour and horizontal and vertical segregation of women. For some time, feminists have been attempting to deconstruct and reconstruct the U.K. academy. A central finding on gender equality in the academy is that both formal interventions, such as policies, and informal structures, including networks and sponsorship, play important roles in both reproducing and challenging inequalities (Morley, Kwesiga, & Lihamba, 2005). Studies on gender equality in U.K. higher education all confirm the difficulties at the policy, institutional, organizational, and micropolitical levels of putting into place strategies for social inclusion in institutions of higher education (Bagilhole, 2002; Howie & Tauchert, 2002; Morley, 1999, 2003a; Deem, 2003).

Equality issues have had a fairly tenuous connection with U.K. higher education. Compared to the rapid neo-liberal transformation, policy development for equality in general has been slow. In 1986, an investigation in Britain for the Commission for Racial Equality discovered that 20 out of the 42 universities replied by citing only their charters as sufficient evidence of their commitment to equal opportunities; the researchers also found that former polytechnics were more likely to have policies than were established universities (Heward & Taylor, 1993). Enquiries of the Commission on University Career Opportunity (CUCO) in the late 1980s suggested that while over 90% of universities had formally adopted equal opportunities policies, a little over half had examined their criteria for appointments, promotions, and regrading, but only 37% had devised implementation plans (CUCO, 1994; Davies & Holloway, 1995). In their study of the representation of ethnic minority groups in 53 university prospectuses in the academy, Jewson et al. (1991) concluded that four-fifths of universities did not offer any sort of equal opportunities statement, either explicit or implicit, in their prospectus.

The situation is beginning to change, however. Higher education in the United Kingdom now needs to address recent legislation in the forms of the Race Relations Amendment Act (2000) and the Special Educational Needs and Disability Act (2001). These laws have heightened awareness of aspects of inequality that have been fairly under-represented in the past. U.K. universities are now required by their funding bodies to have policies on a wide range of inequalities for both students and staff and which must be incorporated in wider human resource and reward strategies.

Gender and Diversity

An important consideration is gender in relation to diversity. The concept of diversity has been more researched and applied in industry (Kandola & Fullerton, 1994; Lorbieki, 2001) than it has in fields such as education where concepts of equal opportunities, equity, and social inclusion have been more frequently use – textually at least, if not in practice. Yet conceptualizing diversity is now slowly entering higher education with gender being intersected with other structures of inequality, including race, social class, disability, age, ethnicity, and sexual orientation (Deem, Morley, & Tlili, 2004).

The theoretical and policy challenge is how to avoid setting up hierarchies of oppression, competitions, and oppositions while at the same time not diluting or diverting attention from specific characteristics and formations of oppression. Traditionally, in the United Kingdom, government organizations have been formed to implement single pieces of legislation, so separate bodies have existed for race, gender, and disability. However, nationally, the Equal Opportunities Commission is set to merge with the Commission for Racial Equality. In U.K. public services, the move is slowly being made towards making diversity policies (Equality Challenge Unit/Joint Negotiating Committee for Higher Education Staff, 2003).

More recently, concern has been demonstrated about how different structures of inequality can be challenged in a coordinated and non-hierarchical way. Higher education research has been conducted on representation of ethnic minorities (Modood & Acland, 1998), people with disabilities (Gibson, 1996; Riddell, 2005), and sexual orientation (AUT, 2001b). In 1999, the ATHENA project, a special project to foster the prospects of women science academics, was also established, funded by the Higher Education Funding Councils and the government's Office of Science and Technology (Bebbington, 2001). To form policy, the Universities UK (the organization that represents university vice-chancellors) has an Equality Challenge Unit that includes gender in a portfolio of equity and diversity concerns.

However, questions persist as to what drives change. Traditionally, in the United Kingdom, social movements have led change agency and curriculum reform in the academy. Innovations, including women's studies, black studies, and gay and lesbian studies, came about through activism rather than from equalities legislation. Now, in the United Kingdom, it is largely the EC framework for equal treatment in the Employment Directive of 2000 that has shaped policy for public bodies, including educational institutions, in areas such as ethnicity and disability. A cynical view is that higher education institutions in the United Kingdom address equality issues only when the law requires them to do so. Even then, policy activity in one area of the academy does not necessarily transfer to debates on values, purpose, and the overall conceptualization of higher education. There is still a belief that products and processes of higher education are largely universal, gender-neutral, and based on a concept of meritocracy.

Gender appears to be a disqualified discourse in higher education policy in the United Kingdom, certainly compared to other national locations (Morley, Kwesiga, & Lihamba, 2005). This silence is strange as major gender inequalities still exist. For example, women staff are still concentrated in the caregiving and service areas and are a minority in the areas in higher education where power is exercised and decisions are made. However, it is assumed by policy makers that gender is no longer an issue as undergraduate representation of women is now over 50%. The under-representation of women in senior roles is left untheorized by the policy makers.

The exclusion of women from powerful areas of academic life can be theorized nevertheless using a variety of approaches. One approach suggests that denial of women's capability is a form of oppression (Sen, 1994). Another approach argues that women's under-representation in senior and decision-making roles is not merely symbolic; rather, it is a form of status injury. The lack of women in senior positions is both cultural misrecognition and material and intellectual oppression (Fraser, 1997). However, the situation is conceptualized, it remains a mystery as to why some inequalities persist.

The issue of *persistent inequalities* in higher education is frequently debated and documented (Husu & Morley, 2000). For example, in Britain, a woman first became an academic in 1893, and a woman was first appointment professor in 1894. By the 1970s, the proportion of women academics was virtually the same as it was in the 1920s. Despite potent advocacy and inquiry combined with equity legislation, patriarchal power appears hard to denaturalize in the U.K. academy.

When gender equity initiatives do exist, strong sense of limits and counter-hegemonic challenges operate within powerful hegemonies (Morley, 1999). In other words, equality policies have traditionally occupied an oppositional status. Deem, Morley, and Tlili (2004) note how there has been little integration of equality measures into mainstream higher education policy development. This is particularly the case with gender. In terms of gender, post-feminist rather than feminist theory shapes the U.K. higher education policy. Post-feminism suggests that battles have been fought and won and that women and men now have equal opportunities. It reconceptualizes gendered power and suggests a new type of citizenship in which agency and individual choice are explanatory variables rather than structures, social relations, and hegemonies (see figure 9.1).

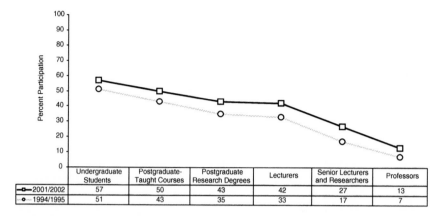

Figure 9.1 Representation of Women among Students and Academic Staff in the United Kingdom

Sources: Higher Education Statistics Agency. (1996). *Higher Education Statistics for the UK, 1994–1958*. Cheltenham: HESA and Higher Education Statistics Agency. (2003). *Higher Education Statistics for the UK, 2001–2002*. Cheltenham: HESA.

Devaluing Women

The devaluing of women has become a normalized social relation in the academy even within the changing political economy of higher education (Morley, 2003a). As staff, women are more likely to be in junior positions, as students, they earn less (Bett, 1999), and their qualifications are worth less in the labour market (Hogarth et al., 1997). Whereas the employment market, particularly at senior levels in elite professions, still favours men, it is important to note that gender equality is not just about quantitative change in the academy and access to the labour market. It should include the quality relating to the working and learning environments. It should also be concerned with the expansion of rights and entitlements for women as a group. One right that appears to be breached persistently is that of equal pay. In spite of legislation in the United Kingdom since 1970, academic women's time and capital are still worth less than that of their male counterparts, breaching the European Union Directives regarding equal treatment on pay (Bett, 1999). Analysis of data from the Higher Education Statistics Agency (HESA) by the Association of University Teachers (AUT, 2001a) shows that while women academics in the United Kingdom earned on average 15% less than men earned in 1995, by 2000 the gap had actually widened slightly to 16%. In other words, for every pound earned by a male academic, their female colleagues earned only 84 pence. Institutions at the top of the quality league tables also had higher gender pay gaps, with women at the London School of Economics earning 21% less than what their male counterparts earned.

Material inequalities are potent symbols of wider power relations. They can also act as a form of 'hard' evidence to demonstrate a gendered occupational hierarchy. The highly influential White Paper *The Future of Higher Education* (DfES, 2003) does not include gender as a category of analysis in strategies to enhance participation or the graduate earnings premium that is so commonly cited as a rationale for introducing tuition fees. For example, the calculation is that graduates will earn over £400,000 more in a lifetime than will non-graduates. However, this figure overlooks gender inequalities in the labour market. Research has consistently demonstrated that women graduates earn less (Joshi, 2000) and are more likely to be underemployed than male graduates. Connor (1999, p. 96) found that male graduates more than female graduates are likely to be in professional or managerial occupations whereas female graduates are more likely to be in secretarial/clerical occupations. Nevertheless, students in this key policy document are presented as undifferentiated by gender.

None of this should come as a surprise. The academy forms part of a more complex matrix of gender relations with gender inequality omnipresent in the wider civil society. For example, 66% of the world's illiterates are women. On average, women's salaries are 25% lower than those of men, and politically and globally, women represent only 10% of parliamentarians (UNESCO, 1999). Macro inequalities lead to micro practices. Universities can act as amplification devices for gender inequalities.

Innovation and Change

It is intriguing that, internationally, the political economy of higher education is rapidly changing. The global higher education scene appears to be governed by a logic of iterability, with rapid developments in borderless provision and the knowledge economy, and yet some areas of academic life seem slow to change, for example, the under-representation of women in subjects of science and technology or as senior and managerial academic staff.

The situation is full of contradictions. Boundaries between the economic and social now appear porous. The market economy now moves towards audit, accountability, user-pay, and the enterprise culture. The relationship of higher education with globalization and wealth creation has been accompanied by debates on democratization and human rights (Morley, 2003a). Knowledge and its growth are equated with greater efficacy and greater freedom rather than with emancipatory politics (Peters, 2001). In a context of post-welfare market, the emphasis is on the economy of individual and organizational performance and the capitalism of knowledge rather than on social identity. Democratization and human rights usually enter the frame only in relation to student access, not in staffing issues. Deem, Morley, and Tlili (2004) discovered that for many academic and administrative staff, equal opportunities policies and practices were perceived as relating only to the student body. In a market economy, policies have been reduced to marketing devices to attract more 'non-traditional' students and hence meet government targets.

Gender silences are noticeable in debates on innovation and change in higher education. There is a burgeoning literature in higher education studies on new formations, the enterprise culture, and the market economy (Clark, 1998). There is writing on the emergence of new competitions, new markets, and new sites of learning, including the workplace and the community (Williams, 2002). Considerable policy and critical attention is paid to off-shore, online, distance, franchised, and private forms of higher education (Garrett, 2005; King, 2003; Middlehurst, 2000). However, debates on borderless universities, e-learning, and the expanding global reach of higher education remain ungendered. There are few questions about the gendered implications of new forms of higher education or whether these forms indeed provide opportunities or constraints for women.

Gender is also a silence in teaching and learning. The professionalization of higher education teachers has become a major policy initiative and has expanded the market. Literature is proliferating in the United Kingdom on learning theory, learning styles, and effective teaching (Entwistle, 2003; Prosser & Trigwell, 1999; Ramsden, 2003). Yet within these texts, learning is often constructed as a socially decontextualized cognitive process. The gendered identity of teachers and learners remains unproblematized, and no intellectual attention is paid to knowledge produced by earlier feminist scholars on inclusive and non-discriminatory pedagogies (Morley, 2002). The move away from the social towards the cognitive is part of a wider paradigm shift. Higher education is being reduced to a private good, with notions of collective empowerment eclipsed by individualistic engagements (Howie, 2002; Morley, 2003b; Singh, 2001). In a post-feminist terrain, women are no longer members of an oppressed collective or international social movement for change but are individual self-maximizing and self-interested actors in a market economy.

Quality and Equality

Women staff are being allowed into certain less popular areas of the academy, which in the United Kingdom can translate into managing quality assurance procedures! Quality assurance is a major regime of power in U.K. higher education as the U.K. higher education is the most audited in the world (Cowen, 1996). Audits exist both for teaching and learning quality and for research productivity. The former consists of inspections organized by the Quality Assurance Agency of programmes of study. The latter, known as the Research Assessment Exercise (RAE), consists of an audit of quality and quantity of publications and research grants organized by the Higher Education Funding Council. Results in the RAE determine an organization's research funding. Both systems have scoring mechanisms that are relayed into the public domain and contribute to national league tables. The league tables are also frequently used as marketing devices.

Other major equality silences are found in the way in which quality is assured in U.K. higher education. Equality issues have not been performance indicators in quality audits, and there is limited ideological debate about what signs of quality are audited and promoted. Excellence is represented as value-free. The politics of knowledge are overlooked. Students tend to be treated as a social bloc, fairly undifferentiated by gender, race, social class, disability, sexual orientation, religion, or age. Equity and diversity issues in employment are not perceived as quality concerns. Quality assurance has complex and contradictory implications for women (Morley, 2001, 2005). Quality assurance precipitates organizational and professional change, but it is questionable whether it incorporates an understanding of equity.

There are several arguments connecting quality and equality (Blackmore, 2000a, 2000b). One argument relates to equity in terms of service delivery. Equity issues are not automatically considered performance indicators in quality audits. In taxonomies of effectiveness, the organizational world is presented as an orderly, rational surface, untainted by the mess and chaos of unequal power relations in which the lived world is constituted. When gender equity in higher education is included, it is invariably represented by quantitative signifiers of change, relating to the student body rather than to staff.

A second argument relates to gendered employment regimes in the academy (Blackmore & Sachs, 2001; Brooks & Mackinnon, 2001). The morality of quality can be profoundly gendered, with women heavily responsibilized for student-focussed services (Morley, 2003a). Women's career ambitions appear to be easily tied to domestic arenas. There has been some sex role spillover, as women's socialized patterns of caring are appropriated by the teaching quality movement. The psychic economy involved in quality assessment is part of a gendered care chain.

A third argument connecting quality to equality is that the two accounting systems, that is, teaching and learning quality and research quality, are in hierarchical and oppositional relationship to each other with accompanying gendered implications. An area of concern expressed by some feminist commentators is that while women are well represented as reviewers and managers of teaching quality, they are under-represented both as producers and reviewers of research quality (Morley, 2003a). Leonard (2001, p. 17) points out how, according to the 2001 RAE, fewer than one in four panel members and only one in seven of the panel chairs were women; the panels chaired by women were responsible for allocating less than 10% of RAE funding. Furthermore, men were almost twice as likely to be entered in the RAE than were women (Knights & Richards, 2003). The point about transparency in the appointment of assessors has caused so much concern that it has been noted as a recommendation in the recent Roberts' Review of the Research Assessment Exercise (2003): 'The funding councils should monitor and report upon the gender balance of sub-panel members, sub-panel chairs, panel chairs, moderators and senior moderators' (p. 40). Now, organizations have to factor in equality issues into their returns for the 2008 Research Assessment Exercise by confirming that they developed, adopted, and documented an appropriate internal code of practice in preparing submissions and selecting staff for inclusion in RAE submissions. The chairs of assessment panels are also briefed on equal opportunities and the implications of recent equalities legislation.

A fourth argument relates to the possibilities for subversion or rearticulation, which suggests that the quality agenda can be appropriated to enhance the rights of less powerful groups, such as students with dyslexia (Luke, 1997). In Britain, quality assessment of teaching and learning has been popular with the National Union of Students, as they believe that it has provided them with opportunities for influence and 'voice' (Morley, 2003b). Thus, marginalized groups have been brought under the auditing gaze. Externality has traditionally been an important driver for change for equity issues (Glazer-Raymo, 1999). Luke (1997) argues that accountability measures, the 'institutional economies' of quality assurance, and the new contractualism can be harnessed for equity ends. Blackmore (1999, p. 47) also suggests that 'equity can be built into all contractual arrangements ... Top management commitment can be gained on the grounds that equity is more "productive." '

A fifth argument is that quality accolades do not necessarily coincide with equity achievements. Some of the most elite research organizations in Britain with consistently high scores in the RAE also have the worst record on gender equity. For example, Cambridge did not allow women graduates full status until 1947. Women are already disproportionately concentrated in areas and institutions with the lowest levels of research funding (Lafferty & Fleming, 2000).

A sixth argument relates to women and research, with questions about whether gender discrimination is institutionalized via employment practices and career trajectories. In the United Kingdom, the Wellcome Trust and six of the United Kingdom's Research Councils commissioned an independent report from the National Centre for Social Research (NCSR) to analyse application and award rates. Some 3,090 academic staff from 44 institutions of higher education were surveyed between October 1999 and February 2000. Of the women questioned, 50% had applied for research grants in the previous five years compared to 59% of men. This work showed that women not only made a smaller number of applications but were also less likely to be the principal applicants; they sought lower levels of funding than did their male counterparts and generally applied for grants for shorter lengths of time. In addition, only 46% of women applied to the Research Councils or the Welcome Trust for their grants compared to 65% of men (NCSR, 2000). Women are awarded only 33% of ESRC grants, and from the British Academy, they received 25% of the large research grants and 38.7% of small research grants.

These circumstances create a vicious circle: women are too busy teaching or administrating, too junior, and too precariously employed to gain major research grants. They are then ineligible to apply for senior posts, as they have no major research grants. In addition to these structural barriers, there are attitudinal barriers. In Sweden, Wennerås and Wold (1997) found that eligibility criteria were gendered and that women needed to publish two and a half times more than did their male counterparts to get the same rating for scientific competence. The networks between the successful male applicants and members of the panel caused such a scandal that the entire board was sacked!

Audit has both creative and oppressive potential for gender equality. Theoretically, quality assurance could provide new governance frameworks through which issues of equity can be mobilized. However, equity is frequently absent as a category of analysis in organizational arrangements for quality assurance. Furthermore, via their engagement with quality assurance, women academics and managers are being incorporated into a neo-liberal managerial discourse. Micro-level analysis of the effects of audit and the evaluative state seem to suggest that hegemonic masculinities and gendered power relations are being reinforced by the emphasis on competition, targets, audit trails, and performance (Morley, 2003a) even though there is a new cadre of quality managers, and many of these are women. Additionally, current policy concerned with the quality of teaching and learning is, at one level, promoting visibility of a traditional area of women's work.

In Britain, audit is conducted as a gender-neutral activity (Morley, 2003a). Yet audit relies heavily on women's social and emotional capital, and the danger exists that women's labour is being appropriated to legitimate a regime of power that may not serve their long-term interests. Women could be squeezed out of high status research work, which has implications for women's career development. The exclusion of many women from research opportunities might account for why so many women are incorporated into quality assurance procedures for teaching and learning. For some of them, this placement provides a welcome opportunity to be included and valued. Involvement in quality management creates career opportunities for women while simultaneously pushing them into a career pathway strongly associated with organizational housekeeping.

Gender Mainstreaming

A strong argument, originally from feminist academics and women's studies scholars and even more recently from international organizations, is that access needs to be accompanied by changes in organization and curriculum. At the Fourth United

Nations Women's Conference in Beijing in 1995, both a gender equality declaration and an action programme were adopted. In the Beijing document, gender mainstreaming was highlighted as a strategy to promote gender equality. Gender mainstreaming is now an initiative supported by international organizations, including the European Union, the Commonwealth Secretariat, and UNESCO (Leo-Rhynie & the Institute of Development and Labour Law, University of Cape Town, South Africa, Law 1999; UNDP, 2002; UNESCO, 2002). It is a strategy that claims to make women's and men's experiences an integral dimension in the design, implementation, monitoring, and evaluation of policies and programmes. It is the process of assessing the implications for women and men of any planned action, including legislation, policies, or programmes in any area and at all levels.

Gender mainstreaming is highly controversial. Some think of it as the successful integration of gender into institutional development. The curriculum, forms of pedagogy, and 'best practice' have increasingly been perceived as value-laden, context-specific, and norm-related. A contradictory view is that it is a deradicalization of feminist goals, a bland form of contract compliance. In this construction, feminism is no longer considered a disruptive challenge to patriarchal organizations but is diluted to yet another tedious example of new managerial regulation possessing diagnostic authority and suggesting formulaic solutions. Others question areas of exclusion from gender mainstreaming and the nature of the good that is being mainstreamed. However, very little activity relating to gender mainstreaming is taking place in Britain, compared to extensive activity elsewhere in Europe and in the Commonwealth (Bishop-Sambrook, 2000). A question is how to challenge the gendered hidden curriculum of higher education.

Conclusion

The establishment of a knowledge market means that women are entering the academy in Britain in large numbers as students, but their representation as staff, particularly in senior positions, is still problematic. Elite organizations are continuing to favour white, middle-class students and male senior postholders. When women are promoted, particularly to senior management, questions arise about their incorporation into the evaluative state and audit society that might work against women's interests. Innovation, change, and policy development in higher education ignores gender as a category of analysis. The discourse of social inclusion often fails to recognize or redistribute gendered opportunities. Britain still has a long way to go in terms of how the expansion of higher education impacts the expansion of rights and material benefits for women in wider civil society because the accountability so beloved by the United Kingdom's audit culture is rarely extended to equity and social inclusion. In a political period of intense U.K./U.S. proximity and neo-liberal policy borrowing, Britain needs the liberalization of the European Union to ensure that gender is intersected with other structures of inequality in higher education policy in order to ensure that women's interests are firmly on the political agenda.

References

AUT (Association of University Teachers) (2001a) *The gender pay gap*. London: AUT.
——— (2001b) *Lesbian, gay and bisexual participation in UK universities*. Retrieved August, 2003, from http://www.aut.org.uk/index.cfm? articleid=160.

Bagilhole, B. (2002) Challenging equal opportunities: Changing and adapting male hegemony in academia. *British journal of sociology of education, 23*(1):19–33.

Bebbington, D. (2001) *Women scientists in higher education: A literature review.* London: ATHENA Project.

Bett, M. (1999) *Independent review of higher education pay and conditions: Report of a committee chaired by Sir Michael Bett.* London: Stationery Office.

Bishop-Sambrook, C. (2000) The logical framework as a tool for gender mainstreaming in university. *Gender and Education, 12*(2):239–247.

Blackmore, J. (1999) Localization/globalization and the midwife state: Strategic dilemmas for state feminism in education? *Journal of Education Policy, 14*(1):33–54.

—— (2000a) More power to the powerful: Mergers, corporate management and their implications for women in the reshaping of higher education. *Australian Feminist Studies, 15*:65–98.

—— (2000b) Warning signals or dangerous opportunities? Globalization, gender and educational policy shifts. *Educational Theory, 50*(4):467–486.

Blackmore, J., & Sachs, J. (2001) Women leaders in the restructured and internationalised university. In A. Brooks, & A. McKinnon (Eds.), *Gender and the restructured university* (pp. 45–66). Buckingham: Open University Press.

Brooks, A., & MacKinnon, A. (Eds.) (2001) *Gender and the restructured university: Changing management and culture in higher education.* Buckingham: Open University Press.

Clark, B. R. (1998) *Creating entrepreneurial universities: Organizational pathways of transformation.* Oxford: Pergamon.

Connor, H. (1999) Different graduates, different labour market. In M. Henkel, & B. Little (Eds.), *Changing relations between higher education and the state* (pp. 90–104). London: Jessica Kingsley.

Cowen, R. (1996) Performativity, post-modernity and the university. *Comparative Education, 32*(2):245–258.

CUCO (Commission on University Career Opportunity) (1994) *A report on the universities' policies and practices in employment.* London: CUCO.

Davies, C., & Holloway, P. (1995) Troubling transformations: Gender regimes and organizational culture in the academy. In L. Morley, & V. Walsh (Eds.), *Feminist academics: Creative agents for change* (pp. 7–21). London: Taylor and Francis.

DfES (Department for Education and Skills) (2003) *The future of higher education.* London: DfES.

Deem, R. (2003) Gender, organisational cultures and the practices of manager-academics in UK universities. *Gender, Work and Organisation, 10*(2):239–259.

Deem, R., Morley, L., & Tlili, A. (2004) 'The equity in European higher education debate in the twenty- first century: Preliminary findings from an investigation of staff experiences of current equality policies in UK higher education institutions'. Paper presented at the European Conference on Educational Research, Crete, September.

Entwistle, N. J. (2003) *Research-based university teaching: Encouraging a deep approach to learning.* Basingstoke: Palgrave Macmillan.

Equality Challenge Unit/Joint Negotiating Committee for Higher Education Staff (2003) *Partnership for equality: Action for higher education.* London: Universities UK.

Fraser, N. (1997) *Justice interruptus: Critical reflections on the 'postsocialist' condition.* New York: Routledge.

Garrett, R. (2005) Fraudulent, sub-standard, ambiguous: The alternative borderless higher education. *The Observatory on Borderless Higher Education, 24.*

Gibson, R. (1996) Deaf women academics in higher education. In L. Morley & V. Walsh (Eds.), *Breaking boundaries: Women in higher education* (pp. 67–77). London: Taylor and Francis.

Glazer-Raymo, J. (1999) *Shattering the myths: Women in academe.* Baltimore: John Hopkins University Press.

Heward, C., & Taylor, P. (1993) Effective and ineffective equal opportunities policies in HE. *Critical Social Policy, 37* :75–94.

HEFCE (Higher Education Funding Council for England) (2001) *Strategies for widening participation in higher education: A guide to good practice*. Bristol: HEFCE.

HESA (2003) *Resources of higher education institutions 2001/02*. Cheltenham, UK: HESA.

Hogarth, T., Maguire, M., Pitcher, J., Purcell, K., & Wilson, R. A. (1997) *The participation of non-traditional students in higher education*. Warwick: University of Warwick Institute for Employment Research.

Howie, G. (2002) A reflection of quality: Instrumental reason, quality audits and the knowledge economy. *Critical Quarterly, 44*(4):140–148.

Howie, G., & Tauchert, A. (Eds.) (2002) *Gender, teaching, and research in higher education: Challenges for the 21st century*. Aldershot: Ashgate.

Husu, L., & Morley, L., (Eds.) (2000) *Higher education in Europe-special edition on academe and gender: What has and what has not changed?* Bucharest: UNESCO.

Jewson, N., Mason, D., Bowen, R., Mulvaney, K., & Parmar, S. (1991) Universities and ethnic minorities: The public face. *New Community, 17*(2):183–199.

Joshi, H. (2000) *Production, reproduction and education: Women, children and work in contemporary Britain*. London: Institute of Education.

Kandola, R., & Fullerton, J. (1994) *Managing the mosaic*. London: Institute of Personnel and Development.

King, R. (2003) *The growth of private higher education: Regulating for diversity or homogeneity?* London: Association of Commonwealth Universities.

Knights, D., & Richards, W. (2003) Sex Discrimination in UK Academia. *Gender, Work and Organization, 10*(2):213–238.

Lafferty, G., & Fleming, J. (2000) The restructuring of academic work in Australia: Power, management and gender. *British Journal of Sociology of Education, 21*(2):257–267.

Leonard, D. (2001) *A woman's guide to doctoral studies*. Buckingham: Open University Press.

Leo-Rhynie, E., & the Institute of Development and Labour Law, University of Cape Town, South Africa (1999) *Gender mainstreaming in education*. London: Commonwealth Secretariat.

Lorbieki, A. (2001) Changing views on diversity management: The rise of the learning perspective and the need to recognize social and political contradictions. *Journal of Management Learning, 32*(3):345–361.

Luke, C. (1997) Quality assurance and women in higher education. *Higher Education, 33*: 433–451.

Middlehurst, R. (2000) *The business of borderless education*. London: CVCP/ HEFCE.

Modood, T., & Acland, T. (Eds.) (1998) *Race and higher education: Experiences, challenges and policy implications*. London: Policy Studies Institute.

Morley, L. ——— (1999) *Organising feminisms: The micropolitics of the academy*. London: Macmillan.

——— (2001) Subjected to review: Engendering quality in higher education. *Journal of Education Policy, 16*(5):465–478.

——— (2002) Lifelong yearning: Feminist pedagogy in the learning society. In G. Howie & A. Tauchert (Eds.), *Gender, teaching, and research in higher education* (pp. 86–98). London: Ashgate Press.

——— (2003a) *Quality and power in higher education*. Buckingham: Open University Press.

——— (2003b) Reconstructing students as consumers: New settlements of power or the politics of assimilation? In M. Slowey & D. Watson (Eds.), *Higher education and the lifecourse* (pp. 79–92). Buckingham: Open University Press.

——— (2005) Opportunity or exploitation: Women and quality assurance in higher education. *Gender and Education, 17*(4).

Morley, L., Kwesigard, J., & Lihamba, J. (2005) *Gender equity in selected Commonwealth universities*. Research report to the Department of International Development. London: DFID.

NCSR (National Centre for Social Research) (2000) *Who applies for research funding?* London: National Centre for Social Research.

Peters, M. (2001) National education policy constructions of the 'knowledge economy': Towards a critique. *Journal of Educational Enquiry, 2*(1):1–22.

Prosser, M., & Trigwell, K. (1999) *Understanding learning and teaching: The experience in higher education.* Buckingham: SRHE and Open University Press.

Ramsden, P. (2003) *Learning to teach in higher education.* London: Falmer.

Riddell, S. (2005) *Disabled student and multiple policy innovations in higher education.* Presentation at CHES Seminar Series. London: Higher Education in Transition Seminars, Institute of Education, University of London, May.

Roberts, G. G. (2003) *Review of research assessment.* Report by Sir Gareth Roberts to the U.K. funding bodies, issued for consultation, May.

Sen, A. K. (1994) *Beyond liberalization: Social opportunity and human capability.* London: London School of Economics and Political Science/STICERD.

Singh, M. (2001) 'Re-inserting the "public good" into higher education transformation'. Paper presented at the SRHE Conference Globalisation and higher education: Views from the south, Cape Town, South Africa, March.

UNESCO (United Nations Educational, Scientific and Cultural Organization) (1999) *Gender and higher education: A sea change.* Report on the debate entitled 'Women in higher education: Issues and perspectives held at the World Conference on Higher Education'. Paris: Swedish International Development Cooperation Agency.

———— (2002) *UNESCO: Mainstreaming the needs of women.* Paris: UNESCO.

UNDP (United Nations Development Programme) (2002) *Gender mainstreaming: Learning and development pack.* New York: UNDP.

Wennerås, C., & Wold, A. (1997) Nepotism and sexism in peer review. *Nature, 387*:341–343.

Williams, G. (Ed.) (2003) *The enterprising university: Reform, excellence and equity.* Buckingham: Open University Press.

Chapter Ten

Personal Learning on Professional Doctorates: Feminist and Women's Contributions to Higher Education

Miriam E. David

Using feminist sociological ideas and methodologies of personal reflections, I reflect on how feminist values about the personal have become embedded in learning and teaching, pedagogies, and research practices of higher education through the contributions that women have made to the academy. How have notions of personal development and reflective practice developed in higher education and how might they develop in the twenty-first century academy?

While higher education has been transformed over the past three decades, a key factor in this changing landscape has been the contribution and critiques of women and feminists in the academy (Leonard, 2001; Morley, 2003). Political, social, economic, and neo-liberal ideas have had major implications for changes in families, labour markets, and the economy in the context of changes in information technology and global transformations (David, 2003). These changes have led to moves towards 'a knowledge economy' (Peters, 2001) contested through these concepts and one in which feminist values and 'knowledges' play a key part (Blackmore, 2002).

The expansion of higher education has indeed been built on the increasing involvement of women as students and academics within higher education. Whereas the expansion of higher education has not led to the creation of universities for the masses, it has led to massive universities in which women are now critical participants (Langa Rosado & David, 2006). These extensive changes have led to a changing balance between undergraduate and postgraduate education and an expansion of the academic labour market. In all aspects, women are now a key element. Women are the majority of all undergraduate students or students pursuing first degrees (53%) (Social Trends, 2004, as cited in Langa Rosado & David, 2006). 'Female students are now in the majority, comprising 54.8% of all postgraduates, compared with 48.5% in 1995/6. However, they are still in the minority of overseas students studying in the UK; this difference has narrowed from 36% to 43.7% over this period 1995/6 to 2001/2' (HESA, 2003, as cited in Woodward & Denicolo, 2004, p.12). Women also make up a significant minority of academics: 39% (AUT, 2004, as cited in Sanders, 2004; Court, 2004). 'Despite a surge in promotions for women (*Times Higher*, June 25,

2004), they are still outnumbered by men in top jobs. They make up 13% of professors in old universities, with success highly dependent on subject' (Sanders, 2004, p. 60).[1] Their presence remains extremely rare in the top echelons and management of British universities, however (David & Woodward, 1998; Morley, 2003; Woodward & Ross, 2002).

I will consider how these involvements reflect more global, economic, familial, and social transformations and the values on which they are based. I will also provide a case study of my personal involvement as a feminist sociologist in some of these changes and especially in recent developments in postgraduate doctoral education. I will focus on the development of a professional doctorate in education in which personal and critical reflections are a key pedagogy and methodology, drawing on feminist ideas. I will also consider how these mesh with new ideas about personal development and learning from other arenas and draw some conclusions about the contributions of feminist values and methodologies for future directions in the practices of higher education. I argue that the future in higher education is likely to be based on such pedagogies and research practices.

Feminist Values and Sociology of the 'Personal'?

This chapter draws on the themes and feminist methodology of my recent book *Personal and Political: Feminisms, Sociology and Family Lives* (David, 2003). The book is a personal reflection, in feminist fashion, of the development of feminist theories and methodologies within academic sociology, drawing on a range of international literature on feminist values of care. I review these developments from their embryonic beginnings over three or four decades and periods of what I call *liberalism*, namely social democracy, economic liberalism, and neo-liberalism, contested though these notions may be.

I argue that the theoretical and methodological developments within sociology as part of the emergent social sciences and cultural studies are such that the *boundaries*, or distinctions between sociology as a discipline and the subdisciplines of sociology of education and policy sociology, are now relatively porous and permeable. What constitutes each subject/discipline is highly contested and dependent upon changing theories and methodologies of which feminist theories and values are critical.

In particular, I am interested in the shifts in notions of *personal and political* from *second wave*[2] feminist attempts to embed an innovative approach to learning and teaching in the centrality of women's experience to the ways in which personal, subjective, and qualitative accounts are now entrenched within sociology and/or education through transformations within the social sciences and cultural studies, especially with post-structuralism and educational ethnographies. Whether these perspectives and values can now be claimed as *feminist* alone is rather more problematic since a relatively recent approach to education and pedagogies is that of demonstrating *personal development* through plans and portfolios. Indeed, in Britain, there is now a major New Labour government commitment to developing what are called forms of *personalized learning*.

Feminist Personal and Critical Reflections

The notion of personal and/or critical reflections has been gaining currency over the past decade or so within the social sciences and cultural studies within the global academy. These ideas emanate from several sources but in particular draw upon feminist values, concepts, and methodologies as they have been developed within academic sociology (David, 2003). These notions may also be derived from ideas about reflective practice as they have been considered within educational theories. Drawing upon Schon's work (1987, 1991) and the notions from psychology of personal construct theories (Denicolo & Pope, 1997, 2001), these considerations have contributed to personal development as a method within the social sciences and even beyond. More generally, they also draw upon what has been called the *social and cultural turn* (Jones, 2003) or the *biographical turn* within the social sciences (Chamberlayne, Bornat, & Wengraf, 2000). Most recently, in Britain at least, the ideas of personal learning have become the subject of debate with respect to learning and teaching or pedagogies of education, from schooling through postgraduate and doctoral education.

These all entail a methodological focus on notions of the subject and the self, known as *the project of the self* (Rose, 1998), including auto/biography (Stanley, 1992), rather than on traditional and social scientific subject/object distinctions hitherto. Giddens (1992) has also emphasized how the self in relation to a more reflexive *risk society*, drawing on Beck's ideas (1992), has become endemic to high or late modern societies. In other words, the moves have been great from forms of social protection and state involvement towards more individualization. However, these ideas have been highly contested even among feminist sociologists (Oakley, 2000). Nevertheless, they have led to changing practices in social and educational research methodologies (Oakley, 2000) and to critiques of traditional approaches to social scientific knowledge and methodologies, and they have moved away from positivism towards more experiential, ethnographic, and qualitative approaches (Fine & Weis, 2003; Drake & Owen, 1998; St Pierre & Pillow, 2000; Weis & Fine, 2000).

At the same time, the rich diversity of sociology has also led to notions of reflexivity as an epistemological break with the past within sociology and extended developments in critical theory (Bourdieu, 1992; Giddens, 1990, 1992; Beck, Giddens, & Lash, 1996). All of these trends have contributed to changes within the practices, theories, and methodologies of sociology and education. Moreover, the distinctions between substantive areas within sociology, such that the sociology of education as a subdiscipline has developed an approach that can be distinguished from sociology as a discipline in itself, is far more difficult to sustain. It has become rather fashionable across all the social and political sciences to develop personal, biographic, and narrative accounts of personal experiences (Stanley, 1997; Drake & Owen, 1998; St Pierre & Pillow, 2000; Kamler, 2001).

While this approach has become endemic within the social sciences extending the notions from purely feminist ones as a part of the social and cultural turn, this has been particularly the case from the perspective of women of my generation internationally. We became involved in the academy and the social sciences, sociology, and/of education as part of the generation who benefitted from the expansion of educational opportunities in the post-war period (Arnot, David, & Weiner, 1999). Many of these women in Britain became conscious feminists valuing equality and have reflected upon their experiences more recently (Deem, 1996; David & Woodward, 1998; Stanley, 1992; Walkerdine, 1997; Weiner, 1994; Williams, 1999; David, 2002c). Oakley (2003), while contesting the methodological developments, has also contributed a rich and detailed analysis from her own feminist perspective of developments in academic sociology. This phenomenon has occurred internationally with evidence from the Anglophone literature of such critical and personal reflections from inter alia Australia (Curthoys, 2000; Kenway & Bullen, 1997; Blackmore, 1999), New Zealand (Middleton, 1998) and North America (Britzman, 2002; Luttrell, 2003).

Personal and Political: Feminist Values and Pedagogies

The notion that *the personal is political* was key to the second wave women's movement as it developed in the late 1960s and early 1970s. It entailed the notion that personal, private, and intimate family matters nevertheless were highly *political* in the sense that they relied upon deep power relations between men and women. In other words, women's private family experiences were not unique but were the product of wider power relations between men and women in society, ones in which women were subordinate and not equal. At first, these became the ideas that influenced the burgeoning women's liberation movement as a political movement, but later they began to influence academic developments, especially in sociology, as women entered the academy and became involved as academics.

The term *feminist* was not in the lexicon of academe until the 1970s when such women became involved as academics, although the word had been used in the late nineteenth century as a political concept. The ideas were highly contested as academic subjects such that women's studies initially developed outside of conventional undergraduate courses and extramurally for mature women students as part of life-long learning. However, as more women became involved as academic sociologists, sociologists of education, or other social and political scientists, they began to develop and transform the ideas based on feminist values and develop feminist theories, methodologies and/or pedagogy, and *knowledge*.

Indeed, the growth and development of such theories and methodologies within social and cultural studies reveals the complexities and transformations of these concepts (Ramazanoglu, 2002). A key transformation has occurred in notions of personal and political in the sense that the centrality of women's personal experiences viewed as deeply 'political' has shifted to the 'gaze' now centrally focused upon the manner in which the political is suffused with the personal. In other words, there has been a major shift from *outsider* and objective approaches and accounts to more subjective and *insider* approaches.

One hallmark, however, of these various feminist perspectives was the centrality of women's personal experience to understandings and the development of *knowledge*. It is also a hallmark of feminist pedagogy (Morley, 1999; Kamler, 2001). This involves an exploration of personal experiences, reflections, and narrative or biographical accounts of both professional and personal developments as part of the approach to learning and teaching the *curriculum* and the *knowledge* created.

As higher education has also expanded, these ideas have become embedded in wider pedagogical practices and can be seen now as a form of continuing/personal professional development (C/PPD) as well. Indeed, they have spread to forms of professional education not only within the studies of education in higher education but within wider forms of educational developments and practices of learning and teaching such that the notion of personal experience is no longer the preserve of feminist pedagogy and practice. There are also some key developments in the idea of personal development as part of professional development and training as linked to lifelong learning. It remains important to account for these developments in both pedagogy and practices in sociology and educational studies by referencing the new *knowledge society or economy* (Blackmore, 2002; David, 2003).

The notions of personal and political have indeed become deeply embedded within the theories and methodologies of many of the disciplines/subjects of the social sciences and humanities. The ways in which they have been adopted and adapted have also been associated with feminist and post-structural or post-modern theories and methodologies.

Personal and Feminist Values in the Changing Landscape of Higher Education

By the beginning of the 1990s, the process of *massification* of higher education had begun in earnest and was accelerated by the creation of a new system of universities in Britain. From 1992, this resulted in a doubling of the number of universities in Britain and a changing subject or disciplinary base. Many of the humanities, arts, and social science disciplines or subjects expanded, and women's studies along with media and cultural studies became key subjects. More importantly, women's involvement in higher education continued to grow both as students and as part of the transforming academic labour market. Widening participation to higher education along class, ethnicity/race, and gender lines became, in the early 1990s, a key feature of government policies. At the beginning of the twenty-first century, issues around new forms of access to higher education, including lifelong learning, have contributed to these developments and have entailed further increases in women's involvement. Thus, over the decade from 1994 to 2004, there has been a massive transformation in the balance of undergraduate and postgraduate higher education, creating massive universities although the evidence for these being universities for the masses remains elusive (Langa Rosado & David, 2006).

'Over the past 20 years, total student numbers have grown from 863,000 in 1982/3 to 1,444,000 a decade later, despite government restrictions applied in the mid-1990s, and by 2001/2 they stood at 2,086,075 (HESA, 2003) ... The rate of growth in postgraduate student numbers has outstripped undergraduate expansion ...' (Woodward & Denicolo, 2004, p. 12). The expansion of higher education, by doubling the number of higher education institutions, also allowed for the massive increase in postgraduate studies compared with undergraduate education. Each university, from 1992, had its own regulations and formal and informal procedures for awarding their own doctorates. It also ensured that even those higher education institutions that were not yet universities had to be engaged in PhD supervision in order to become eligible to change their status to become universities. An interesting irony, however, of the more recent moves to further expand higher education through New Labour policies in the twenty-first century is the removal of research degree awarding powers as a criterion of university status. This was one of the key features of the government proposals on the future of higher education (DfES, 2003). However, by 2004, 'the graduate school has become the dominant model for the organization of graduate education across the sector. Two-thirds of the institutions responding to the (UKCGE) survey now have graduate schools' (Woodward & Denicolo, 2004, p. 3).

Moreover, women as both academics and students have become engaged at every level of education, from schools and further to higher education, and are increasingly involved within educational studies not only with initial teacher education but also with a variety of forms of professional development and practice. In other words, there is complexity and diversity in forms of educational studies and research, including feminist perspectives, theories, methodologies, pedagogies, practices (Ramazanoglu, 2002).

In particular, the development of postgraduate professional and doctoral education has been the hallmark of this period. For instance, developments in doctorates have entailed expansion of traditional PhDs, what are still called *research degrees* in Britain, and the growth of professional doctorates, especially but not only in education (Leonard, 2001; Scott et al., 2004). There have been contradictory developments in doctoral education versus training. On one hand, the main emphasis with respect to traditional PhDs has been *research training* rather than education. This is a growing prerequisite as part of the quality assurance movement and has resulted in numerous publications about quality in postgraduate research degrees (Woodward & Denicolo, 2004).

Similarly, there have also been moves towards what have recently been called *new route PhDs* based upon North American and some European experiences, including those through the Bologna agreement for the harmonization of European postgraduate studies. These programmes involve one year of taught courses programmes as a prelude to the production of a research thesis on traditional lines, including full-time individual study. On the other hand, there has been a rapid growth of professional doctoral education, modelled more on Commonwealth, particularly Australian, experiences (David, 2002b; McWilliam, 2002; McWilliam et al., 2002). These programmes are mainly part-time and involve periods of intensive blocks of teaching and study usually in cohort groups. Questions have also been raised as to the kinds of knowledge involved in professional education, namely distinctions between academic and professional practice (Scott et al., 2004). There is also an overlapping question of whether professional doctorates are about practice as opposed to traditional academic knowledge and about teaching or learning as opposed to research.

The process of massification of doctoral education is also indicated by the recent increase in numbers and is accompanied by the increased autonomy and potential variation among the universities in which doctoral students study. By the end of 2000, there were over 101,000 doctoral or so-called research students in U.K. universities both full-time and part-time in a total of 129 institutions (Woodward & Denicolo, 2004). More than 10,000 new students started their PhDs in 1998–1999 compared to just over 3,000 in 1992. In excess of 14,000 candidates are currently awarded doctorates annually. With the advent of 'professional, taught and practice-based doctorates', 'new route and traditional Ph.D.s', and general credential inflation, those undertaking 'research-based degrees' represent a quarter of all postgraduates and include many overseas students (Woodward & Denicolo, 2004, p. 5). Moreover, postgraduate students number over a third of all students in higher education (Morley, Leonard, & David, 2002).

In my study with Leonard and Morley (Morley, Leonard, and David, 2002), our interests as feminists were in the transformations; we felt that although the massification of doctoral studies had opened up possibilities for women as doctoral students on an unprecedented scale, it also limited the further creation of *feminist knowledge.*

Moreover, although there have been massive transformations, the procedures for realizing quality and even more so for sustaining or developing equality and fairness have not been addressed fully.

Under the current New Labour administration, there has been a new stress on the doctorate as research training rather than as scholarship or original knowledge. Through the various quality assurance procedures and reports of the different research councils, it gradually has become accepted practice to require postgraduate research students to undertake a programme of research training in their preparation to undertake a research thesis. The first such programme was an MRes, or masters in research, in the physical and biological sciences as a prelude to a doctorate. More recently, this requirement has been generalized to all doctoral studies and has necessitated the completion of methodology courses or a preceding specialist master's course in research. These degrees have become the criteria for awards or bursaries from the various different research councils across the sciences and social sciences.

These requirements have also inspired a proliferation of bodies and organizations concerned with monitoring or ensuring standards of postgraduate degrees and qualifications. Chief among these are the UK Council for Graduate Education, founded in 1994 (Woodward & Denicolo, 2004), the UK GRAD, founded by the government's funding body for higher education (HEFCE), and the research councils that fund postgraduate and research studies. This body provides opportunities for research training across all the regions of the United Kingdom for doctoral students, not only those funded by the various government funding bodies.

However, despite the emphasis in New Labour's innovative approach to evidence-based policy and practice (David, 2002a; Thomas & Pring, 2004), the *evidence base* for these various policy changes and developments have been quite sparse: rather inadequate statistical records, self-report studies, and documentary analysis and narratives (Delamont, Parry, & Atkinson, 1998; Delamont, Atkinson, & Parry, 1997/2005; Eggleston & Delamont, 1983). Nevertheless, what has been called *new managerialism* in the United Kingdom (see chapter 9 in this book by Louise Morley) has transformed the priorities, culture, and practices of the academy. In keeping with developments in new forms of management and forms of reflective and feminist practice, studying this constitutes a new research agenda and could contribute to equity procedures within universities. I move now, therefore, to a case study of the developments in professional doctoral education from a feminist perspective. I shall look briefly at the opportunities afforded by professional doctorates in education for imparting some of the insights of feminist theories and knowledge and developing aspects of both feminist pedagogies around the personal as well as those more central notions of personal development and portfolios that are now accepted as part of the pedagogies and practices of learning and teaching in higher education.

Professional Doctorates in Education: The Case of Feminist Knowledge and Pedagogies

Using my own experiences again in traditional feminist fashion (David, 2002c, 2003), I shall focus on developments in the professional doctorate in education around gender and feminist values, knowledge, and pedagogy. At the time of writing, I was appointed six years earlier to Keele University specifically to develop a professional doctorate in education (David, 2002b, 2003). Although I had supervised numerous traditional PhD students in the social sciences, many with a feminist perspective, and had been a feminist sociologist committed to developing new curricula and pedagogies around feminist values, I had not been involved with professional doctorates in education. Thus, these developments represented a very new challenge to me. They also represented a new challenge for Keele University as a way to expand its postgraduate student clientele in the context a rapidly changing political and social environment for higher education.

Moreover, Keele University was a relatively small traditional university catering mainly to undergraduate students. Its distinctiveness was to provide dual honours in undergraduate studies, and it had pioneered foundation years for undergraduate degrees. The university had been founded in 1960 as part of what became a considerable degree of university expansion in the 1960s known then as a new wave of universities on green field sites or campuses (David & Woodward, 1998). This kind of expansion concentrated on undergraduate students with the aim of extending provision to a wider range of social classes and implicitly targeting gender. Keele decided to use the model of American undergraduate degrees as its focus. However, by the end of the 1990s, given the pressures and changing nature of national higher education policies, the university was unable to sustain these four-year degrees and moved into traditional three-year degrees. It had a very small number of postgraduate students. In keeping with many traditional universities, it had created a graduate school but specifically for the social sciences the year that I arrived (Woodward & Denicolo, 2004). Indeed, the social sciences, including education, comprised almost half of the university. Pioneering developments in postgraduate and doctoral education within the social sciences was clearly a key task, given the balance of subjects. Indeed, the social sciences and research in these areas was seen as a major basis for either expansion or survival.

The vice-chancellor of the university, appointed three years previously, was herself a liberal feminist sociologist and was eager to develop women's studies and postgraduate research in the social sciences. She convened a number of discussions to develop and promote these ideas and activities and so set the conditions for the emergence of these programmes. Although the university had several feminist academics within the social sciences and humanities, there was neither much collaborative work nor any specific undergraduate courses offered in gender or women's studies. The concentration was far more on traditional kinds of social science research. Developing feminist values and pedagogies for a professional doctorate was clearly a major challenge within the context of a small university with a small group of feminist and pro-feminist colleagues committed to such an endeavour and therefore was a relatively neutral environment for such developments. The wider political context was also becoming more competitive, and opportunities for forms of expansion were more difficult to locate.

Moreover, the Education Department to which I was appointed was relatively small and heterogeneous. It provided large courses for postgraduate teacher education and some forms of continuing professional development, although it did not have many traditional research programmes. Its research effort was mainly linked with a very small number of those colleagues who were also involved with teaching on undergraduate courses in educational studies. Thus, the doctorate in education was originally meant to contribute to the suite of programmes for professional development and mainly for senior teachers and administrators. The scene had been set for this development on my arrival and the initial programme had had initial internal approvals. However, I set about giving wider consideration to how to develop this initial programme (David, 2004).

As a background to our development of the professional doctorate, I move now to consider briefly some of the contradictory and challenging features of professional doctorates in education. Whereas we have seen how the massification of doctoral education has not been clearly linked to new public management, it has opened up new potentialities. Some of these possibilities draw particularly on international experiences, especially in the Anglophone and Commonwealth countries, such as Australia and New Zealand (Middleton, 2001; Green, Maxwell, & Shanahan, 2001; McWilliam et al., 2002). McWilliam and colleagues were particularly intrigued by the contribution that professional doctorates might make to mandatory research training in Australia as the degrees were becoming increasingly popular as a form of provision in Australia at the turn of the twenty-first century and, by implication, also for Britain.

Whereas the emphasis on research training in Britain has also been embedded in all forms of doctoral education, including in professional doctorates, it has varied considerably, and none of it has yet become mandatory. Moreover, some professional doctorates focus more on the practice-based knowledge than on the development of academic knowledge, especially in areas or disciplines such as art or music, and thus even professional doctorates in education vary in their emphasis and perspectives (Scott et al., 2004). Thus, variety has also emerged in respect to professional doctorates and the expectations of content and assessment. The massive growth in professional doctorates, and education doctorates in particular, over the past decade has emulated earlier practices in Australia, New Zealand, and Canada (McWilliam et al., 2002). Indeed there have been four biennial conferences on professional doctorates organized in Australia.

There are over 30 professional doctoral programmes in education in Britain, loosely coordinated through a group of directors of education doctoral programmes, the first having started at the University of Bristol in the early 1990s. They all have certain key features, namely, they contain many taught elements or coursework units in addition to the writing of a thesis or dissertation, and they are attended mainly on a part-time basis. These developments in coursework or taught elements pre-dated and may have actually prefigured some of the more recent developments in research training and skills for the traditional PhD in Britain. Another feature of professional doctorates is that they tend to be taught on a cohort basis to groups of students. A usual criterion of entry is involvement in a professional activity, and thus the majority of students are mature (adults) rather than undertaking study immediately after undergraduate degrees. They can be seen as part of the process of lifelong learning and continued professional development. They are also designed for a particular market of students, namely professional educators, who are either teachers in schools, further or higher education, or lifelong learning, or they are administrators and managers within aspects of education and related areas.

In exploring my own reflections on professional doctorates in education, I decided to conduct a small survey of such doctorates, using what became 'an opportunity sample'. In the spring of 2003, I wrote to all directors of doctorates in education involved in a network in Britain. I also tried to develop some view of the same issues in Australia but received formal replies only from one university that had been deeply engaged in developing the broader issues around research training. However, both anecdotal and collegial evidence from Australia, Canada, and New Zealand would suggest similar developmental trajectories. I was particularly interested in whether or not gender was a feature of these doctorates, especially the balances between men and women as both students and doctoral graduates from such programmes. I also wanted to gain a sense of the extent to which new styles and forms of pedagogy around the personal and/or feminist had been used, but I have only a more informal or anecdotal sense of this.

Fourteen of the 30 university directors replied and confirmed my initial supposition that women were in a majority in such programmes, although not as dramatically as I had initially supposed. Out of students enrolled on the programmes in the summer of 2003, 56% were women and only 44% were men. Similarly, of those students who have graduated as doctors of education (and these are currently very small numbers as the programmes remain relatively new), 53% were women and 46% men.

Given these figures, although the study was neither representative nor did it cover a range of subjects and issues, there are indications that professional women educators are taking up opportunities for forms of professional development. From the kinds of studies written about Australia and New Zealand particularly (Middleton, 2001; McWilliam et al., 2002), it seems clear that women and feminist involvement is developing here as well. However, it is also evident from this that the question of women's involvement and developments in new types of pedagogy including feminist methodologies depends upon the orientation of the academics and researchers involved at the institutional level. For example, the doctorate in education in Lincoln, a very new university, seems to have targeted men rather than women, as only a third of their graduates are women.

The Keele Doctorate in Education: Gender and Education Management

In the case of the education doctorate at Keele University, we developed a particular market niche for the doctorate in education. We recognized what was implicit rather than explicit in the other professional doctoral programmes in Britain that a majority of the students in professional education were likely to be women. Given the evidence accumulated over the past 30 years about women's growing involvement in education and higher education as forms of professional work, we assumed that there would be a market for studies that made the issues of gender explicit. Indeed, it quickly became evident that a majority of students in doctoral programmes in education were not just women from school-based education or local management and administration where men held the more senior positions but were women from the rapidly expanding sectors of further and higher education.

In particular, they included a preponderance of women in education administration and in the new forms of higher education, particularly the new universities. We recognized and adopted an approach targeting the majority of students wishing to undertake such programmes in Britain who were professional women, especially those already in higher education requiring a doctorate for professional development.

The initial doctorate in education at Keele had been planned to complement the critical policy research focus of the department and its links with the British New Labour government's attempts to develop an innovative approach to policy making, namely an evidence-based approach (Thomas & Pring, 2004). However, given that we found that the majority of our first students in the evidence-based policy and practice programme were women who were attracted to consideration of various critical, theoretical, and methodological developments, we decided to revise the programme. We adapted our scheme and resubmitted it for course review to the internal committee structures of the university – first, a faculty course development subcommittee followed by the university main committee. Given that we had been very successful in recruiting our first cohort of students and were able to demonstrate a clear market for this programme, the university committees quickly approved our revisions around gender and education management. In any event, the university was eager to maintain and expand student numbers wherever they could. Moreover, we were able to show that our team had sufficient expertise and experience in both research and teaching to develop this strand effectively.

The majority of our students on the first four cohorts of the gender and education management (GEM) strand of our doctorate in education were either female administrators or academics from the post-1992 universities, teaching across a range of subjects from business studies to psychology. We also had a small number of administrators from the further education sector, augmented by a very small number of senior administrators in local authority educational management. In addition, we had a number of health educators chiefly developing paramedical education in higher education, including nurse educators and physiotherapists, from both the pre- and post-1992 universities.

We thus tailored our learning and teaching strategy specifically for these students who were mainly women. We focussed especially on providing feminist knowledge through the use of feminist and personal pedagogies. As far as we are aware, this approach was unique in the United Kingdom, although it may not have been with respect to other countries, especially not with respect to Australia (McWilliam et al., 2002). We developed this unique strand to our doctorate in education around feminist theories and methodologies and used personal reflections and feminist pedagogy. Our original approach to the initial evidence-based policy and practice (EPP) strand, modelled on the approaches to doctoral education taken by other universities in Britain, was to develop the notion of reflective practice as it applies to both professional issues and to notions of research on professional issues in education. However, we also remained committed to a research-based degree while aiming to dovetail research training for traditional PhDs with our doctorate in education.

We drew initially on Schon's foundational work (1987, 1991). However, we subsequently modified it to take account of feminist scholarship and practices around reflexivity and experiential perspectives (Drake & Owen, 1998; David, 2002c, 2003). In particular, we introduced feminist approaches to being reflective researchers and practitioners, and we used such models of academic reflexive researchers by David (2002c) and Deem (1996). Our practices and pedagogies were also modelled on these notions, and we drew out personal and professional experiences within the classroom as well as within the required assignments. We also have developed explicitly feminist perspectives on research concepts and methodologies as well as feminist theories drawing on feminist insights around post-structuralism (St Pierre & Pillow, 2000).

Moreover, we have also used feminist post-structuralism to critique ideas about gender, masculinities, and femininities. Here Lingard and Douglas's (1999) *pro-feminist* work has been salient. This feminist perspective is threaded through both the substantive course units or modules on educational theories and the research-'training' elements. Our overarching pedagogical practice builds upon traditional feminist practice but aims to integrate social science transformations through biography, narratives, and voices (Pitt, 2003; Britzman, 1998; St Pierre & Pillow, 2000).

We found thus far, that is, at the time of writing and over three years into the doctoral programme for gender and education management (GEM), that this was by far the more popular strand, and each course unit was evaluated very highly by all the students as part of the regular form of quality assurance required by the university. Indeed, several of the students who initially registered for our other strand on EPP asked to transfer to GEM. Thus, we began to integrate our two approaches and provide only separate tutorials for the twin strands.

The British system of quality assurance requires a system of external examiners. In the case of our doctorate in education, we have had two external examiners for the coursework elements, one for the EPP strand and one for the GEM strand. Both have been involved over the past three years in moderating all of the coursework on the programme. Students are required to complete five pieces of coursework before undertaking their thesis, the final one of which is a summative assessment in the form of a thesis proposal examined orally and in writing. Students have to do a presentation at a thesis proposal conference in order to progress to their actual thesis. Both the external examiners have commented each year on the excellent theoretical, methodological, and ethnographic work that the students manage to achieve in their first two years in the programme.

We were also eager to see the fruits of our feminist and pro-feminist practices and have found that our students were very responsive to these gendered approaches, especially the elements of reflective and critical research practices. Their enthusiasm has been such that they have used their personal experiences as ways to critique not only their past practices but centrally as part of their research endeavours and methodologies of critical and/or feminist ethnographies as well. Indeed, writing about their personal and professional developments are required initial pieces of coursework, but the students are extremely enthusiastic to use this kind of approach in all of their work, and often it serves as the hallmark of how they have developed first their coursework components and subsequently their actual thesis. Several of the students are now at the stage of completing their theses, and the key to their work is the use of their personal perspectives linked to their own professional development within higher education especially. For instance, one male student has developed a pro-feminist critique of his own practice of developing management courses for students in China who are primarily women. Another has developed a strong feminist critique of the development of auditing and quality assurance procedures in British universities, given her base as a university teacher of accounting. A third has developed her work as a lecturer in health education, studying HIV/AIDS and sex education from a black feminist perspective.

Conclusion

As women have entered the academy in increasing numbers and over the generations, the academy itself has been transformed. These changes over the past 30 years in British higher education have been associated with changing forms of liberalism and their justification in relation to technological and labour market changes in the economy. Developments towards a knowledge society or economy have also entailed developments and diversity in women's education and forms of largely professional employment. A key feature, rarely noticed or acknowledged, has been women's contributions and engagements with such developments. Particularly intriguing and important are the ways in which feminist values, theories, methodologies, and pedagogies have contributed to the complexity and diversity of the changes, providing challenges to future developments in higher education.

Feminist theories, methodologies, and research practices have grown from within sociology and/of education to the social sciences more generally and have combined with other epistemological changes within social and cultural studies. This has happened over a lengthy 30- to 40-year period, in association with broader social and political changes, linked with transformations in forms of so-called liberalism. Thus, there is now a complexity and diversity of theoretical and methodological changes to which feminist and critical theories contribute. Indeed, it can be argued that, as part of the social and cultural turn, feminists within social and educational studies, among others, theorize the political as personal and contribute to the pedagogical shifts towards the personal that is now relatively endemic in higher education. Moves towards personal reflections and reflective professional practices have influenced not only undergraduate studies and research practices, contributing to rich and complex educational research ethnographies but also to developments in postgraduate and professional education.

Most recently, under neo-liberalism, the majority of higher education changes have led to a massification of postgraduate and doctoral education and constraints on equity, originality, and creativity through quality assurance mechanisms; at the same time, there have been great opportunities for women's involvement and the development of feminist values and knowledges as part of the new knowledge economy (Blackmore, 2002). Feminist values around the ethic of care and personal development are now deeply embedded in pedagogical practices at levels of higher education. This seems to have been the case especially with respect to professional, doctoral education rather than in research training for traditional doctorates (David, 2004).

Indeed, feminist values around an ethic of the personal and practices of care, knowledge, and pedagogy from the early second wave feminist political movement initiating feminist values, knowledges, and theories may have prefigured these developments in doctoral education in the new knowledge economy, and feminist pedagogies may contribute to developing innovative practices in professional doctoral education. The development of feminist pedagogies within and across higher education and especially doctoral education, including personal and critical reflections and experiences, have become embedded in the practices and pedagogies of higher education more generally.

On the basis of a personal reflection, I have argued that feminist values and sociological methodologies have made, and will continue to make, important contributions to the development of new knowledge and innovative approaches to learning and teaching in higher education generally and in postgraduate professional and doctoral studies in particular. The moves towards the personal in social and educational research and in pedagogical practices, such as personal development plans and portfolio assessment, in higher education have been critical to the wider transformations in higher education, such as widening participation and access to higher education. However, current changes in higher education policies and practices may militate against such transformations for future generations, especially in relation to postgraduate studies. Nevertheless, women's engagement in higher education, the changing work/life balance, and the theorization of the personal will continue to make important contributions for understandings in the future. Hopefully, there will be greater recognition of feminist ethics of care and concern in wider policy developments for education and higher education in particular, modifying the class, race, and gender imbalances currently in practice (Reay, David, & Ball, 2005) in the global society and knowledge economy. Such concerns would ensure a greater commitment to how the personal and political are entwined in all of our lives.

Notes

1. The old universities are all those universities that were created and established before the 1992 Higher Education Act and are sometimes referred to as the pre-1992 universities to distinguish them from those universities created as a result of the 1992 Act. These latter are sometimes called new universities or post-1992 universities.
2. *Second wave* feminism refers to the ways in which the women's movement as a social and political movement in the 1960s and 1970s began to develop academic and theoretical notions that were developed and eventually adopted within the academy.

References

Arnot, M., David, M.E., & Weiner, G. (1999) *Closing the gender gap: Post-war education and social change.* Cambridge: Polity Press.

Beck, U. (1992) *The risk society: Towards a new modernity.* London: Sage.

Beck, U., Giddens, T., & Lash, S. (1996) *Reflexive modernisation.* Cambridge: Polity Press.

Blackmore, J. (1999) *Troubling women.* Buckingham: Open University Press.

———— (2002) Is it only 'what works' that 'counts' in new knowledge economies? Evidence-based practice, educational research and teacher education in Australia. *Social Policy and Society, 1*(3):257–267.

Bourdieu, P. (1992) *Reflexive sociology.* Cambridge: Polity Press.

Britzman, D. (1998) *Lost subjects, contested objects: Towards a psychoanalytic inquiry of learning.* Albany, NY: SUNY Press.

———— (2002) *After-education: Anna Freud, Melanie Klein and psychoanalytic histories of learning.* Albany, NY: State University of New York Press.

Chamberlayne, P., Bornat, J., & Wengraf, T. (Eds.) (2000) *The biographical turn in the social sciences.* London: Routledge.

Court, S. (2004) *The unequal academy.* London: Association of University Teachers.

Curthoys, A. (2000) Adventures in feminism: Simone de Beauvoir's autobiographies, women's liberation, and self-fashioning. *Feminist Review, 64*:3–18.

David, M. E. (2002a) Evidence-based policy as a concept for modernising governance and social science research. *Social Policy and Society, 1*(3):213–215.

David, M. E. (2002b) Feminist contributions to doctoral education in Britain: Feminist knowledge in the new knowledge economy. In E. McWilliam (Ed.), *Fourth international biennial conference on professional doctorates research training for the knowledge economy conference proceedings* (pp. 39–53). Brisbane, Australia: Queensland University of Technology.

———— (2002c) From Keighley to Keele: Personal reflections on a circuitous journey through education, family, feminism and policy sociology. *British Journal of Sociology of Education, 23*(2):249–271.

———— (2003) *Personal and political: Feminism, sociology and family lives.* Stoke-on-Trent: Trentham Books.

———— (2004) Feminist sociology and feminist knowledges: Contributions to higher education pedagogies and professional practices in the knowledge economy. *International Studies in the Sociology of Education, 14*(2):99–125.

David, M. E., & Woodward, D. (1998) *Negotiating the glass ceiling: Senior women in the academic world.* London: Falmer Press.

Deem, R. (1996) Border territories: A journey through sociology, education and women's studies. *British journal of sociology of education 17*(2):5–19.

Delamont, S., Atkinson, P., & Parry, O. (1997/2005) *Supervising the Ph.D.: A guide to success* (2nd ed.). Buckingham: Open University Press and Society for Research in Higher Education.

Delamont, S., Parry, O., & Atkinson, P. (1998) Creating a delicate balance: The doctoral supervisor's dilemmas. *Teaching in higher education*, 3(2):157–172.

Denicolo, P., & Pope, M. (Eds.) (1997) *Sharing understanding and practice.* Farnborough: EPCA Publications.

——— (2001) *Transformative professional practice: Personal construct approaches to education and research.* London: Whurr Publishers.

DfES (Department for Education and Skills) (2003) *The future of higher education* (White Paper). London: HMSO.

Drake, P., & Owen, P. (Eds.) (1998) *Gender and management issues in education: An international perspective.* Stoke-on-Trent: Trentham Books.

Eggleston, J., & Delamont, S. (1983) *Supervision of students for research degrees, with special reference to educational studies.* Crewe: British Educational Research Association.

Fine, M., & Weis, L. (2003) *Silenced voices and extraordinary conversations: Re-imagining schooling.* New York: Teachers College Press.

Giddens, A. (1990) *The consequences of modernity.* Cambridge: Polity Press.

——— (1992) *The transformation of intimacy.* Cambridge: Polity Press.

Green, B., Maxwell, T. W., & Shanahan, P. (2001) *Doctoral education and professional practice: The next generation?* Armidale: Kardooriar Press.

Jones, K. (2003) *Education in Britain since 1944.* Cambridge: Polity Press.

Kamler, B. (2001) *Relocating the personal: A critical writing pedagogy.* State University of New York: SUNY Press.

Kenway, J., & Bullen, E. (2002) *Consuming children.* Buckingham: Open University Press.

Langa Rosado, D., & David, M. E. (2006) 'A massive university or a university for the masses: Continuity and change in higher education in Spain and England'. *Journal of education policy*, 3(3):343–363.

Leonard, D. (2001) *A woman's guide to doctoral studies.* Buckingham: Open University Press.

Lingard, B. & Douglas, P. (1999) *Men engaging feminisms: Pro-feminism backlashes and schoolig.* Buckingham: Open University Press.

Luttrell, W. (2003) *Pregnant bodies; Fertile minds.* London: Routledge.

McWilliam, E. (Ed.) (2002) *Fourth international biennial conference on professional doctorates research training for the knowledge economy conference proceedings.* Brisbane Australia: Queensland University of Technology.

McWilliam, E., Thomson, P., Green, B., Maxwell, T., Wildy, H., & Simons, D. (2002) *Research training in doctoral programs: What can be learned from professional doctorates?* Canberra: ACT Commonwealth of Australia Department of Education, Science and Training.

Middleton, S. (1998) *Disciplining sexuality: Foucault, life histories and education.* New York: Teachers' College Press.

——— (2001) *A doctorate in the house?* Hamilton, New Zealand: Waikato Press.

Morley, L. (1999) *Organising feminisms: The micropolitics of the academy.* Houndsmill, Basingstoke: Macmillan.

——— (2003) *Quality and power in higher education.* Buckingham: Open University Press.

Morley, L., Leonard, D., & David, M. E. (2002) Variations in Vivas: Quality and equality in British Ph.D. assessments. *Studies in higher education*, 27(3):263–273.

Oakley, A. (2000) *Experiments in knowing.* Cambridge: Polity Press.

——— (2003) *Gender on planet earth.* Cambridge: Polity Press.

Peters, M. (2001) National education policy constructions of the 'knowledge economy': Towards a critique. *Journal of educational enquiry*, 2(1):1–31.

Pitt, A. (2003) *The play of the personal: Psychoanalytic narratives of feminist education.* New York: Peter Lang.

Ramazanoglu, C. (with Holland, J.) (2002) *Feminist methodology: Challenges and choices.* London: Sage.

Reay, D., David, M. E., & Ball, S. J. (2005) *Degrees of choice: Class, gender and race in choices of higher education.* Stoke on Trent: Trentham Books.

Rose, N. (1998) *Governing the soul.* London: Routledge.

Sanders, C. (2004) Casual culture props up academe. *Times higher education supplement, 1660* (60) (October 1), http://www.thes.co.uk/search/story.aspx?story_id=2016170. Retrieved 25 August 2006.

Schon, D. (1987) *Educating the reflective practitioner.* San Francisco: Jossey-Bass.

——— (1991) *The reflective turn: How professionals think in action.* NewYork: Teachers' College Press.

Scott, D., Brown, A., Lunt, I., & Thorne, L. (2004) *Professional doctorates: Integrating professional and academic knowledge.* London: Open University Press.

St Pierre, E. A., & Pillow, W. (Eds.) (2000) *Working the ruins: Feminist post-structuralist theory and methods in education.* London: Routledge.

Stanley, E. (1992) *The auto/biographical I.* Manchester: Manchester University Press.

——— (Ed.) (1997) *Knowing feminisms.* London: Sage.

Thomas, G., & Pring, R. (Eds.) (2004) *Evidence-based practice in education.* Buckingham: Open University Press.

Walkerdine, V. (1997) *Daddy's girl.* London: Macmillan.

Weiner, G. (1994) *Feminisms in education.* Buckingham: Open University Press.

Weis, L., & Fine, M. (2000) *Speed bumps: A student friendly guide to qualitative research.* New York: Teachers College Press.

Williams, F. (1999) Good enough principles for welfare. *Journal of Social Policy, 24*(4): 667–689.

Woodward, D., & Denicolo, P. (with Hayward, S., & Long, E.) (2004) *A review of graduate schools in the UK.* Retrieved 25 August 2006 from the U.K. Council for Graduate Education Website, www.ukcge.ac.uk/files/Graduateschools.pdf.

Woodward, D., & Ross, K. (2002) *Managing equal opportunities in higher education.* London: SRHE and Open University Press.

Chapter Eleven

Gender Equality in the American Research University: Renewing the Agenda for Women's Rights

Judith Glazer-Raymo

This chapter assesses the role and status of American women in their efforts to achieve gender equality in higher education. It examines the economic, political, and social framework of policies that have contributed to women's advancement in the United States, the complex interrelationships of the federal, state, and institutional decision makers, and the mechanisms and strategies for assuring the autonomous status and access to power of women in the academy as faculty and administrators. It is informed by the recognition that all American women are experiencing the ungendering of public policy. The strategy seems to be threefold: (1) raising the level of policy making from the state to the federal level while also proclaiming the sanctity of constitutional guarantees for states' rights; (2) turning to the courts, through the appointment of conservative judges, to rule on controversial policies on constitutional grounds; and (3) using threats to world peace as weapons for abrogating civil liberties and instilling fear and distrust among Americans. These tactics manifest themselves in a more polarized society characterized by social justice concerns that affect women's ability to attain full equality. In that context, the role of the higher education community should be to provide independent leadership; however, economic and political uncertainties constrain their actions. What do these uncertainties and altered priorities portend for women, including women of colour? And what can be done to build a more inclusive agenda for women's rights?

The Research University in Context

American higher education is unique in its complexity, variety, and organization, setting it apart from most other nations and making comparability of cases a difficult task. Its diversified and unsystematized structure reflects the multiple influences on its historical development and the decentralization of responsibility to each of the 50 states rather than to the federal government. As a result, an array of diverse centres of learning has originated, representing distinctive levels of control and financing, academic missions, and organizational structures.[1] Public institutions predominate, generally structured as complex hierarchical systems with research universities as their 'flagships', governed by elected or appointed boards of trustees or regents, and comprising 76.5% of all enrolments. Private institutions, governed by largely self-perpetuating boards dominated by corporate executives, civic leaders, alumni, and wealthy donors, account for 24.5%. Operating budgets and capital expenditures are derived from a combination of state tax funds, private contributions, federal student aid, tuition and fees, and grants and contracts. In 2003, appropriations of state tax funds for operating expenses of higher education in the 50 states totalled $60.3 billion, a decline of 2.1% from the previous year and indicative of a trend to decrease public reliance on state and federal tax dollars (Arnone, 2004). Throughout the latter half of the twentieth century, as the federal contribution to higher education grew, the 50 states engaged in massive capital construction programmes, employing an economic rationale for burgeoning multicampus systems, portraying their institutions as major corporate enterprises of central importance to the development of each state's geographic regions. The corporatization of American universities can be seen in the escalating budgets for administrative and managerial positions and the multiplicity of job functions, ranging from development, communications, human resources, and legal counsel to accounting and finance, real estate, information systems, physical plant, and security. Business-industry consortia, comprehensive health centres, global networks, and intercollegiate athletics also contribute to the revenue-producing operations of the research university. Although these occupations expand opportunities for non-academic employment of women and minorities, their justification often places them in competition with the heart of the enterprise – faculty, students, academic programmes, and scholarship.

As a small proportion of higher education institutions, research universities comprise 260 (6.4%) of the 4,074 institutions: 64% public and 36% private (*Chronicle of higher education almanac 2004–5*, 2004, p. 16). Though small in number relative to four-year or two-year colleges, they are the primary beneficiaries of public and private largesse. In 2002, revenues from alumni, corporations, foundations, and religious organizations totaled $24 billion; research universities generated an impressive two-thirds (62%) of this total, with the average of $73 million per institution (*Chronicle of higher education almanac 2004–5*, 2004, p. 30). Further evidence of their dominance is indicated by the fact that, in 2000, 18 federal agencies obligated $20 billion for academic science and engineering activities with more than a third (36%) awarded to 20 research universities (Bennot, 2002). The increasing dependence of the research university on governmental and private resources has played a significant role in their support of programmes to end sex, race, and other forms of discrimination on their campuses. And as the historical record shows, anti-discriminatory policies in higher education as in other organizations, gained credence through the determined efforts of civil rights and women's rights groups demanding greater representation, inclusion, and a voice in the political process.

Enacting a Women's Rights Agenda

In 1961, President John Kennedy issued Executive Order 10925, mandating that federal contractors take *affirmative action* in treating minorities without regard to race, creed, colour, or national origin and granting investigatory powers to an Equal Employment Opportunity Commission in the Department of Labor ('sex' was not part of this order). However, another executive order (10980) issued that year established the nation's first Presidential Commission on the Status of Women (PCSW). Kennedy was persuaded that by establishing this commission, he would co-opt feminists in the National Women's Party who sought his support for an Equal Rights Amendment (ERA). Opposition to a constitutional ERA came from an unlikely quarter, the Women's Bureau in the Department of Labor, which argued that an ERA would subvert protective labour laws that had historically differentiated between men's and women's employment.[2] Under the leadership of Eleanor Roosevelt as commission chair, the PCSW began a dialogue on women's issues that involved Congress, business, labour, and civic leaders. Rather than support the ERA, it recommended that the equal protection clause of the constitutional Fourteenth Amendment, which already applied to race by the courts, be extended to protect both sexes. As Kessler-Harris observes, its position reflected 'the tensions inherent in its continued adherence to traditional assumptions about women and family life and its unwillingness to see sex and race as equally the targets of invidious discrimination' (2001, p. 232). Ultimately, it successfully pressured Congress to pass an Equal Pay Act (EPA) in 1963.

In 1964, nationwide civil rights protests in support of racial integration led President Lyndon Johnson, Kennedy's successor, to enact the Civil Rights Act. Title VI of this act reaffirmed equal employment opportunity guarantees and the role of the EEOC (Equal Employment Opportunity Commission) in barring ethnic and racial discrimination in programmes receiving federal assistance; Title VII of the Civil Rights Act became the first federal law to include 'sex' in its prohibition of employment discrimination. By linking sex and race in this legislation, which made support of racial segregation a criminal act, feminists recognized an opportunity to engage in similar strategies as a means of ending sex segregation as well. Johnson also issued two Executive Orders: EO11246 (1965) mandated a continuing programme of equal employment opportunity regardless of race; and under pressure from women's groups, in 1967, he issued EO11375 adding 'sex' to this mandate. Title VII of the Civil Rights Act and EO11246, as amended by EO11375, that provided the initial legal basis for affirmative action for women in employment in the U.S. affirmative action programmes seeks to remedy past discrimination against women, minorities, and others by increasing the recruitment, promotion, retention, and workplace opportunities in employment and by removing barriers to admission to educational institutions (Feminist Majority Foundation, n.d.). Most affirmative action programmes have been directed towards improving employment and education opportunities for women and minorities by expanding the pool of job or admission applicants through vigorous recruitment strategies and through professional development programmes that increase the occupational mobility of employees. Affirmative action programmes have been instituted voluntarily or as the result of state and federal laws, EEOC enforcement, or court decrees.

State commissions on the status of women, the National Organization for Women, and the Federation of Business and Professional Women joined forces in demanding that the EEOC issue strict guidelines to end protective labour laws, removing discriminatory provisions from the statutes, and investigating charges of sex bias. In 1969, the EEOC acquiesced, stating that laws prohibiting or limiting women's employment conflicted with provisions of Title VII, that women were entitled to equal benefits, and that employers could no longer use such reasons as 'inadequate physical facilities' for failing to hire or promote women (Kessler-Harris, 2001, p. 267).

Grassroots organizing energized a new generation of women academics when they realized that the Civil Rights Act of 1964 did not apply to institutions of higher education. It was ultimately the leadership provided by women in the U.S. Congress that resulted in passage of an omnibus Higher Education Act in November 1971. This act extended Title VII to higher education employees under the Equal Employment Opportunity Act, giving the EEOC investigative authority and oversight of institutional affirmative action plans, including workforce analyses of universities' good faith efforts to employ women and minorities. It also extended the Equal Pay Act to executive, professional, and administrative employees. Perhaps the most far-reaching of these laws was Title IX of the Education Amendments, signed into law in 1972 but not implemented until 1975. It stated, 'No person in the United States shall, on the basis of sex, be excluded from participation in, be denied the benefits of, or be subjected to discrimination under any education program or activity receiving Federal financial assistance'. A symbolic message was sent by the U.S. Congress in which it granted compliance responsibility to the Office of Civil Rights, the same bureau that monitored compliance with civil rights regulations. Also in 1972, the Congress approved the Equal Rights Amendment for ratification by two-thirds of the states. It failed to win ratification by three states and lapsed in 1982.[3]

Other actions also tipped the balance of power towards the federal government in the 1970s, notably the adoption of need-based financial aid for undergraduate college students and the advent of a cabinet-level Department of Education (a campaign promise to the nation's teachers by President Jimmy Carter). Starting modestly enough, student financial assistance now accounts for $14.4 billion, including direct student aid, student loans, and work-study programmes that serve to offset tuition and fees and subsidize operating budgets.[4] The Federal Pregnancy Discrimination Act of 1978, which is now part of Title VII and is enforced by the EEOC, requires employers to provide the same institutional benefits for pregnancy and childbirth as for any other physical disability. Physicians routinely certify six to eight weeks for which women are entitled to be paid. Some states go beyond federal law and require pregnancy disability leaves, regardless of the availability of other disability leave policies. The Family and Medical Leave Act of 1993 requires employers with 50 or more employees to provide up to 12 weeks of unpaid leave a year to women and men for care of newborn or newly adopted infants or for care of children, spouses, or parents with serious health conditions.[5]

Enacting a Diversity Agenda

U.S. Supreme Court rulings on affirmative action have been instrumental in restructuring its boundaries. In 1978, the Supreme Court ruled in *Bakke v. University of California-Davis* that race may be taken into consideration as one of several factors used to admit minority students to medical schools. That landmark decision, narrowly approved 5–4 by the Court, developed into the template for tailoring undergraduate and graduate minority admission policies, acknowledging the practicality of a diversity rationale in states without a history of racial segregation and in response to the demands of historically under-represented groups. The defeat of Jimmy Carter by Ronald Reagan in 1980 ushered in a conservative era, however. Among the casualties were women's rights and civil rights. Divisive attacks on Title IX, affirmative action, social welfare and health care measures adopted in the 1960s and 1970s worked to fracture a diverse American society. For women, Reagan's legacy and that of his successor, George H. W. Bush, were highlighted not only by their supply-side economic policies and the termination of social welfare programmes but also by the appointments to the Supreme Court of two conservative justices, Antonin Scalia and Clarence Thomas, tipping the judicial balance of power away from women's rights, gay rights, and civil rights.

Throughout the 1990s, privately funded think tanks led by the Heritage Foundation and the Center for Individual Rights (CIR) intensified attacks on affirmative action policies initiated in the 1960s and 1970s. Although affirmative action and anti-bias laws and regulations extended to all public agencies, state research universities became the combat zone for a conservative, well-financed campaign to invalidate policies that weighed race in its admission and hiring decisions. Support for this campaign came from neo-conservatives who likened affirmative action to quota systems that had denied access to members of ethnic or religious groups or to reverse discrimination that singled out white males. The diversity rationale that had formed the basis for the *Bakke* decision acquired greater immediacy as universities sought to justify scholarship, admissions, employment, and contracting policies. Legal actions raised the stakes for compliance, and in the process the importance of affirmative action for women got lost in the discourse. In fact, the redirection of university policy from equality to diversity was an incremental process, fragmenting advocates of affirmative action hiring into a multiplicity of competing interest groups.

The state-by-state strategy to overturn affirmative action began in California in 1995, when the University of California's Board of Regents (of which the governor was a member) approved by 10–8 a decision to end affirmative action in admissions. This resolution was subsequently extended to all state agencies as a Civil Rights Initiative and was approved by California's voters in 1996 (Proposition 209). Two years later, the State of Washington followed suit when its voters approved Proposition 200. The Center for Individual Rights also challenged the constitutionality of affirmative action admissions policies at flagship universities in Texas, Georgia, and Michigan, charging that 'racial preferences' violated the equal protection clause of the Fourteenth amendment to the Constitution that states, 'No state shall make or enforce any law which shall ... deny to any person within its jurisdiction the equal protection of the laws'.

On April 1, 2003, efforts to elevate affirmative action from a state to a federal issue culminated in arguments before the U.S. Supreme Court on the constitutional legality of the University of Michigan's admissions policies for its law school and its undergraduate college of arts and science. Once again, the Supreme Court rendered a split decision. In the key judgement, *Grutter v. Bollinger*, the Court upheld 5–4 the Law School's affirmative action programme, stating that there is a 'compelling interest in a diverse student body ... at the heart of the Law School's proper institutional mission' and that 'the law school's educational judgment that such diversity is essential to its educational mission is one to which we defer' (O'Connor, 2003, p. A24). In its companion case, *Gratz v. Bollinger*, the Court rejected Michigan's undergraduate admission policy for assigning a point system to all minority applications, and, in the view of the majority, 'violating the Equal Protection Clause of the 14th Amendment' (Rehnquist, 2003b, p. A24). Universities, professional associations, and corporate leaders had filed amicus curiae (Friends of the Court) briefs in support of affirmative action, and these ultimately influenced the Court's decision.[6] The one-vote margin permits the continuation of affirmative action, but it underscores the need for vigilance by its proponents. Affirmative action remains the law of the land in university admissions, 'providing a safe harbor for a policy that Justice Sandra Day O'Connor's majority opinion described not as something to be grudgingly tolerated but as close to a moral imperative' (Greenhouse, 2003, p. A1). Feminists are rather wary, however, that the conservative tilt of the Supreme Court, which splits its vote 5–4 in many key decisions, sets an ominous tone for future debates on both race and gender equality.

Although George W. Bush stated his acceptance of the Court's judgement in the Michigan decision, his judicial appointments have been uniformly conservative, and he has equated affirmative action with quota systems. The American Association of University Professors' Associate Counsel Ann Springer observes that, unlike southern and border states, Michigan has no history of segregation and therefore had to use the diversity rationale in its defence rather than as a remedy for discrimination (2003, p. 5). She has also pointed out that the use of this rationale will affect faculty employment policies. If this is the case, women can anticipate a reordering of priorities to align faculty hiring with diversity goals and timetables. Regardless of actions taken within the university, opponents of affirmative action have promised more legal challenges 'as colleges and universities work towards implementing the details of the Court's decision and as affirmative action opponents broaden the focus of their legal and political attacks' (Springer, 2004, p. 1).

Affirmative action is not the only domestic policy in jeopardy. Since 2001, President Bush has also overseen billions of dollars in tax cuts for corporations, farmers, and wealthy individuals, the appointment of conservative federal judges, the redirection of public policy to support religious-based educational programmes (in violation of the constitutional separation of church and state), denial of support for women's reproductive rights, stem cell and other research initiatives, and the start of a process to privatize public institutions, including health care, education, and social security. The elimination of federal support for social welfare, health, and educational programmes has compounded the economic problems confronting state legislatures, and the 'trickle-down' effect has been disastrous in many states already facing budget shortfalls. As a consequence, tuition and fees have been increased, remedial programmes curtailed, salaries frozen, and high-cost programmes eliminated. In 2004, seven states continued to freeze or reduce spending. Oregon announced a 12% budget cut for higher education; California reduced its appropriations for its research universities by 6% and for its state system by almost 8% (*Chronicle of higher education almanac 2004–5*, 2004). In Ohio, however, the Governor committed the state to $1.1 billion in loans and grants to support research at state universities as part of an ambitious economic development plan for this depressed state.

The Demographics of Gender in Higher Education

As public and private universities expanded their graduate and professional schools and actively recruited women students, the number of women with PhDs seeking academic positions increased proportionately. Tenure policies, which are viewed as fundamental in protecting academic freedom and job security, are now in jeopardy. In 1940, the American Association of University Professors (AAUP) and the Association of American Colleges and Universities (AAC&U) issued a joint Statement of Principles on Academic Freedom and Tenure.[7] In gender-neutral language (equated at the time with fairness and objectivity), the statement called for a maximum period of probation not to exceed seven years for all faculty, with service beyond that period constituting continuous appointment or tenure (Glazer-Raymo, 2001a). Throughout the ensuing decades, this statement served as the prototype for subsequent policy declarations with a salutary impact on faculty governance and the protection of faculty rights. By the 1960s, academic freedom and tenure had become institutionalized as the optimum faculty employment standard in American higher education. Typically, tenure recommendations are made in accordance with person-nel policies and procedures that may vary among institutions but typically weigh scholarship, publications, teaching evaluations, and community service in recom-mendations to the president and Board of Trustees of the institution. The decline of tenure-track positions in recent years and the concomitant increase in part-time and non-tenure-track contingency hiring at a time when more women are in the aca-demic pipeline is a source for serious concern. Other obstacles also compromise their positions, even at senior levels and in prestigious research universities. Evidence of the problematics of gaining resources, access to senior leadership, and professional recog-nition, including grants, named chairs, and higher salaries, can be seen in recent reports compiled by women's commissions at research universities, including Ohio State University, Stanford University, Princeton University, and MIT.

One argument to discount the persistence of gender inequities arises when statis-tics on student enrolments by gender are used to demonstrate women's majority sta-tus. Of the 15.9 million students now enrolled in higher education, over 8 million or 56% are women; they also earn 56% of all academic degrees. The number of women students has exceeded the number of men since 1984, and women are in the majority at all levels – undergraduate, graduate, full-time and part-time. Between 1990 and 2000, the percentage of male full-time graduate students increased by 17% compared to a 57% increase for full-time women students; the proportion of male part-time graduate students decreased by 3% compared to a 11% increase for women. These dis-parities have led critics of affirmative action and Title IX to assert that gender pro-grammes should address the stasis in male enrolments rather than support mechanisms for expanding women's participation. Women thereby become victims of their own success, having benefited from laws and regulations that are now being called into question.

When states reduced their support for higher education, the impact on salaries and benefits was not good news. In 2003–2004, the average faculty salary increase regardless of rank was 2.1%, 'the lowest annual increase in nominal average salaries in more than three decades' (Ehrenberg, 2004, p. 23). In 2003–2004, at least two pri-vate research universities that are among the highest-paying in the nation – Stanford and New York universities – froze faculty salaries at their 2002–2003 levels. Nevertheless, the AAUP survey for 2003–2004 shows that faculty at private doctoral universities fare better than at public ones where, for example, full professors average only 77.4% of their colleagues at private universities.

Each year, the AAUP conducts a survey of member institutions to measure the economic status of the professoriate. The current survey shows continued disparities between men and women faculty in salaries, tenure rates, and overall representation (Ehrenberg, 2004). In 2003, 38% of all faculty in the AAUP American Association of University Professors survey were female compared to 62% male, an increase of less than 2% in one year. Fourteen percent are people of colour, defined as born or naturalized American citizens who identify racially or ethnically with one or more under-represented groups in the United States, for example, people of African, Latino, Asian, and Native American descent. Women comprise 47% of all tenured faculty compared to 66% of men; 77% of women faculty are on the tenure track compared to 88% of men. Women continue to earn less than do men, a gap that has been relatively unchanged in the past 15 years; in research universities, at the highest rank of full professor, women earned an average of 90% of the salaries of male full professors (p. 23). This gender pay gap extends to women in the general labour force where women earn 77 cents for every dollar earned by men (Rose & Hartmann, 2004).

A secondary analysis of AAUP data of women faculty at 85 research universities found that the percentage of women tenure-track faculty increased from 17% to 25% between 1988 and 1997 (Hornig, 2003, p. 45). When analysed by rank, the percentage of women full professors increased from 8% to 14% but for women assistant professors from 32% to 45% (p. 47). This analysis also showed that in 1997 41% of all women faculty at Yale University were not on the tenure track, 16% had contractual appointments, and only 12% were tenured (p. 48). At Rutgers University, the flagship university of the New Jersey State system, 43% of women faculty were not on the tenure track, a similar percentage had tenure-track appointments (42%), and one-fourth were tenured. At Harvard University, where tenure tends to be granted only to those hired from other universities, not to those who come up through the ranks, 13% of tenured faculty were women, 28% were off the tenure track, and 32% held 'ladder' appointments. Apropos of this finding, 26 senior women professors from 17 departments in the faculty of arts and science at Harvard filed a letter of complaint with its president, Lawrence Summers, over the fact that in 2003–2004 women received only 4 of 36 tenure offers in arts and science, and only 1 of those 4 women accepted (Wilson & Fogg, 2004). The letter states that the elimination of the position of dean of affirmative action position signals that 'steady progress for women and minorities is no longer a major decanal concern' (Wilson & Fogg, p. A14). In response, Harvard noted that it has a $25 million outreach fund to recruit women and members of minority groups, and that, in 2004–2005, 40% of new hires at the junior faculty level are women. Summers ignited another firestorm in January 2005 when he commented at a conference of the Bureau of Economic Research that women's under-representation in the top echelons of science and mathematics may be due to innate differences from their male counterparts. The ensuing controversy led to the formation of two panels at Harvard: a Task Force on Women Faculty to increase the appointments of women to leadership positions and a Task Force on Women in Science and Engineering to seek ways to remove barriers to women's success in the sciences (Fogg, 2005).

A comparative analysis of 1993 and 1999 data reported by the National Survey of Postsecondary Faculty (NSOPF) provides further evidence of the slow rate of progress for women faculty in American research universities. As shown in figure 11.1 women continue to make impressive gains in the conferral of master's (+10%) and doctoral (+8%) degrees. However, these gains appear to be in inverse proportion to their recruitment as faculty in research universities with their greatest representation as instructors/lecturers (generally non-tenure-track positions) or as assistant professors. The most impressive increases are occurring at the rank of associate professor (+8.4%) with smaller increases at the senior rank of full professor (+5%).

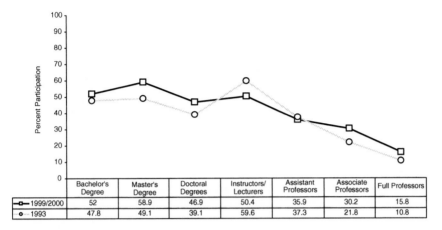

	Bachelor's Degree	Master's Degree	Doctoral Degrees	Instructors/ Lecturers	Assistant Professors	Associate Professors	Full Professors
1999/2000	52	58.9	46.9	50.4	35.9	30.2	15.8
1993	47.8	49.1	39.1	59.6	37.3	21.8	10.8

Figure 11.1   Representation of Women among Students and Faculty in U.S. Research Universities

Source: Snyder, T., & Hoffman, C. (2000). *Digest of education statistics, 1999*. Washington, DC: Government Printing Office.

That women full professors in the NSOPF-99 survey account for only 15.8% of all women faculty in research universities despite their conspicuous presence in the faculty pipeline and at lower ranks focuses attention on structural barriers to institutional change within the professoriate.

The growth of a part-time, non-tenure-track workforce in which women maintain a disproportionate share of contingency teaching positions is symptomatic of a decline in national commitment to tenurable positions (Glazer-Raymo, 2003). The policy of hiring part-time faculty began in the 1970s as a temporary measure – a university response to Title VII and EEOC compliance criteria. The rationale was twofold: universities viewed part-time and non-tenurable positions as a strategy for demonstrating good-faith efforts to recruit women faculty and administrators; they were also wary of expanding their commitment to women whose demands included spousal hiring, campus childcare, and access to health and pension benefit plans. In this construct, the family-values argument weighs in heavily. By the mid-1980s, research universities had adopted corporate approaches, restructuring their faculties to be more closely aligned with the marketplace through the recruitment of 'stars' for named chairs, alliances with business and industry, mergers and acquisitions of other institutions, and an array of entrepreneurial degrees to capture the adult and continuing education clientele. Part-time hiring became an acceptable device for controlling faculty size, regulating personnel expenditures, terminating high-cost/ low-enrolment programmes, and responding to unforeseen changes in the economy. Part-time, clinical, and other forms of non-tenure-track appointments are now entrenched policies, resulting in a resurgence of union activism at public and private research universities as academic positions for the growing number of women doctorates diminish year by year. They now account for 43% of all faculty, although the ratio of full-time to part-time faculty is typically greater at research and doctoral institutions than at four-year or two-year colleges (Berger et al., 2002). One-third hold consulting positions apart from their institution and three-fourths hold additional non-consulting jobs.

It is ironic that laws and regulations designed to protect women and minorities now serve to inhibit their prospects for permanent employment in higher education systems that support part-time, non-tenure-track appointments. The rise of for-profit universities that rely almost entirely on part-time faculty, the lack of universal childcare, and the decline in tenure-track positions in all fields further problematizes the situation. Since the mid-1990s, part-time and adjunct faculty at research universities have unionized as a means of gaining greater job security including assurances of continued employment, health benefits, higher salaries, and better working conditions. A similar trend is evolving among the ranks of graduate students who feel disenfranchised in their complex roles of student-teacher-research associate. As Hearn and Anderson (2001) observed in a study of clinical faculty in schools of education, the part-time nature of clinical contracts may serve to further reify hierarchical systems of faculty work – some teach, some do research, and some supervise students – further weakening the tenure system and making units that employ this mechanism more vulnerable to institutional retrenchment (p. 134). This negatively impacts efforts to achieve gender and race equality within the professoriate.

Enacting a University Women's Rights Agenda

One strategy that has gained in popularity, particularly in research universities, is the presidential commission, a political mechanism for defusing contentious policy questions. Since the advent of President Kennedy's Commission on the Status of Women in 1961, and its replication in many states, universities have adopted this model as a political mechanism for defusing contentious policy questions and meeting the demands of campus interest groups. Task forces or ad hoc groups have also been organized by women students, faculty, and administrators to collect data on compensation, campus climate, and related personnel concerns. They have gained credibility within the professoriate as women seek leadership roles and administrative action regarding tenure, compensation, benefits, and a range of campus climate issues. Women legal scholars within research universities have been in the forefront of efforts to end discriminatory personnel practices affecting women and minorities. Catherine MacKinnon, whose compelling work *Sexual Harassment of Working Women* (1978) contributed to the substantiation of sexual harassment as a legal claim under sex discrimination law in the United States, demonstrates the important role played by feminist legal scholars in establishing that 'sexual harassment [is] neither incidental nor tangential to women's inequality, but a crucial expression of it [and] a central dynamic in it' (p. xi). In the two decades since its publication, many cases alleging sexual harassment have been argued in federal court. U.S. Supreme Court decisions in the 1980s and 1990s continue to define the meaning and extent of sexual harassment law in the corporate workplace and in governmental and academic institutions (Glazer-Raymo, 1999, 2001b). In 1982, Bernice Sandler published the first of several reports on 'the chilly climate' for women in higher education.[8] Two decades later, sexual harassment, hostile environment, and campus safety continue to rank among the highest priorities of women's groups. A Glass Ceiling Commission Report issued by the U.S. Department of Labor (1995) heightened awareness among policy makers of the impermeability of barriers to women's advancement; however, it did little to change the structure or priorities of major corporations, the target of its recommendations, and eventually it sank without a trace. By 2004, only 6 of the Fortune 500 companies were headed by women who were also only 13.6% of the 435 members of the U.S. Congress and 6 of the 50 state governors (Rose & Hartmann, 2004).

In the 1990s, women's commissions that had lapsed after the initial flurry of feminist activism were reconstituted or created de novo to produce diversity action plans that considered gender, race, ethnicity, sexual orientation, and disabilities. Meanwhile, feminist epistemologies had become so diffuse that women scholars no longer spoke with a unified voice. Women's studies programmes were being recast as gender, ethnic, cultural, or gay, lesbian, bisexual, and transgender (GLBT) studies. Critiques of commission reports questioned the ability of women's commissions to challenge authority and bring about substantive changes in administrative policies, given the risks of asserting independent or contradictory viewpoints (Glazer-Raymo, 1999) and the unintended consequences of policy discourses that constructed women as outsider supplicants, passive victims, or deficient in professional skills and training (Allan, 2003). The difficulty of overcoming sexism and racism and gaining more than cosmetic changes in existing policies underscored the need for structural and attitudinal changes beyond the ability of task forces, commissions, and committees to accomplish. Nevertheless, by speaking truth to power, these coalitions have served an important purpose in revealing persistent inequities and problems that interfere with women's ability to be full partners in the academic enterprise.

Speaking from her real-life experience as president of Smith College from 1975 to 1985, Jill Conway has noted the, at times, rather puzzling nature of public discourse. In the third volume of her memoir, *A Woman's Education* (2001), she recalls, 'Answering questions from politicians and corporate leaders on standard feminist goals – equal pay, for instance – taught me that most people thought about women's advancement as a zero-sum game. If women gained equal pay, there would be less for men. ... To most people, changing the segregated workforce and giving women opportunities to learn and advance over a lifetime career wasn't a productivity issue, it was just a transaction in a zero-sum game' (2001, p. 120). As the liberal-conservative debate over affirmative action intensified following passage of Proposition 209 in California in 1996, national support dwindled for a women's rights agenda. Women's organizations found themselves on the defensive in making the case for gender equality as a viable goal.

In 1999, at the Massachusetts Institute of Technology, where Conway is a resident scholar, tenured women scientists documented gender bias in the School of Science for women seeking tenure, laboratory assignments, grants, and other perquisites of being a tenured research scientist (Committee on Women in the School of Science, 1999). Another series of reports, commissioned by the provost and undertaken by the Massachusetts Institute of Technology (MIT) Committees on the Status of Women Faculty, revealed comparable inequities in the schools of humanities, management, architecture, and engineering (Council on Faculty Diversity, 2002). Prior to issuance of the second report, MIT's President Charles Vest convened a meeting of presidents, chancellors, and 25 women professors from 9 research universities, including the California Institute of Technology, Harvard University, Stanford University, the University of Pennsylvania, and the University of California at Los Angeles. The nine university presidents issued a statement following this meeting in which they acknowledged that 'barriers still exist to the full participation of women in science and engineering' and agreed to pursue a goal of full equity for women faculty, to be more attentive to compensation, resource distribution, and family responsibilities, and to collect and monitor data on an annual basis (MIT News Office, 2001). The influence of the MIT report extended to the U.S. Congress, which commissioned a review by the General Accountability Office (GAO) of Title IX compliance by the departments of Education and Energy, the National Aeronautics and Space Administration, and the National Science Foundation. It found that only the Department of Education was monitoring its grantees by conducting agency-initiated assessments of grantees to determine the extent of Title IX compliance. Among the promising practices it cited were programmes to encourage women to pursue graduate study in science and engineering, to expand the recruiting pool for jobs in these fields, making them more attractive to women, and to provide workload reduction as a means of improving the balance of work-family roles (GAO, 2004). Most notable has been the appointment in 2004, by MIT's Board of Trustees, of its first woman president and first non-engineer – Susan Hochfield, a neuroscientist and provost at Yale University.

Research universities have made other potentially significant changes in leadership in this decade, including a former Yale provost as the first woman Vice-Chancellor of the University of Cambridge (United Kingdom) and women presidents at Princeton, Brown, Syracuse University, the University of Michigan, Ohio State University, the University of Pennsylvania, and Indiana University. In at least two of these institutions, Princeton and Ohio State universities, women CEOs have also appointed women provosts as their deputies, and Brown has the distinction of appointing Ruth Simmons as the first African-American woman to be president of a research university. Nevertheless, women still comprise only 21% of all presidents of colleges and universities, 13% at research/doctoral institutions. Since it is the governing boards that appoint the presidents and interact with them in the policy arena, their composition is also critical. Women hold the minority of these voluntary, unpaid positions in both public and private universities and colleges: 26% on private boards and 30% on public boards. The smallest percentage of women serve on the boards of research universities (15%) and the largest percentage on boards of baccalaureate liberal arts (33%) and two-year colleges (34%) (Scollay, Bratt, & Tickamyer, 1996). Women trustees are still more likely to serve by appointment of a church body or order whereas men are more likely to be selected by an institutional president or governor (Scollay, Bratt, & Tickamyer, 1996).

At Stanford University, ten years after release of a critical report on the status of women faculty at that institution, and as a result of participating in the MIT conference in 2001, Stanford's provost appointed an Advisory Committee on the Status of Women Faculty. Its report, issued in 2004, compared the experiences of men and women faculty at Stanford with collateral data on recruitment and retention of women faculty, compensation, resources, and recognition (including non-salary forms of compensation and support for research), and on the quality of life at Stanford (professional satisfaction, workload, campus climate, discrimination, harassment, and work/family concerns) (p. 6). Among their findings were heightened concerns among women faculty regarding greater workload pressure related to advising and mentoring, particularly among women of colour, and greater levels of work/family stress related to the availability and affordability of quality childcare. They underscored the low representation of women of colour in certain fields and divisions of the university. Among women full professors, they found cumulative disadvantages based on gender, exclusion, and undervaluation of their contributions, difficulties of reconciling their personal and professional lives, compounded by financial pressures and inadequate quality childcare. The committee recommended that Stanford's schools adopt 'best practice' policies and strategies: (1) outreach efforts and targeted funds for recruiting women in under-represented fields and divisions; (2) adequate hiring and retention packages that consider childcare, spousal employment, family leave, and tenure policies; (3) retention policies that provide individual support, recognition, and gender equity among faculty; (4) periodic evaluation of compensation packages to ensure appropriateness and equity; (5) inquiries and initiatives to address sexual harassment and discrimination claims that do not result in formal complaints; and (6) appointment of a faculty panel and senior level administrator to focus on gender equity concerns, collecting data on a regular basis, collaborating with other institutions to gain more understanding of gender equity challenges and responses and to assess the effectiveness of particular strategies, for example, reduced workloads, extended family leaves, formal mentoring, and diversity and harassment training (pp. 9–10).

The Faculty of Arts and Science at Rutgers University also assessed the status of its women faculty, focusing its attention on faculty compensation, hiring, promotions, research support, and the campus climate for women (FAS Gender Equity Committee, 2002). It found that women are more visible and better represented than in previous generations, although they are still under-represented in the sciences when compared to doctorate production and continue to experience salary disparities. As in other research universities, the higher the rank, the fewer the women: in 2001, they were only 9% of 170 senior professors and 8% of 48 special professors. Women humanists were more likely to be in leadership positions than were women in the social and behavioural sciences; in the sciences, only one woman had chaired a department since the early 1980s. Subtle biases in how departmental chairs, faculties, and deans managed the promotion process were viewed as deterrents to women. Discretionary funds also advantaged men, who were more likely to earn summer money, have larger research accounts, and better startup packages. In their interviews with women faculty, the research team reported that women perceived themselves as 'victims of discrimination, albeit less blatant forms than they remember from earlier years'. The report's recommendations, like those of the MIT and Stanford surveys, stressed the importance of decanal leadership in affirming the Faculty of Arts and Science commitment to gender equity by working with department chairs, monitoring promotion procedures, and ensuring that women have access to influential positions. They identified a series of strategies to increase hiring of women faculty, provide oversight of departmental policies, improve mentoring, and collaborate with Rutgers' central administration on whose goodwill women continue to rely for corrective action (pp. 4–6).

What else can women do to end discrimination given the political and economic context in which they work and the difficulties of changing organizational cultures? How can they make the diversity rationale work to their advantage? It is obvious that coalition building is necessary and that women have to turn their attention outward to their external environment and communicate across disciplinary and institutional boundaries. The AAUP cites the Equal Protection Clause of the Fourteenth Amendment to the Constitution, Titles VI and VII of the Civil Rights Act of 1964, and case law interpreting them as the 'primary legal benchmarks in employment discrimination law' (Springer, 2003, p. 2). Its policy manual provides excellent guidelines for informing institutions that 'the Constitution and federal statutes require employers to eliminate discrimination on the basis of race or sex', that employers can be sued under these laws for individual discrimination, referred to as 'disparate treatment', or policies and practices that create disparities of women and minorities in the workplace, referred to as 'disparate impact', and that 'some federal laws require employers to provide diversification (affirmative action) plans as tangible proof of their efforts' (p. 2).

Gender Equity in the United States: Are We There Yet?

The ungendering of public policy necessitates that women reaffirm a women's rights agenda. For one decade, the nation has moved from a state-by-state to a federal strategy in threatened reversals of anti-bias and affirmative action statutes and regulations. Now there is some indication that this strategy may change in response to the Supreme Court's decision in the Michigan case. These laws are of greatest significance to higher education with admission policies at the heart of the national debate. Allegations of racial preferences, quotas, and affirmative discrimination have undermined carefully crafted admission procedures and their support from governing boards, legislatures, and funding agencies. Opponents of affirmative action have resumed state-by-state legal challenges to overturn this policy, buoyed by the fact that propositions making affirmative action illegal in California and Washington State apparently remain unaffected by the Supreme Court decision (Schmidt, 2003). In the state of Washington, following passage of Proposition 200 in 1998, banning race-conscious affirmative action in the public sector, the University of Washington announced that it would suspend consideration of race and gender in admissions. Making gender and race the basis for such either-or arguments invariably leads to questions about qualifications, commitment, and motivation, reinforcing gender and race/ethnicity stereotypes, and ultimately lulling the public into renewed acceptance of the status quo. The family values argument that dominates much of the political rhetoric also contributes to the widening gap between the public and private, the personal and the professional, emphasizing the bimodal character of women's lives and their marginalization in male-dominated fields. Now that the discourse of sex and race equity has been replaced with the diversity rationale, it is more imperative than ever that women construct a policy discourse that sustains both gender and race equity. In rejecting the view that women can gain equality through their assimilation into alienating institutional structures, a new academic generation of women may find it necessary to adopt a more activist view of themselves as agents of social change.

Campus commissions have contributed to the dialogue through their efforts to increase women's representation, voice, and role in academic governance. The campus culture has been altered through the implementation of federal mandates, diversity guidelines, sexual harassment and equal employment policies and programmes. Efforts to restructure hiring, tenure, and promotion policies have faltered as universities have increased part-time and non-tenure-track hiring. Efforts to reform the benefit structure by resolving family/work concerns, supporting subsidized childcare, and closing the gender pay gap have also had mixed results on a state-by-state basis. The Supreme Court decisions set a new standard for universities in defining what is permissible in the name of affirmative action, and in deferring to the universities that, according to the majority opinion in the *Grutter v. Bollinger* decision, 'occupy a special niche in our constitutional tradition' (O'Connor, 2003), setting new conditions.

In writing that opinion, Justice O'Connor acknowledged the significance of the briefs that were filed by corporations, universities, professional associations, and the military when she asserted that 'context matters when reviewing race-based governmental action under the Equal Protection clause'. But she put a time limit of 25 years to achieve race equity in American society.

To what extent this decision will have an impact on gender equity remains to be determined. I would argue that if women are to thwart reversals in policy initiatives, greater transparency is needed to increase the ease of availability of data analyses by interested women's organizations and policy makers. In an extensive review of the Supreme Court and women's rights, the National Women's Law Center (2003) cautions that 'just one new Justice who does not support women's rights to equal protection of the law could mean a dramatic erosion of the right to choose, but also of women's rights to equal protection of the law and to be free from discrimination in education, employment, health, and other arenas' (p. 1).[9] The reintroduction of the Equal Rights Amendment in 2002 by 183 members of the House and 20 members of the Senate should not be dismissed as symbolism. It is as relevant today as it was 20 years ago in validating every woman's right to constitutional protection against all forms of discrimination. Taking Title IX as one example, an Equal Rights Amendment would provide the constitutional basis for all such statutes that are meant to provide gender equity.

The twenty-first-century research university operates in the context of a politically and economically volatile climate, both nationally and in each of the 50 states. The Supreme Court, in its decision on May 29, 2003, that state employees can sue for damages under the Family and Medical Leave Act, showed that 'it is sympathetic to gender-based claims [and that] states are not immune to suits ...' ('Upholding Family Leave', 2003, p. A22). In her analysis of the decision, Greenhouse (2003) observed that the conservative majority on the Court continues 'on a campaign to extend states' rights by limiting Congress's power to legislate' (p. A1). The experience of senior women scientists at MIT indicates that issue definition at the highest levels frequently begins when prestigious research universities are confronted by evidence of inequities from ad hoc groups that demand immediate and positive action on the part of those in positions of authority. The challenge for feminists in other institutions is to let grassroots activism inform feminist theory rather than the other way around, participating more actively in problem solving at a time when the backlash against feminism goes beyond affirmative action in law school admissions and the size of science laboratories at elite institutions to more general attacks on universal childcare, public education, family planning, and environmental protection. Women need to analyse more closely the implications of eliminating women's educational equity from the federal agenda, the appointment of conservative judges to the federal judiciary, and continued threats to affirmative action and anti-discrimination laws and regulations. To do this systematically will mean revisiting the laws and judicial decisions that are now embedded in institutional policies and practices. It will also necessitate monitoring how the decisions that were recently rendered by the Supreme Court play out in the Congress and in the research universities.

Notes

1. The Carnegie Foundation for the Advancement of Teaching devised a higher education classification system in 1970 to facilitate the collection and disaggregation of data by the federal government. A restructured system was adopted by Carnegie in 2000 and has taken effect

in 2005 (Basinger, 2000). The current hierarchical taxonomy consists of seven categories: research I and II, doctoral I and II, master's, baccalaureate, and two-year colleges. The proposed system would consolidate doctoral and research universities into two rather than four categories, an effort to place greater emphasis on teaching and to discourage competition for resources, rankings, and recognition (Basinger, 2000). Institutions would be categorized as doctoral/research universities-extensive and intensive, master's (comprehensive) colleges and universities I and II, baccalaureate colleges (liberal arts and general), associate's colleges, specialized institutions (professional schools), and tribal colleges and universities. At least 148 institutions (3.8%) would be in the doctoral/research universities-extensive category, based on conferral of a minimum of 50 doctorates a year in at least 15 fields, and another 2.9% as doctoral/research universities-intensive based on conferral of at least 10 doctorates annually in 3 or more disciplines (Basinger, 2000).

2. See A. Kessler-Harris (2001, pp. 239–267) for a detailed historical account of how implementation of the Civil Rights Act of 1964 led to the demise of federal and state protective labour laws that had differentiated by sex in women's employment.

3. The ERA states, 'Equality of rights under the law shall not be denied or abridged by the United States or by any state on account of sex'. It was reintroduced in 2001 by a coalition of congressional supporters, and in 2003, Illinois became the thirty-sixth state to ratify the ERA. Arizona, Florida, and Missouri, three states that rejected it in the 1970s, are now targeted by ERA supporters. Opposition comes from conservative legislators who use the family-values argument to mobilize their base. Ironically, the argument that women would be required to take part in military combat, one of the original causes for opposition in the 1970s has been refuted in the Iraq War where women are fully engaged.

4. See the *Digest of educational statistics, 2002–3* (Washington, DC: National Center for Educational Statistics, 2004) for data on federal appropriations for major programs by state. See also Center for Higher Education & Educational Finance (2004), which publishes the *Grapevine: A National Database of Tax Support for Higher Education*.

5. Ten years after passage of the FMLA by Congress, the Supreme Court ruled that states do not have constitutional immunity in protecting employees' federally guaranteed rights to take time off for family emergencies, and that this law applies equally to men and women (Rehnquist, 2003a, p. A18).

6. In the case of *Grutter v. Bollinger*, which involved a constitutional issue and was argued before the U.S. Supreme Court, the petitioners of the amicus curiae brief, or Friends of the Court, were associations or businesses with expertise and a substantial interest in the outcome of this decision but were not aggrieved parties to this case.

7. The American Association of University Professors (AAUP), founded in 1915, serves the academic profession and has as its members faculty, librarians, and academic professionals in two- and four-year accredited public and private colleges and universities. Current membership is about 45,000, with over 500 local campus chapters and 39 state organizations. Its main purpose is the advancement of academic freedom and shared governance and the development of standards and procedures to maintain quality in education and academic freedom in American colleges and universities. Its amicus briefs before the U.S. Supreme Court and federal and state appellate courts address significant issues of academic freedom. See also www.aaup.org for further information, including articles contained in *Academe*, the AAUP journal.

8. See Sandler & Hall (1993) for an update on the original report.

9. The National Women's Law Center, founded in 1972, is a non-profit advocacy organization working to advance the progress of women, girls, and families with emphasis on employment, education, reproductive rights and health, and family issues. See www.ncrw.org for information on its projects, activities, and a review of its position papers.

References

Allan, E. J. (2003) Constructing women's status: Policy discourses of university women's commission reports. *Harvard educational review, 73*(1):44–72.

American Association of University Professors (2001) *Policy documents and reports* (9th ed.). Washington, DC: Author.

Arnone, M. (2004) State spending on colleges drops for first time in eleven years. *The chronicle of higher education, 50*(19):A24.

Basinger, J. (2000) A new way of classifying colleges elates some and perturbs others. *Chronicle of higher education, 46*:A31.

Bennot, R.J. (2002) Federal academic science and engineering obligations increased 10% in FY 2000. *Info brief NSF* 02–310. Washington, DC: National Science Foundation. Retrieved October 20, 2005, from the National Science Foundation Website, http://www.nsf.gov/statistics/nsf02310/.

Berger, A., Kirshstein, R., Zhang, Y., & Carter, K. (2002) *A profile of part-time faculty: Fall 1998*. Washington, DC: U.S. Department of Education, Office of Educational Research and Improvement.

Center for Higher Education & Educational Finance (2004) Fifty state summary table (based on FY04 data). In *Grapevine: A national database of tax support for higher education*. Normal, IL: Illinois State University. Retrieved September 22, 2004, from the Illinois State College of Education Website, http://coe.ilstu.edu/grapevine/50state.htm.

Chronicle of higher education almanac 2004–5 (2004) The 50 states & the District of Columbia. Retrieved from the *Chronicle of Higher Education* Website, http://chronicle.com/free/almanac/2004/.

Committee on Women in the School of Science (1999) A study on the status of women faculty in science at MIT. *The MIT faculty newsletter, 9*(4). Retrieved from The Massachusetts Institute of Technology Website, http://web.mit.edu/fnl/women/ women.html.

Conway, J. K. (2001) *A woman's education: The road from Coorain leads to Smith College*. New York: Alfred Knopf.

Council on Faculty Diversity (2002) *The status of women at MIT: Reports from the Schools of architecture and planning; engineering; humanities, arts, and social sciences; and the Sloan School of Management*. Retrieved July 3, 2003, from The Massachusetts Institute of Technology Website, http://web.mit.edu/faculty/reports/overview.html.

Ehrenberg, R. G. (2004) Don't blame the faculty for high tuition: The annual report on the economic status of the profession, 2003–04. *Academe, 90*(2):21–33.

FAS Gender Equity Committee (2002) *A study of gender equity in the faculty of arts and sciences in New Brunswick-Rutgers University*. Retrieved April 4, 2004, from the New Brunswick-Rutgers University Website, http://fas.rutgers.edu/info/gender.shtml.

Feminist Majority Foundation (n.d.) *Affirmative action information center: Origins of affirmative action for women*. Retrieved December 6, 2004, from the Feminist Majority Website, http://www.feminist.org/other/ccri/aafact1.html.

Fogg, P. (2005) Harvard's president wonders aloud about women in science and mathematics. *Chronicle of higher education, 5*(21) (January 28):A12.

GAO (General Accountability Office) (2004) *Gender issues: Women's participation in the sciences has increased, but agencies need to do more to ensure compliance with Title IX*. Washington, DC: General Accountability Office.

Glass Ceiling Commission (1995) *Good for business: Making full use of the nation's capital*. Washington, DC: U.S. Department of Labor.

Glazer-Raymo, J. (1999) *Shattering the myths: Women in academe*. Baltimore: Johns Hopkins University Press.

——— (2001a) The fragmented paradigm: Women, tenure, and schools of education. In W. G. Tierney (Ed.), *Faculty work in schools of education: Rethinking roles and rewards for the twenty-first century* (pp. 169–188). Albany: State University of New York Press.

——— (2001b) Sexual harassment in the academy: A review essay. *Review of higher education, 23*(4):491–500.

——— (2003) Women and part-time employment: The impact of public policy. In B. Ropers-Huilman (Ed.), *Gendered futures in higher education: Critical perspectives for change* (pp. 97–110). Albany: State University of New York Press.

Greenhouse, L. (2003) In a momentous term, justices remake the law, and the court. *The New York Times*, July 1, pp. A1, A18.

Hearn, J. C., & Anderson, M. S. (2001) Clinical faculty in schools of education: Using staff differentiation to address disparate goals. In W. G. Tierney (Ed.), *Faculty work in schools of education: Rethinking roles and rewards for the twenty-first century* (pp. 125–150). Albany: State University of New York Press.

Hornig, L. S. (Ed.) (2003) *Equal rites, unequal outcomes.* New York: Kluwer/Plenum.

Kessler-Harris, A. (2001) *In pursuit of equity: Women, men, and the quest for economic citizenship in 20th century America.* New York: Oxford University Press.

MacKinnon, Catherine, *Sexual harassment of working women: A case of sex discrimination.* New Haven: Yale University Press.

MIT News Office (2001) Leaders of 9 universities and 25 women faculty meet at MIT, agree to equity reviews. *MIT News,* January 30. Retrieved July 3, 2003, from the MIT News Office Website, http://web.mit.edu/newsoffice/2001/gender.html.

National Women's Law Center (2003) *The Supreme Court and women's rights: Fundamental protections hanging in the balance.* Washington, DC: National Women's Law Center.

O'Connor, S. D. (2003) Excerpts from justices' opinions on Michigan affirmative action cases: From the decision by Justice O'Connor. *The New York Times,* June 24, p. A24.

Provost's Advisory Committee on the Status of Women Faculty (2004) *Report on the status of women faculty at Stanford University.* Retrieved July 3, 2003, from Stanford University Website, http://www.stanford.edu/dept/provost/womenfacultyreport/.

Rehnquist, W. (2003a) Excerpts from court's ruling on personal leave. *The New York Times,* May 28, p. A18.

———— (2003b) Excerpts from justices' opinions on Michigan affirmative action cases: From the decision by Chief Justice Rehnquist. *The New York Times,* June 24, p. A24.

Rose, S., & Hartmann, H. (2004) The unequal society: The long-term gender gap. *Challenge,* 47(5):30–50.

Sandler, B. R., & Hall, R. (1993) The campus climate revisited: Chilly climate for women faculty, administrators, and students. In J.Glazer-Raymo, E. M. Bensimon, & B. K. Townsend (Eds.), *Women in higher education: A feminist perspective* (pp. 175–204). Needham Hts, MA: Ginn Press.

Schmidt, P. (2003) Foes of affirmative action in Michigan plan to take their battle to the ballot. *Chronicle of higher education, 49*:A1.

Scollay, S. J., Bratt, C. S., & Tickamyer, A. R. (1996) *Gender and college and university governing boards: Final report of a grant from the Gale Fund.* Lexington: University of Kentucky.

Springer, A. (2003) *How to diversify faculty: The current legal landscape.* Retrieved May 4, 2003, from the American Association of University Professors Website, http://www.aaup.org/Legal/info%20outlines/legaa.htm.

———— (2004) *Update on affirmative action in higher education: A current legal overview.* Retrieved October 20, 2004, from the American Association of University Professors Website, http://www.aaup.org/Issues/AffirmativeAction/aalegal.htm.

'Upholding family leave' (2003) *The New York Times,* May 8, p. A22.

Wilson, R., & Fogg, P. (2004) Female professors say Harvard is not granting tenure to enough women. *The chronicle of higher education, 51*(6):A14.

Chapter Twelve
Academic Excellence and Gender Equality at Ohio State University

Mary Ann Danowitz Sagaria and Pamela S. Van Horn

In an effort to reassert their legitimacy, public research universities in the United States are experiencing a shift from entities of social good to industries or quasi-corporations. This case study of the Ohio State University (Ohio State or OSU) illustrates some of the consequences associated with academic restructuring, a form of organizational change that creates departments for the purpose of exploiting core competencies in order to enhance the university's competitiveness. It also focusses on policy discourses and efforts to incorporate equality to improve the status of women. Placing academic restructuring alongside the equality initiatives provides insight into multiple dimensions of organizational change and why increases in the representation of women faculty over the past decade have been only modest.

From Social Good to Quasi-Corporate: Consequences for Gender Equality and Diversity

U.S. public colleges and universities are transforming into an economic sector requiring an industrial or quasi-corporate model of production that demonstrates responsiveness to market forces and demands for relevance. Thus, they are expected to increase their prominence as competitors in a knowledge industry through research, grants and contracts, publications, and other scientific accomplishments (Gumport, 2000). Dill and Sporn (1995) assert that universities wanting to function successfully in an international market must develop the capacity to employ university personnel, resources, and programmes in a more flexible, efficient, and adaptive manner.

As universities intensify efforts to compete in the knowledge marketplace, they also continue to strive to maintain their standings as social institutions by preserving 'essential educational legacies', such as improving equality in society, socializing citizens, increasing students' chances for upward social mobility, and cultivating interests for the general social welfare (Gumport, 2000, p. 71). In the past, the *social good* argument has been the most important legitimizing claim for universities. Their existence has been linked to their record and potential for improving people's capacity to fully engage as citizens and therefore contribute to the sustainability of the United States as a democratic society (Gurin et al., 2002).[1] Thus, efforts to achieve gender equality and greater racial and ethnic diversity within universities have been linked to the good of the larger society. Despite the scientific and sometimes legal argument that equality and diversity are compelling interests or conditions to sustain a democratic society, U.S. universities have few external requirements or incentives in the past decade to infuse a social good orientation, such as incorporating measures to achieve equality, into their principle agendas. In contrast, economic justification and neo-liberal forces have become more pervasive and have bolstered a quasi-corporate logic in university decision making. The shift in the legitimizing rationale from higher education as a social good to a higher education as a quasi-corporate entity provides a lens for understanding organizational change at Ohio State University. This case study draws upon institutional policies and research, committee reports, and the first author's accounts as a participant-observer to provide a picture of Ohio State's responses to growing market pressures and their implications for gender equality between women and men in the university community.[2]

The University

Founded in 1870, the Ohio State University is a land-grant institution that has committed itself to serve the state's agricultural community and to generate and apply research to benefit the state and its citizens.[3] Its main campus, the focus of this study, is located in Columbus, the state capital, and six regional campuses are located across Ohio, a Midwestern state. In 2005, 57,748 students attended the university, of whom 50,504 were enrolled in Columbus, making it the second largest campus in the United States. There, women comprised 49.2% of the student body, and students of colour accounted for 15% (OSU, 2005).[4]

Ohio State University is highly effective in garnering external funds. In 2005, the university ranked nineteenth in the country in fund-raising, having generated $203 million the previous year with $72.8 million, or 36%, of those funds coming from corporations ('Counting Gifts', 2005). That same year, OSU directed $123.5 million to research (OSU, Research Foundation, 2005).

Like other U.S. higher education institutions, Ohio State has been adapting to align with the dominant legitimating expectations to generate revenue, establish its preeminence in research and innovation, and shift its overall institutional direction to compete more effectively with other research universities. Moreover, the confluence of an unfavourable national economy, a continuing deterioration of the state's manufacturing-based economy, and the redirection of state resources from higher education to other services, such as heath care and corrections, have resulted in less state funding for all public higher education institutions, including Ohio State, so that by 2005 the state funded only 15% of the university's budget (Holbrook, 2005).

The university is autonomous, governed by a lay board of trustees whose members are appointed by the governor of the state. The board appoints a president, the chief executive responsible for the total administration of the university over which he or she may delegate authority. A presidential planning cabinet of senior administrators make or contribute to many of the university-wide decisions. The university faculty exercises its authority to establish educational and academic policies through the university senate, a governance body elected by faculty peers. Faculty members hold appointments in one or more of 98 tenure-initiating units of departments and schools located in the 17 colleges of the university. During the past 15 years, Ohio State has had three presidents: Gordon Gee served from 1990 to 1997, William Kirwan served from 1998 to 2002, and Karen Holbrook followed as the first woman president of Ohio State. Because of this turnover at the top, different and at times conflicting leadership priorities have affected the direction of excellence and equality at the university.

Representation of Women

A comparison of the percentages of women graduates by level and faculty rank in 1993/1994 and 2004/2005 shows that the representation of women has increased slightly. As figure 12.1 shows, women students have comprised the majority of bachelor's and master's degree earners since 1993. The largest increase in representation was a gain of 6.6% at the doctoral level. Among the faculty, the percentage of women has increased only slightly, with the number of associate professors increasing by 8.8%. The percentage of assistant professors, however, has remained virtually unchanged, and there has been but a very modest increase of 6.3% among full professors. In short, across the university, women students have achieved parity in representation for the first two degrees, and they appear to be moving towards equality in representation at the doctoral level. Nevertheless, across all faculty ranks, men continue to predominate, with women having made modest gains but by no measure coming close to achieving equality.

These changes in the representation of women over the past decade provide a point of departure to examine the gender dynamics at the university. Examining the total number of women by each rank in relationship to the total number of tenure-track faculty positions, however, offers more insight into the relative sphere of women's influence and potential qualitative differences in the experiences of men and women. Figure 12.1 shows that women made up a mere 17.4% of the full professors in 2004. Figure 12.2 places that percentage in the context of total tenure-track faculty numbers: 33%, or 957, of the 2,899 tenure-track faculty members at the

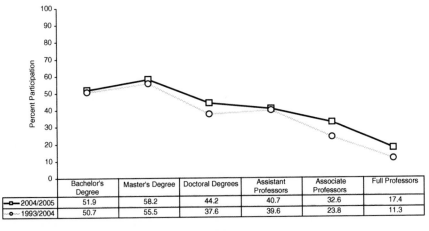

Figure 12.1 Representation of Women among Students and Faculty at the Ohio State University

Source: OSU Registrar, 2005; OSU OHR, 2005.

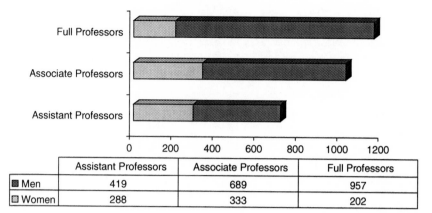

	Assistant Professors	Associate Professors	Full Professors
▨ Men	419	689	957
▨ Women	288	333	202

Figure 12.2   OSU 2005 Tenure-Track Faculty
Source: Office of Human Resources, Ohio State University, 2005.

university are male full professors. Women full professors account for 7% (202) of the total faculty, while women associate professors comprise 11.5% (333) of the faculty, and women assistant professors make up 10% (288). These numbers indicate an extreme power imbalance between male full professors and female faculty across all ranks, a condition that has major implications for the academic culture. It is the full professors who decide most policy matters, who act both as gatekeepers for hiring and promotion and as evaluators for awards, grants, and who consequently shape the institutional culture. Moreover, they maintain the institutional patriarchal support system (Bagilhole & Goode, 2001) as well as the networks and recognition (Morley, 1999; Currie, Theile, & Harris, 2002).

Whereas women's faculty representation has remained steady between 1993 and 2005, women have made progress in administrative leadership positions. Most noteworthy are the facts that both the current president and the vice-president and provost are women, and the percentage of female vice-provosts has increased from 33% (2) in 1993 to 66.7% (4) in 2005. There has also been a slight increase in women deans from 20% (5) to 28% (7). However, among department chairs and school directors, the numbers have decreased slightly from 16.5% (19) to 15.5% (15). The increased representation of women at the provost and vice-provost level can be explained by the commitment of leaders at the top. Appointments of vice-provosts are made largely at the discretion of the president and provost and may or may not include an open public recruitment and search process. One explanation for the decrease in women department chairs and school directors is the large percentage of male full professors and the importance of the faculty vote in recommending an individual to the dean, who then makes the decision to appoint a head of a department or school.

Policy Discourses on Women, Gender, and Racial Equality

The changes in the representation of women and the policy gender dynamics at Ohio State can be understood in relation to women's collective formal efforts to improve their status in recent university-wide policies. At Ohio State, as at many other U.S. universities, women have actively constructed their status by generating equity policy and issuing reports by women's commissions. These commissions, conceptualized within a liberal feminist framework, have generally served three related purposes: (1) to demonstrate administrative support for the improvement of women's status; (2) to give women a collective voice on campus (Allan, 2003); and (3) to serve as a sounding board for women's concerns (Glazer-Raymo, 1997). In particular, they function by 'clarifying issues, setting priorities, collecting data, making recommendations, monitoring activities, and influencing the policy agenda' (Glazer-Raymo, 1999, p. 66).

For the past 35 years, Ohio State women have studied their situation and described not only the weaknesses and achievements of the university's affirmative action programmes but also the need for the university to recognize women's abilities and achievements. Formal documentation of women's efforts to improve their conditions began with the release of the Ad hoc Committee on the Status of Women's *Report on the OSU Status of Women* in 1971. This report was followed by the creation of a Commission on Women and Minorities directed by the Board of Trustees, which released a major two-volume report by the Commission on Women and Minorities in 1977 (see OSU, Commission on Women and Minorities, 1977). Fifteen years later, having accepted a charge from the university President Gordon E. Gee, the President's Commission on Women issued the 1992 *Report of the President's Commission on Women*.

The theme that the university has failed to acknowledge women's talents and accomplishments has been echoed in reports for the past 30 years. For example, a 1991 letter to President Gee, the chair of the Commission on Women summarized the commission's conclusions about the campus climate at that time:

> The major and most general finding of the Commission is that the campus climate for women at The Ohio State University is virtually unchanged from that described in the Report of the 1977 Ohio State University Commission on Women. Indeed, for women of color, the climate may well have worsened. Women still confront an environment that ignores critical gender differences, places impediments in the ways of women striving to reach their full potential, and fails to recognize and respect women's professional abilities and achievements. (OSU, President's Commission on Women, 1992, p. 23)

In 1996, the infrastructure for monitoring and advocating for equality radically changed with the creation of a Diversity Committee to address all aspects of equity at Ohio State. The group combined the University Senate Committee on Women and Minorities with the President's Committee on Diversity. Although members of the long-standing Committee on Women and Minorities of the university senate opposed dissolving their group for fear that the university would lose its focus on women and minorities to broader issues, the Board of Trustees created the Diversity Committee to end overlapping activities of the two previous committees. The new committee was charged with monitoring the university's non-discrimination policy and recommending ways to foster civility, tolerance, and mutual respect as well as advising the president and other senior administrators on climate issues, policies, and priorities.

The year 2000 was a watershed year for reports on equality with the release of three major documents the *SRI Report on Retention of Women and Minority Faculty and Staff at The Ohio State University*, *A Diversity Action Plan for The Ohio State University*, and *Affirmative Action Committee Report*. The first report was prepared by an outside consulting firm 'to deepen institutional understanding of the issues that negatively impact the climate for retention of women and minorities' (OSU, Committee on Retention of Women and Minority Faculty and Staff, 2000, p. 1) The study identified salient issues that the university must address if the climate for women and minorities were to become more favourable, focusing on the confluence of racism and sexism that faculty women of colour experience. It advanced nine primary recommendations associated with conducting salary reviews for comparability, increasing dialogue concerning diversity, establishing research undertaking involving diverse sets of faculty members, and creating a more 'family-friendly' organization.

The following month, the Diversity Action Committee released *A Diversity Action Plan for The Ohio State University*, which stressed that the university had taken insufficient action to achieve diversity, gender, and racial and ethnic differences:

> A diverse environment at The Ohio State University is central to the mission and to the academic goals that have been set. This belief has long been professed, but the university has not acted aggressively and consistently on this belief. Some progress has been made, especially in the recruitment of women faculty, but, overall, the campus community is not diverse. The profile of faculty, staff, and students is not as diverse as the state of Ohio or the nation. (OSU, 2000, p. 2)

To deal with this critical assessment, the Diversity Action Plan proposed a strategy of accountability designed to improve the campus climate for women and men of colour, white women, and gay and lesbian students, faculty, and staff. The plan delineated points of accountability for the provost, vice-presidents, and college deans, such as establishing diversity sites, training, and workshops; providing curriculum materials and services; installing support mechanisms to handle complaints of harassment and discrimination; developing an internal/external comprehensive marketing campaign to raise awareness of diversity and promote inclusion; creating research grants and programmes for multicultural issues; requiring vice-presidents, deans, and department chairs to report on the progress made towards greater diversity; and making funds available to aggressively recruit women and minority faculty to increase the number of women and minorities by 2005.

The Committee on Affirmative Action released its report in September detailing the viability of diversity strategies associated with students, faculty, staff, and the campus climate. The committee had studied the Diversity Plan, which it supported, but focused on five pressing needs, one of which was to increase racial, ethnic, and gender diversity among faculty members in departments lacking that diversity. It also emphasized the need for the University to take a strong stand to communicate support for affirmative action in anticipation of external legal challenges (OSU, Committee on Affirmative Action, 2000).

Despite both the investment of many faculty members, administrators, and staff in these endeavours and the significant institutional commitment to undertake the faculty retention study of white women and faculty of colour, the reports received little public attention. For example, the university administration expressed no expectations to discuss these findings in academic departments, and initially few measures were implemented. Publicly, they were dwarfed by the launch of the primary strategic initiative, the Academic Plan, in October 2000 (OSU, Office of Academic Affairs

[OAA]). The Academic Plan proclaimed strong support for all the goals of the Diversity Action Plan, yet it included only two of the Diversity Action Plan's goals in a weakened version: to recruit, support and retain to graduation more qualified minority students and to hire at least five to ten women and five to ten minority faculty at senior level ranks with a commitment of $250,000 to $500,000 per year for five years. Thus, the Academic Plan reduced by half the number of hires proposed in the Diversity Plan.

Structures for Gender Equality at Ohio State

The university's innovative programmes, activities, and structures for gender equality and diversity have been incremental and additive. For example, because of campus activism, the university began providing childcare to the campus community in 1972 with flexible hours to meet the needs of student, faculty, and staff. Under President Karen Holbrook, the university also has been progressive in its work policies by implementing some of the recommendations of the 2000 *Report on Retention of Women and Minority Faculty and Staff*. The parental leave policy enables a faculty member to delay a tenure decision by up to two years, an option that has been used by men and women. A flexible workload policy and a dual career-hiring policy are also in place. In the area of curriculum, women studies evolved from a small centre to a strong department that now offers the PhD and has 13 tenure-track faculty and more than 55 associated faculty members. The growth of the Women's Studies Department came about through advocacy, outstanding scholarship, delivering required general education undergraduate courses, and the advocacy of the dean of the College of the Humanities to grant departmental status to the Center for Women's Studies.

In 2000, the university launched a highly visible initiative to improve the status of women through the creation of the Women's Place (TWP), which emerged from efforts of both the Committee on Academic Excellence for Women and grassroots activities. The Women's Place was embraced by President Kirwan, who incorporated it into the Academic and Diversity Plans as a catalyst for institutional change to expand opportunities for women's growth, leadership, and power in an inclusive, supportive, and safe university environment (OSU, TWP, 2005a). The Women's Place has consolidated and expanded resources and support systems for women as an action-oriented, information resource centre, a catalyst for networking, and an entity for identifying problems and finding constructive solutions (OSU, TWP, 2005a). The current director of TWP, a senior faculty member and longtime academic activist, also serves as associate provost for women's policy initiatives and interacts regularly with senior policy makers on university-wide matters.

Early Steps towards Excellence: Ohio State's Selective Investment Program

To fulfil its role for the social good, Ohio State has generated a great deal of activity and publicity regarding its policies of equality and diversity. However, the policies have drawn the attention mainly of white women and men and women of colour, in other words, those who have experienced inequities. In contrast, the Selective

Investment policy initiative implemented in 1997 and the Academic Plan in 2000 attracted the attention of most faculty members across the university. Moreover, the latter two initiatives instituted and redefined university priorities and the academic core while silencing gender and adversely affecting faculty women's representation and status.

In an effort to boost Ohio State's academic stature both nationally and internationally by strengthening its strongest departments, the university launched a three-year Selective Investment (SI) Program in July 1997. Departments were selected if they (1) were central to the academic mission of the university; (2) built on areas of existing strength and held promise of substantial future benefit; (3) showed cross-disciplinary potential; (4) had plans to monitor progress and evaluate achievement; (5) served a larger social good outside the university; and (6) demonstrated commitment of resources from the department and its college (OSU, OAA, 2004). The initiative was intended to support competition, emphasize benchmarking, and create academic and research profit centres that exploit the university's core competencies (Prahalad & Hamel, 1990). As such, it was designed to reflect the efficiency and effectiveness of university resource allocations (OSU, Office of Institutional Research and Planning, 2004).

Each unit chosen for the Selective Investment Program was awarded funds from reallocated continuing university funds. Like the Academic Enrichment Program, the reallocated funding was generated by all departments returning an additional 0.5% of their base budget allocation each year beginning in 1995. Those dollars were then redirected to Selective Investment units. The central funding was also matched with college and departmental funding. Thus, each of the 11 Selective Investment units received $1 million in annual continuing funds. Several of the units also received Academic Enrichment funds for programme development (OSU, OAA, 2004).

During the three years of the Selective Investment Program, 1997–2000, funds were reallocated to 13 recipient units located in six colleges. The programmes were electrical engineering and materials sciences in the College of Engineering; physics, chemistry, and mathematics in the College of Math and Physical Sciences; economics, psychology, and political science in the College of Social and Behavioral Sciences; the College of Law; english and history in the College of Humanities; and the cardiovascular bioengineering and neurosciences in the College of Medicine. We report on 11 of the 13 recipient units and exclude the units in the College of Medicine because they were collaborative efforts involving newly established units that operated differently form traditional departments where the vast majority of faculty work.

The Influences and Consequences of
Selective Investment

The Selective Investment Program produced substantial organizational change both structurally and budgetary through internal reallocations. As a form of academic capitalism (Slaughter & Leslie, 1997) designed to increase market responsiveness, it radically changed the criteria for allocations of university funding and shifted continuing allocations. All academic departments returned funds to the central administration, and all departments funded for Selective Investment had additional funds committed to them from their colleges.

For three years, the Selective Investment Committee, appointed by the provost, reviewed proposals that were submitted by departments and endorsed by their respective colleges. The Committee was comprised of distinguished faculty members who, in years two and three, also substantially represented Selective Investment-funded departments and who made recommendations to the president and provost. Like most award competitions, the ratings were not public. In addition, the ratio of women to men on the Selective Investment Evaluation Committee was 1:6 in 1998, 1:7 in 1999, and 3:5 in 2000 (OSU, OAA, n.d.). Only during the 2000 funding review did women make up more than 30% of group membership as Kanter's (1977) research shows is needed for minority individuals to influence the outcome of situations. In that same year, the only SI proposal mentioning diversity was funded.

University faculty widely supported the SI Program and the committee's decisions in part because they were perceived as legitimate, having been made by a faculty peer-review process rather than by administrators ('The Nation', 2002). Also, the president, provost, and evaluation took steps that have been successful for large-scale change (Kotter and Cohen, 2002). They became a guiding team that communicated with the faculty in order get them to agree to the change and to create momentum for a short-term win or accomplishment. In 2004, OSU communicated the successes of the plan in the *Report on the Impact of Selective Investment and Academic Enrichment Funding at The Ohio State University*. The report focused exclusively on knowledge production from a corporate perspective by highlighting improved examination scores and competitive standings, such as changes in publication rates. It did not mention diversity.

To determine the consequences of the financial investment for men and women, an examination of the percentage of women faculty in each of the Selective Investment departments between 1993[5] and 2005 shows the changes in gender representation. The department as the unit of analysis is used here because it is the location where faculty work and are hired and promoted, where resource allocations are made, and where units have decidedly different cultures that could reflect different attitudes toward men and women. Table 12.1 shows departmental data on faculty positions in 2005: the current total of faculty and change since 1993, the number of men and women hired under the SI Program, and the changes in the percentages and numbers of women from 1993 to 2005.

The majority (8) of the Selective Investment departments grew in size during the period, yet only 5 departments increased their representation of women faculty members. One unit, the Department of Psychology, decreased greatly in size by 14 faculty members including 1 woman but increased its representation of women. Three departments that increased in size (Electrical Engineering, Materials Science, and Economics) decreased their representation of women. Mathematics decreased in size along with its percentage of women. Chemistry did not increase in size, but it significantly increased its representation of women from 2.9% (1) to 11.7% or (4) hiring them through regular rather than Selective Investment lines as were the two women hires in Physics.

Women are more of the minority in Selective Investment departments than in the university as a whole. In 2005, women accounted for approximately 28.5% of the tenure-track faculty at Ohio State (OSU, OHR, 2005). Using 28.5% as the benchmark to determine each department's share of female faculty representation at the university

Table 12.1 Gender Representation in Selective Investment Departments in 1993 and 2005

Department	Positions in 2005	Position Change from 1993	SI Men Hired	SI Women Hired	Women 1993		Women 2005	
					%	No.	%	No.
Electrical Eng.	44	+3	10	0	7.3	(3)	4.5	(2)
Materials Science	23	+4	5	1	5.3	(1)	4.3	(1)
Chemistry	34	0	3	0	2.9	(1)	11.7	(4)
Mathematics	68	−11	4	0	8.9	(7)	5.9	(4)
Physics	57	+8	9	0	4.0	(2)	7.0	(4)
Economics	34	+3	7	1	19.0	(4)	11.7	(4)
Psychology	43	−14	3	3	22.8	(13)	27.9	(12)
Political Science	37	+12	8	4	12.0	(3)	33.3	(9)
English	65	+1	5	1	46.9	(30)	50.7	(33)
History	54	+7	3	4	21.3	(10)	33.3	(18)
Law	45	+10	7	1	22.8	(8)	31.1	(14)

Source: Data extracted from Ohio State Office of Human Resources Diversity Data for Faculty and Staff Unit Level Statistics 1993–2005.

and the presence of horizontal segregation, 7 of the 11 Selective Investment funded units were below the 28.5% benchmark for female representation.

During the Selective Investment Program, these 11 units hired 79 faculty members, yet only 19% (15) were women. Further analysis of Selective Investment hires by rank shows that in those departments 37% of total SI hires were men appointed as full professors, and only 0.5% of the total hires were women at the most senior rank. Thus, the Selective Investment Program, which was designed to improve the research output of the university, has contributed to furthering a male-dominated professoriate, particularly at the full professor level. It has also created a system of male faculty stars, or established distinguished scholars who have increasingly different reward and work conditions from their colleagues. For example, in 2001, the average salary of full professors was $92,000. Individuals hired through the SI Program were given salaries as high as $220,000; in addition, these hires had lighter teaching loads and, in some cases, startup packages of more than a million dollars each ('Ohio State "Taxes" Departments ...', 2001).[6]

Considering the gender outcomes of Selective Investment hiring, women were less likely to be hired through that programme than through a regular hiring process.[7] Only 17.3% (13) of the Selective Investment faculty hires were women as compared to 34.5% of the faculty hires between 1993 and 2004 (OSU, President's Council on Women's Issues, 2005). One explanation for this discrepancy is that many Selective Investment faculty appointments were made as a result of targeted searches wherein the position was not publicized and applications were not solicited. Thus, these procedures differed from the normative practice of an open search in which a position is advertised widely in disciplinary and professional publications in order to recruit the most talented and diverse pool of candidates. In other words, departments relied heavily on networks, personal contacts, and visibility, all factors that are likely to exclude women (Morley, 1999).

During the 2003–2004 academic year, the first author interviewed several heads of Selective Investment units to understand their hiring processes. The interviews indicated that different departmental hiring approaches yielded very different gender outcomes. One department chair who hired all males with Selective Investment funds but increased representation of women through regular hiring of assistant professors explained how the department had used a stealth-like approach to hire a Selective Investment faculty member. The unit identified its choice person and pursued him, 'making an attractive offer without hassles', without requiring him to submit an application, in order to increase the unit's chances of hiring him. Another chair in a department that had decreased its representation of women explained that, with limited resources, emphasis had to be placed on quality and that his department had hired one woman, 'but she could not get along with the faculty, and she left'. A third department chair whose representation of women also decreased, explained that the department members wanted the best talent, and they did not think they could lure women away from higher ranked departments. In reality, they had not tried to do so. The attitude and approach was extremely different in a unit that increased its percentage of women and hired both a white woman and people of colour using Selective Investment funds. The head explained that the unit was diverse before receiving Selective Investment funds, that it was a natural impulse to have diversity as part of every search, and that they relied on networks to identify diverse persons as faculty hires.

In short, in focusing on increasing the research reputation of various departments, heads of units were given the freedom to hire whom the unit chose; thus, the culture of each department was not challenged or supported to identify candidates who were both leaders in their disciplines and women or people of colour. Consequently, male-dominated departments tended to hire men, and departments that had already embraced diversity incorporated that criterion into their recruitment for their Selective Investment appointments as part of the goal to achieve excellence.

The Push towards Academic Excellence: The Academic Plan

In 2002, Ohio State launched an ambitious academic plan guided by the vision 'to become one of the world's great public research and teaching universities' (OSU, OAA, 2000, p. 1). Ohio State administrators, deans, and faculty worked on the five-year plan for more than two years. The core elements of the plan are outlined in 6 strategies and 14 supporting initiatives. The strategies are to (1) build a world-class faculty; (2) develop academic programmes that define Ohio State as the nation's leading public land-grant university; (3) enhance the quality of the teaching and learning environment; (4) enhance and better serve the student body; (5) create a diverse university community; and (6) help build Ohio's future.

In its efforts to create a diverse university community, the Academic Plan incorporated priorities and reaffirmed recommendations of the 2000 Diversity Action Plan:

> To create this rich learning environment, The Ohio State University must recruit and retain greater numbers of women and minorities into faculty, staff, and administrative positions, especially senior positions. Such senior faculty arrive with tenure and serve as role models and mentors for their junior counterparts. ... We must be sure that all groups are represented in campus diversity policy and that the newly established Women's Place receives adequate support. ... Finally, we must ensure that deans,

department chairs, and other leaders are held accountable for their part in increasing campus diversity. (OSU, 2000, p. 14)

As one of its initiatives under the diversity strategy, the Academic Plan included the hiring of at least five to ten women and five to ten minority faculty members at a senior level each year for five years through the Faculty Hiring Assistance Program (FHAP). Funding was made available to departments on a first come first served basis to support three years of salary. For example, in 2004, the provost's office allocated, from that fund, $25,000 for each assistant professor, $30,000 for associate professors, and $40,000 for full professors with the hiring college or department paying the remainder of the salary and benefits for that year and assuming the full cost after three years. A provision was also included that allowed departments to request funds without a national search as might be the case with a dual career-hiring appointment for the second partner (Snyder, 2004). This programme has been helpful, but unlike the Selective Investment Program that offered very high salaries, reduced teaching loads, and research support, units receiving Faculty Hiring Assistance Program funds have had limited success in attracting white women and faculty of colour (OSU, Council on Diversity, 2004).

Conclusion

A commitment to both academic excellence and diversity has been articulated in Ohio State's strategy to become one of the world's great public universities. The developments in this chapter show how the university has pursued quasi-corporate and social good goals, the former through Selective Investment strategies and the latter through special programmes. The strategies and initiatives associated with academic excellence have increased research output, income generation, and improved reputational rankings (OSU, OAA, 2004), suggesting that Ohio State is becoming more competitive in the university marketplace.

By prioritizing knowledge areas, the university has institutionalized a quasi-corporate discourse of selective efficiency and effectiveness. Every faculty member in the university by virtue of his or her unit has been taxed to support targeted departments. However, colleges with the larger numbers of women faculty members and students and with strong linkages to the public good, such as nursing, education, social work, and human ecology, have not been on the receiving end of these centralized funds.

The Selective Investment Program has been agenda setting by producing substantial organizational change in both structure and budget through internal reallocations to increase market responsiveness and competition. The programme changed the university's social structure by creating highly differentiated work conditions and work structures (Hall, 1977) and cultures for Selective Investment units and by modifying its membership patters to hire heavily at the senior ranks using processes that lacked transparency and altered work patterns. The budgetary changes also radically redefined the criteria for allocations of university funding, reallocated funds, and redefined entrepreneurial activities as core.

Although the discourse of the Academic Plan coupled the hiring increase of white women and men and women of colour with the creation of a more diverse faculty, senior administrative leaders have offered little commitment to mainstream gender and diversity into hiring practices. Such programmes as the Faculty Hiring Assistance Program have been additive, layering diversity concerns on existing practices through short-term cash allocations without challenging the fundamental nature of hiring practices. In other words, although they represent special action (Rees, 1998) to redress disadvantage, they have not produced substantial structural, cultural, or budgetary change. As a result, the social good objective associated with diversity and equality have resulted in minimal change compared the Selective Investment Program. When the Diversity Plan was launched in 2000, faculty women comprised 27.7% of the tenure-track faculty positions. Five years later, the target year identified to increase the numbers of white women and women and men of colour, women had increased their represen-tation to 28.6%, a change of less than 1%(OSU, OHR, 2005).[8]

With Selective Investment hiring having ended in 2004, the agenda-setting activity has been a setback for increasing the number of white women and men and women of colour. Like other universities reallocating or retrenching resources (Slaughter, 1993; Volk, Slaughter, and Thomas, 2002), Ohio State's programme has been to the detriment of most of the female-dominated units. Selective Investment units were not held accountable to further affirmative action or equal opportunity at the uni-versity. Consequently, the majority of those units functioned according to their cul-tural dispositions with the majority male-dominated departments becoming even more so through Selective Investment. It is noteworthy, however, that several Selective Investment units with significant female representation, such as English and Law, have become University leaders in addressing diversity issues through curricular change and efforts to attract a more diverse faculty and student population (OSU, Council on Diversity, 2004).

Presidential leadership is a crucial factor in organizational change (Sporn, 1999). Ohio State presidents have had different approaches and degrees of commitment to equality and diversity. President Gordon Gee began the financial reallocation without incorporating equality and diversity into excellence. This agenda-setting decision consequently marginalized equality and diversity. All initiatives to improve the status of women and people of colour have been additive bringing about minimal change in the nature of faculty work or the university culture. President William Kirwan launched the Academic Plan, commissioned two major reports on diversity and affir-mative action, and implemented a diversity-monitoring programme in all colleges and departments. He also created a major lecture series on diversity and an institute on race, which was later named the Kirwan Institute for the Study of Race and Ethnicity in the Americas, and he made diversity and equality issues more prominent within the university by using websites to promote diversity and by increasing access to diversity and equality statistics. With the exception of the expectation of deans to report annually on diversity statistics and activities, other equality measures have not been mainstreamed into policies and procedures.

When President Karen Holbrook assumed the presidency, the Academic Plan was in its second year of implementation. She has embraced the Academic Plan, and much of her public approach to diversity and equality has focused on two much-needed changes: increasing the enrolment and retention of students of colour and implementing policies to reduce family-work tensions for faculty and staff. Under the president's leadership, policies have been enacted for childcare, parental leave, and spousal hiring from which both female and male faculty members have benefited. These human resource provisions have the potential to reduce conflicts between personal/family and professional/career goals in support of an academic career, and they contribute not only by furthering gender equality but also by removing attitudinal barriers within the organization. However, these provisions are additive. They have neither changed the core activities of the organization nor directly affected the nature of academic workplace. They do, however, have the potential to benefit younger scholars and thereby reduce the leaky pipeline problem over time (see chapter 2 in this book by Teresa Rees).

The women in the top two senior administrative positions of the university have legitimized the idea of women as leaders and have brought about incremental change. They have spoken publicly about the need to advance women's careers, have given the Women's Place more prominence, and have stressed audits and efforts to uncover hidden gendered and racist protocols. During the 2004–2005 academic year, they inaugurated the President and Provost's Leadership Institute to deliver leadership training programmes to support and prepare women and under-represented men for agenda-setting roles (OSU, TWP, 2005b). These long-term conditions and measures may change the picture of inequality, however slowly, by making the culture more women-friendly.

In the fall of 2005, President Karen Holbrook, in the annual State of the University Address, highlighted university goals and priorities, mentioned diversity in relationship to the Women's Place, and discussed the need to increase the representation of students of colour and international students. About that time, Provost Barbara Snyder announced that $50 million in central funds would be invested over the next five years for targeted investments in excellence for proposals judged primarily by two criteria: 'one, the program is capable of achieving recognition as one of the top in the field and two, top ranking for the program is likely to have a significant impact on the university's academic structure (Snyder, 2005). Thus, another agenda-setting opportunity has been created to mainstream equality and diversity and to realize the goals and promises of a quasi-corporate university for the social good. There is hope that, with incremental additive changes towards equality and diversity in place and the presence of a highly committed and effective university president, the next agenda-setting initiative will make diversity and equality central to excellence. It may well be that the organizational culture is now more receptive because the foundation has been laid for a bold reinvestment of funding for more white women, and people of colour to strengthen the research enterprise.

Notes

1. Research on university students and adults has supported this position by showing that universities improve individuals' motivation and capacity to participate in a pluralistic and complex society (Gurin, Biren, & Gretchen, 2004). Furthermore, court decisions, such as *California v. Bakke* (1978), have also found diversity in education to be fundamental to developing the skills necessary for success in an increasingly complex labour force even though, as Judith Raymo notes in the preceding chapter, this perspective has not been the dominant position of recent major judicial decisions.
2. With the support of Ohio State Affirmative Action grants, Mary Ann Danowitz Sagaria conducted three comprehensive studies on gender and racial equality for faculty and administrators at the university, beginning with research on female and under-represented male junior faculty members in 1988.
3. OSU is one of 105 public universities and colleges established under federal legislation to provide practical knowledge and information based in scientific research to citizens in rural

and urban areas. These universities are associated with the democratic model for openness, accessibility, and service to people, especially in agricultural research (retrieved December 26, 2005, from OSU OHIOLINK Website, http:ohioline.osu.edu/ lines/grant.html.).

4. In this paper, people of colour are defined as born or naturalized American citizens who identify racially with one or more of the racially and ethnically under-represented groups in the United States. Typically, this definition would include people of African, Latino/Hispanic, Asian, and Native American descent. Faculty whose citizenship is outside the United States are not included under this definition. Nevertheless, their status within American higher education is important and has received attention (Smith, 1992).

5. 1993 was chosen because data were available for comparative purposes despite the fact that the SI Program was first funded in 1998. The Selective Investment Program came shortly after the Academic Enrichment Program, the first centrally funded initiative that ran between 1995 and 2001. Funding was typically directed as an early commitment of resources to 22 promising new programmes. The vast majority of the funding was directed to purchasing equipment and supporting research and education in 22 projects. One female faculty member was hired and funding was directed to eight lead colleges.

6. The salary and startup figures are for the entire university and include the College of Medicine.

7. Although the available pool of women in physical science disciplines such as chemistry and physics and engineering fields are lower than disciplines such as English, history, and psychology, The *2005 Status Report on Women at Ohio State* indicates that women have been underrepresented in hiring in the physical sciences and engineering in relationship to the national pool of women scientists.

8. The percentage of faculty women identifying themselves of colour or ethnicity between 1993 and 2003 increased from 11% (83) of women faculty to 14% (116). It is important to note that ethnicity is self-reported, and the number of persons who choose not to disclose their ethnicity continues to grow each year. For autumn 2003, eight women faculty chose not to disclose their ethnicity.

References

Allan, E. J. (2003) Constructing women's status: Policy discourses of university women's commissions. *Harvard educational review, 73*(1):44–72.

Bagilhole, B., & Goode, J. (2001) The contradiction of the myth of individual merit, and the reality of a patriarchal support system in academic careers: A feminist investigation. *European journal of women's studies, 8*(2):161–180.

Counting Gifts: New Rules Irk Fund Raisers (2005) *Chronicle of higher education, 51*(27) (March 11):A27.

Currie, J., Theile, B., & Harris, P. (2002) *Gendered universities in globalized economies: Power, careers and sacrifices.* Lexington: Lexington Books.

Dill, D., & Sporn, B. (1995) The implications of a postindustrial environment for the university: An introduction. In D. Dill, & B. Sporn (Eds.), *Emerging patterns of social demand and university reform: Through a glass darkly.* Oxford: Pergamon.

Glazer-Raymo, J. (1999) *Shattering the myths: Women in academe.* Baltimore: Johns Hopkins University Press.

Gumport, P. J. (2000) Academic restructuring: Organizational change and institutional imperatives. *Higher education, 39*:67–91.

Gurin, P., Biren, A. N., & Gretchen, L. (2004) The benefits of diversity in education for democratic citizenship. *Journal of social issues, 60*(1):17–34.

Gurin, P., Dey, E. L., Hurtado, S., & Gurin, G. (2002) Diversity and higher education: Theory and impact on educational outcomes. *Harvard educational review, 72*(3):330–366.

Hall, R. H. (1977) *Organizations: Structure and process.* London: Prentice Hall International.

Holbrook, K. (2005) *State of the university address: Progress in fulfilling the promise.* Retrieved March 2, 2006, from The Ohio State University Website, http://president.osu.edu/ pdf/sou_10_2005.pdf.

Kanter, R. M. (1977) *Men and women of the corporation*. New York: Basic Books.

Kotter, J. P., & Cohen, D. S. (2002) *The heart of change*. Boston: Harvard Business School Press.

Morley, L. (1999) *Organising feminisms: The micropolitics of the academy*. London: MacMillan Press.

'The Nation' (2002) *Chronicle of higher education, 49* (1) (August 30). Retrieved December 1, 2005, from the Academic Search Premier database.

Ohio State 'Taxes' Departments to Make a Select Few Top Notch (2001) *Chronicle of higher education, 47*(38) (June 1):A8.

OSU (Ohio State University) (2000) *A diversity action plan for The Ohio State University*. Retrieved November 11, 2005, from http://www.osu.edu/diversityplan/index_1.php.

——— (2005) *Statistical summary*. Retrieved November 18, 2005, from http://www.osu.edu/osutoday/stuinfo.php.

OSU, Ad hoc Committee on the Status of Women (1971) *Report on the OSU status of women*. The Ohio State University archives.

OSU, Commission on Women and Minorities (1977) *Status of Women Report*. The Ohio State University archives.

OSU, Committee on Affirmative Action (2000) *Affirmative Action Committee report*. Retrieved November 18, 2005, from The Ohio State University Website, *http://www.osu.edu/affirmative_action/*.

OSU, Committee on Retention of Women and Minority Faculty & Staff (2000) *SRI report on retention of women and minority faculty and staff at the Ohio State University*. The Ohio State University archives.

OSU, Council on Diversity (2004) *Diversity plans: An analysis 2003–2004*. Retrieved November 19, 2005, from http://www.osu.edu/diversity/reports.php.

OSU, OAA (n.d.) *Centrally funded initiatives: Selective investment*. Retrieved December 1, 2005, from http://oaa.osu.edu/08cfi.html.

——— (2000) *Academic plan*. Retrieved November 18, 2005, from http:// www.osu.edu/academicplan/Acad_Plan.pdf.

——— (2004) *Report on the impact of selective investment and academic enrichment funding at The Ohio State University*. Retrieved December 1, 2005, from http://oaa.osu.edu/Reports/si2004report.html.

OSU, OHR (2005) *Annual Diversity Data 2005*. Retrieved December 1, 2005 from http://hr.osu.edu/miar/diversitydata_home.htm.

OSU, Office of Institutional Research and Planning (2004) *Strategic Indicators*. Retrieved November 18, 2005 from http://oaa.osu.edu/irp/stratind/2004SIreport.pdf.

OSU, President's Commission on Women (1992) *Report of the President's Commission on Women*. The Ohio State University archives.

OSU, President's Council on Women' Issues (2005) *2005 annual report*. Retrieved December 5, 2005, from http://pcw.osu.edu/annual-reports.html.

OSU, Registrar (2005) *Degrees awarded by college offering major by gender and ethnicity*. Retrieved December 1, 2005 from http://www.ureg.ohio-state.edu/ourweb/srs/srscontent/degree/degintrogenmin.html.

OSU, Research Foundation (2005) *Comparative Expenditure Data: FY 2005 vs FY 2006*. Retrieved December 1, 2005, from OSU Research Foundation Website, http://rf.osu.edu/pubrpt/institutional/expend05.htm.

OSU, TWP (2005a) *Mission*. Retrieved December 12, 2005, from the OSU TWP Website, http://womensplace.osu.edu/.

——— (2005b) *The president's and provost's leadership institute: Facilitative leadership training for emerging academic leaders*. Retrieved December 12, 2005, from http://womensplace.osu.edu/Documents/finalleadershipinstituteproposal.pdf.

Prahalad, C. K., & Hamel, G. (1990) The core competence of the corporation. *Harvard business review, 68*(3):79–91.

Rees, T. (1998) *Mainstreaming equality in the European Union*. London: Routledge.

Slaughter, S. (1993) Retrenchment in the 1980s: The politics of prestige and gender. *Journal of higher education, 64*(3):250–282.

Slaughter, S., & Leslie, L. L. (1997) *Academic capitalism: Politics, policies, and the entrepreneurial university*. Baltimore: Johns Hopkins University Press.

Smith, R. M. (1992) *Crossing Pedagogical Oceans: International Teaching Assistants in U.S. Undergraduate Education*. ASHE-ERIC Higher Education Report No. 8. Washington, DC: George Washington University.

Snyder, B. (2004) *Memo of the executive vice president and provost: Faculty hiring assistance program*. December 9. Retrieved January 29, 2006, from The Ohio State University Website, http://oaa.osu.edu/handbook/FHAP.pdf.

———— (2005) *Memo of the executive vice president and provost: Key academic priorities for 2005–06*. Retrieved November 18, 2005 from The Ohio State University Website, http://oaa.osu.edu/KeyAcademicPrioritiesfor2005–06.htm.

Sporn, B. (1999) *Adaptive university structures: An analysis of adaptation to socioeconomic environments of US and European universities*. London: Jessica Kingsley.

Volk, C., Slaughter, S., & Thomas, S. L. (2001) Models of institutional resource allocation: Mission, market and gender. *Journal of higher education, 72*(4):387–413.

Chapter Thirteen

Helping or Hurting Women? The Case of a Dual Career Couple Policy at the University of Kansas

Suzanne Rice, Lisa E. Wolf-Wendel, and Susan B. Twombly

As the number of women earning PhDs has increased in the United States, so too has the number of women seeking faculty jobs. According to Astin and Milem (1997), approximately 40% of women who hold or who are seeking faculty positions are married to other academics. Although there are records of faculty couples as early as the late nineteenth century, until recently academic couples have numbered very few. Now, with women earning a higher percentage of PhDs in many fields, colleges and universities are often faced with the need to consider employment for a spouse or partner regardless of whether the initial hire is a man or a woman.[1] Our own recent study in the United States suggests that most colleges and universities will attempt to do *something* for faculty job finalists who have a spouse or partner. That something may be as simple as sending out resumes or as involved as creating a tenure-track position for a spouse or partner. Such assistance often occurs on an ad hoc basis and depends on the goodwill, knowledge, and wherewithal of individual department chairs. Approximately 25% of colleges and universities have formal dual career couple policies; of these institutions with formal policies, 20% provide the option of finding a tenure-track position for a spouse or partner and outline the procedures that must be followed in order to obtain such a position (Wolf-Wendel, Twombly, & Rice, 2003).

On the surface, such policies – and other accommodation efforts as well – would seem to advantage women. Most colleges and universities give 'hiring more women' as a reason to make hiring accommodations (Wolf-Wendel, Twombly, & Rice, 2003). However, accommodating partners or spouses, especially in tenure-track positions, is complicated. Such accommodations challenge some deeply held academic values regarding faculty quality and how it is assessed through open searches, fairness, and affirmative action. Although an increase in the number of women earning PhDs who seek faculty jobs is one of the main reasons for the addition of such policies, it is not entirely clear to what extent such policies actually benefit women. In our earlier study (Wolf-Wendel, Twombly, & Rice, 2003), we dealt with a number of issues raised by such policies, but we did not deal with the following important gender-related questions: Are institutions more likely to find accommodations for a partner depending on whether the initial hire is a man or a woman? Are women or men who are 'trailing' partners or spouses more likely to end up in non-tenure-track positions? Are receiving departments – departments asked to consider a partner hire – more likely to view the candidate as less qualified depending on the spouse or partner's gender? Do women or men accompanying partners have a more difficult time being accepted among the faculty once hired? Answers to these kinds of questions are essential if dual career couple policies are to contribute to gender-progressive changes in faculty hiring. These are some of the questions we explore in this chapter through a case study of the College of Liberal Arts and Sciences at the University of Kansas.

Conceptual Framework

We have employed what Bensimon and Marshall (1997) call 'emerging methods of policy analysis' (p. 8) in our effort to understand the gender-related implications of accommodation policies. Although we are interested in the effects of a particular policy on gender equity rather than in policy formation per se, we have found emerging views of policy useful and feminist policy analysis especially illuminating. This approach to policy analysis is marked by the following characteristics: (1) it poses gender as a fundamental category of analysis; (2) it is concerned with difference and local context; (3) it privileges the lived experiences of women; and (4) it seeks to be transformative and is itself an interventionist strategy (pp. 9–10). Central to our analysis are the questions (1) who benefits from dual career couple policies; and (2) how might women and men fare differently as a result of these policies?

Existing Literature

There has been little research on dual career-hiring policies in higher education in general and even less research on gender-related aspects of this phenomenon. Most of the attention given to dual career couple hiring in academia has focussed on the experiences of individual faculty members and couples. In fact, in the past several years, over 20 stories about dual career couples have appeared in the *Chronicle of Higher Education* ('Almanac Issue', 2004), the major weekly newspaper in the United States focussing on colleges and universities.

A handful of small-scale studies suggests that institutions are beginning to implement dual career couple-hiring policies or have at least grappled with how to meet the needs of dual career couples. Raabe (1997) concluded, based on a national survey of academic vice-presidents, that 44% of institutions provided some form of job assistance for spouses. An additional 12% of institutions indicated that they were planning to implement a job assistance policy for spouses. Raabe concluded that research universities are the most likely type of university to have a dual career couple policy in large part because they have more resources and more flexibility in creating positions, both academic and administrative, than do smaller institutions. This finding was confirmed by our own national study (Wolf-Wendel, Twombly, & Rice, 2003).

An analysis of the accommodation policy at the University of Illinois at Champaign-Urbana (UIUC) provides some important insights into how that institution has addressed the employment needs of dual career academic couples and the policy's affect on women (Loeb, 1997). UIUC's practice of hiring dual career academic couples began in the early 1980s as an approach to recruiting desired faculty members. According to Loeb, between 1980 and 1994, 90 accommodations took place. Of those accommodated, the so-called primary hire was more likely (77%) to be male. However, as the practice of accommodating spouses at UIUC increased in the 1990s, the cases where women were the primary hire rose to 29% of all accommodations. Loeb reports that some academic units (i.e., the social and behavioural sciences, law, veterinary medicine, agriculture, and education) are much more likely to engage in dual career hiring than are others. This is consistent with Astin and Milem's (1997) study, which also finds that dual career academic couples are more likely in these fields than in others. This finding is particularly important to an examination of the gender-related implications of dual career couple policies and practices because women are more likely to be employed in some disciplines, such as history and English, than others. Further, Loeb reports that while the accommodated partner is more likely to hold a less desirable academic position than the initial hire, most of this difference can be explained in terms of the relative strength of each spouse's credentials. Loeb found no evidence of an accompanying spouse being given a position for which he or she was unqualified merely because of the status of the 'primary hire'. Loeb concludes that the dual career accommodation policy at Illinois is a success in that it has helped the institution recruit and retain faculty it might otherwise have lost.

Our own national survey of dual career couple policies at member institutions of the American Association of Colleges and Universities (AACU) largely confirmed and extended existing findings (Wolf-Wendel, Twombly, & Rice, 2003). In the United States, AACU is the leading national association concerned with undergraduate liberal arts education. AACU is comprised of more than 975 colleges and universities of various institutional types, including research universities as well as smaller liberal arts colleges.

Some of our key findings include the following:

- The needs of dual career couples represent an important concern for colleges and universities.
- Over half of the colleges and universities with existing policies do not have them in writing.
- Even institutions with no policies report assisting couples when possible. The problem with the ad hoc nature of such policies is that they can be unevenly implemented, which could pose a problem for women.
- Accommodations are most likely offered to recruit the initial hire in this order: faculty of color, full professors, and women.
- Domestic partners are often included 'quietly' in institution policies.
- Remaining competitive in faculty recruitment is the key goal of most policies, particularly in the competition for faculty 'stars'. Attracting faculty of colour and women is only slightly less important as a motivation.
- An overwhelming majority of institutions will provide contacts and send resumes to assist a partner or spouse, and about 40% will consider shared academic positions and create non-tenure-track positions, but only 20% will create tenure-track positions.

Method

Data for our current analysis come from several sources. Descriptive information about the University of Kansas (KU), including numerical data about the percentages of women faculty and students were obtained from various university documents generated by the Office of Institutional Research and Planning at KU. Data on the number of faculty accommodated, the nature of their accommodation, and their satisfaction were obtained from the assistant dean in the College of Liberal Arts and Sciences, whose job it is to oversee faculty searches.[2] We conducted interviews with the current dean, one of the associate deans, a former dean who is now senior vice-provost, a vice-provost responsible for various faculty concerns, and three couples who had been accommodated. In selecting couples to interview, we identified one case in which the man was the initial hire and two cases in which the woman was the initial hire. All three couples had been given tenure-track positions for both partners. For one of these couples, however, the accompanying partner, in this case a woman, started in a non-tenure-track position. After several years in that position, she obtained a tenure-track position. We have assigned the couples pseudonyms.

University Background and Characteristics

The University of Kansas is a Carnegie research extensive university and is a member of the American Association of American Universities (AAAU), a select group of 62 public and private research universities that represents excellence in graduate and professional education. The university was founded in 1865. The main campus is located in Lawrence, Kansas, and the Medical Center is located in Kansas City, Kansas. The Lawrence campus itself is in the centre of the U.S. Midwest. Although a politically conservative state, the state has a long tradition of valuing the individual. From its days as a 'border town' before the beginning of the U.S. Civil War in the mid-1800s, Lawrence residents fiercely fought against their Missouri neighbours who wanted Kansas to enter the United States as a slave-holding state. Since then Lawrence, the town in which the main campus is located, has had the reputation of being liberal and of valuing diversity.

The operating budget for the Lawrence campus is approximately $356,453,290 (Office of the Chancellor, 2004). The Lawrence campus is home to the following academic units: the College of Liberal Arts and Sciences and the Schools of Architecture, Business, Education, Engineering, Fine Arts, Journalism, Law, Pharmacy, and Social Welfare. In fall 2003, the university's total enrolment was 29,272 students; of these students, 26,814 were enrolled in graduate and undergraduate programmes on the Lawrence campus, while 2,458 were enrolled at the Medical Center. Of the total student body, 7,485 were enrolled in graduate/first professional programmes. As figure 13.1 shows the participation rate for women students at the University of Kansas in 1989 and 2003 has increased slightly for undergraduates so that women now represent a slight majority among students. In contrast, the representation of women faculty has increased greatly across all faculty ranks so that by 2003, 81% (48) of the instructors, and 56% (143) of the lecturers, 47% (116) of the assistant professors, and 33% (108) of the associate professors were women, and women represented 16% (71) of the full professors (Office of Institutional Research and Planning, 2004). These data suggest that women have achieved numerical equality through the student ranks and through faculty ranks prior to tenure. Even with considerable progress, however, women continue to be under-represented at the associate and full professor ranks.

Administratively, the chancellor is the chief officer of the university and oversees the operations of all campuses. A provost and executive vice-chancellor of the

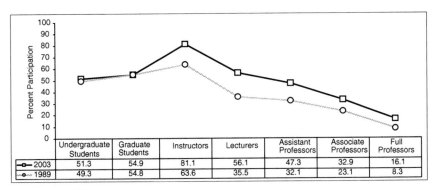

	Undergraduate Students	Graduate Students	Instructors	Lecturers	Assistant Professors	Associate Professors	Full Professors
2003	51.3	54.9	81.1	56.1	47.3	32.9	16.1
1989	49.3	54.8	63.6	35.5	32.1	23.1	8.3

Figure 13.1   Representation of Women among Students and Faculty at the University of Kansas
Source: Office of Institutional Research and Planning, University of Kansas (2004) Profiles.

Lawrence campus serves as the chief administrative office on the Lawrence campus. Functionally, the university is decentralized, meaning that each school, as well as the College of Liberal Arts and Sciences, has considerable control over its own policies and procedures. Such autonomy allows the College of Liberal Art and Sciences to have a dual career couple policy while a university-wide policy is lacking. In the last decade, a number of women have assumed senior administrative positions at KU, including four academic deans in Education, Social Welfare, Journalism, and the Graduate School and International Programs. For a while during 1990s, the dean of the College of Liberal Arts and Sciences was a woman. Currently, the senior vice-provost is a woman, and there are three other women vice-provosts on the Lawrence campus (faculty development, information and technology, and student success/affairs). With perhaps the exception of the vice-provost for information and technology, senior women administrators are in areas traditionally regarded as being 'women-friendly'.

KU is recognized by its faculty and staff as a collegial university that places high value on teaching as well as on research. The university boasts that the populist sentiment of early Kansas, with its faith in the virtues and wisdom of the common person, still fuels KU's commitment to equity and diversity. Women have been represented as students and faculty since the university opened its doors in 1867. Because anti-nepotism (rules against hiring and supervising one's relatives) are a common argument against dual career couple-hiring policies, it is important to note that KU has no such rule. However, there is an official policy preventing supervisors from evaluating or assigning salary increases to anyone with whom they have any sort of relationship, romantic or otherwise, that might inhibit objectivity.

The College of Liberal Arts and Sciences (the College), the focus of this chapter, is by far the largest of the academic units on campus. The College has 53 departments and programmes that enrol approximately 15,000 students. Of its 18 programmes and centres, 5 are headed by women, 3 out of 14 humanities departments are chaired by women, 1 out of 9 departments/divisions in the natural sciences is chaired by a woman, and 1 out of 10 departments in the social sciences is chaired by a woman. One of four associate deans is a woman. In 2001, 20% (41) of the full professors (13% in 1996), 31% (49) of the associate professors (34% in 1996), 47% (61) of the assistant professors (38% in 1996), and 72% of instructors and lecturers (50% in 1996) were women. The distribution of women in faculty ranks in the College is similar to that in the university as a whole.

The Official Policy

The College of Liberal Arts and Sciences created a formal dual career couple policy in the early 1990s as a result of a large influx of couples seeking tenure-track appointments at the same, or nearby, institution. Administrators in the College felt the need to respond proactively to the demands of the market and thus created a formal written policy concerning the hiring of dual career academic couples. The College is the only unit within the larger university that has such a policy. According to the dean of the College, 'The University views this as a school issue rather than as a University-wide effort, which is consistent with how things get done at KU. It works okay with us because we are big enough to make internal accommodations – we don't often have to go out of the college to assist spouses or partners'.

The policy states explicitly that the College has a 'tradition of working to accommodate domestic partners' and that the purpose of this policy is to help the College 'recruit the best possible candidates for tenure-track faculty positions'. The policy applies to both married and unmarried and same-sex and heterosexual couples. According to the dean, the important aspect of the policy is that we have 'created a culture in which the guiding assumption in the Dean's office is that we will try to do what we can for a couple. It's our default position – though trying may mean a number of different results'. He adds, 'The culture is more important than the written policy. Is it an administrative strategy or part of the culture of helping people? I think it is the latter'.

Three guidelines regulate the process of making initial appointments under the policy:

- All candidates for 'tenure-track' positions are informed of the College's willingness to entertain requests for employment and the procedures followed in that process. Tenure-track positions are those that ensure job security for faculty who have successfully completed a probationary period, typically of five or six years, capped by an extensive performance review involving the academic department, the school or college, and the university.
- The needs of the College and the academic unit in which an accompanying partner seeks employment are paramount in employment decisions.
- Offers of employment are contingent on the applicants' qualifications and the availability of resources. These qualifications must be systematically reviewed in light of the standards held by the unit, the College, and the university.

The Policy in Practice

When a candidate is invited to campus for an interview, he or she is informed in writing of the following: 'Any candidate who has a partner whose employment might affect the desirability of an appointment in the College of Liberal Arts and Sciences at the University of Kansas should feel free to discuss those issues during the on-campus interview without risk of potential bias'. In practice, relatively few candidates mention the need for accommodation before an offer has been made. The procedure for trying to accommodate a partner is typically set in motion when a candidate has been offered a faculty position. At that time, he or she informs the dean of the College that a partner is also seeking an academic appointment. The dean then requests a copy of the partner's credentials (curriculum vita, etc.), which upon receipt are reviewed by the relevant unit within the College. This review is intended to ensure that the partner can meet a need of the unit and that he or she is academically qualified for employment in the unit. Assuming these two conditions are met, the partner may be invited for an on-campus interview with the appropriate units. The college unit will forward its recommendation for appointment (either for or against) to the dean, who will then examine the budgetary implications and make a decision. In cases when a candidate for a position in the College seeks a faculty appointment for his or her partner outside the College, then the dean of the College will request a copy of the partner's credentials and forward them to the dean of the relevant school for consideration.

In terms of how the policy actually works, the dean of the College has suggested that the whole system hinges on 'how much we want the initial recruit. We will do a lot more if the person is an A+ than if he or she is a B+'. At the same time, the College administrators are clear that they would never force a department to hire a faculty member and that the accompanying spouse or partner 'must be of high quality and fill a need of the department'.

Outcomes of the Policy

Between 1998 and 2003, the College hired 184 tenure-track faculty members, of whom 43%, or 80, were women. Within the 184 tenure-track faculty members hired, 25%, or 46, were given some type of accommodation for a spouse or partner. Six of the couples accommodated were in same-sex relationships. Further, of the 46 accommodations completed, 25 of the accompanying spouses or partners were either immediately or eventually granted full-time tenure-track appointments, the vast majority of which were in the College of Liberal Arts and Sciences. The remaining 24 accompanying partners were in temporary, part-time, administrative, or 'other' positions. There is no record of the number of partner accommodations requests that were ultimately unsuccessful.

There are very few gender differences of note when examining the nature of the accommodations. As demonstrated in table 13.1, there were 22 cases in which the initial hire was female and 24 cases in which the initial hire was male. The partners of both sexes were equally likely to end up in either a tenure-track or non-tenure-track appointment.

Whereas the official policy is designed only for recruitment purposes, in reality, dual career couple accommodation in the College is used for both recruitment and retention purposes, and this is where we do see some gender differences. In 21 of the cases, accommodation occurred as part of the recruitment of an initial hire while in 25 of the cases the accommodation was part of the effort to retain faculty. It appears that when the initial hire is a woman, the accommodation is more likely to occur during the recruitment phase. The partners of male initial hires are more likely to be hired as the result of a retention effort (see table 13.2).

Table 13.1 Number of Accompanying Faculty Granted Either Tenure-Track or Non-Tenure-Track Appointments by Gender of Initial Hire

Faculty Appointment	Woman as Initial Hire	Man as Initial Hire
Tenure-track appointment for partner	11	14
Non-tenure-track appointment for partner	11	10

Table 13.2 Number of Accompanying Faculty Appointments by Gender of Initial Hire and by Recruitment/Retention Motives

Recruitment or Retention Motive	Woman as Initial Hire	Man as Initial Hire
Recruitment	14	7
Retention	8	17

One potential explanation for these differences is that these men began their careers before KU began accommodating academic couples. Now established in their careers, they are seeking to take advantage of the relatively new policy to obtain positions for their wives and partners who have been in non-tenure-track positions since their arrival at KU. Presumably, these partners, primarily women, were not considered for tenure-track appointments earlier and thus have 'settled' for positions below that for which they were initially qualified. Another likely explanation is that spouses or partners of the men in question came to the KU without having completed the PhD, and now that they have done so, they seek tenure-track appointments. There are probably more of these women at KU who have yet to seek out or receive an accommodation by the College. The question of whether these spouses or partners should be 'accommodated' now in tenure-track positions is an interesting one – and a question that more likely directly affects women than men. Some long-term tenure-track faculty members think it is unfair to offer partner accommodations to new faculty but not to established faculty and their partners. As a College administrator put it, 'How far back are we going to do it?' These are questions that the current administration has not answered except to note that, even though the formal policy does not address retention, in practice, the policy is utilized for both recruitment and retention purposes.

It is also interesting to note that in 25 cases where the accompanying spouse or partner was given a tenure-track position, the partners of women (in most cases men) were more likely to be offered a tenure-track position as a condition of recruitment, whereas the partners of men were more likely to be offered a tenure-track position as a condition of retention (see table 13.3). Similarly, the partners of male initial hires (mostly women) are more likely to be offered a non-tenure-track appointment as a result of a retention request than are the partners of their female counterparts (see table 13.3). A tentative conclusion is that women are either more willing to settle for non-tenure-track positions or they are given little choice but to do so.

We asked key administrators in the College to indicate whether they thought the various accompanying partners who had been accommodated in non-tenure-track positions were content or whether they actually were seeking tenure-track appointments. We labelled these individuals as 'content' or 'striving'. There was a remarkable degree of

Table 13.3 Number of Accompanying Faculty Offered Appointments by Gender of Initial Hire and by Recruitment/Retention Motives

Faculty Appointment and Motive	Woman as Initial Hire	Man as Initial Hire
Tenure track for recruitment	9	6
Tenure track for retention	2	8
Non-tenure track for recruitment	5	1
Non-tenure track for retention	6	9

Table 13.4 Satisfaction of Accompanying Faculty Granted Non-Tenure-Track Appointments by Gender of Initial Hire

Satisfaction	Woman as Initial Hire	Man as Initial Hire
Content	6	5
Striving	4	6

consistency among those we queried as to how to categorize these individuals. The data in table 13.4 reveal no gender differences.

We also sought to determine if there was a gender-related pattern associated with decisions by faculty members to leave the employment of KU. The provost's office attempts to contact faculty members who are leaving the university for reasons other than retirement to determine the nature of their decision. In 1999, the only year for which these data exist, of the 23 faculty members who left the institution, 11 were women. Faculty do not appear to leave for lack of tenure-track positions for a partner. Only one woman and three men reporting leaving KU because the institution was unable to find a tenure-track position for a spouse or partner.

Administrators at both the university and the College level believe that the policy is successful in helping to strengthen the faculty at KU. According to the senior vice-provost, the policy is useful because 'we can get people we wouldn't have gotten otherwise if we didn't offer them a job together. Because both members of a couple can both come here, then we are able to keep them'. She adds, 'Most of the couples have been pretty successful, good hires. It is a lot of work to make this work, but it is worthwhile. [Because of the accommodation] a lot of people stay who otherwise would have gone away because both members of the couple can be successful and satisfied'.

Beyond the Numbers

We interviewed three faculty couples in hopes of gaining insights into the gender-related dynamics that were not apparent in the numerical data of this study. Our hope was that these interviews would reveal (1) whether departments treat male and female accompanying spouses and partners differently when they are given tenure-track positions; (2) the extent to which men and women may respond differently to non-tenure-track appointments; (3) the fairness of having a policy focussed primarily on recruitment and used sparingly for retention; (4) and the extent to which a new university policy stemming from the dual career policy could lead to gender inequality. Each of these questions is explored based on our interviews.

Do departments treat male and female accompanying partners differently? We found no direct evidence to suggest that faculty members who were hired as a result of the dual career couple policy were treated differently because of their gender. The current dean noted, 'Departments all feel like spouses are "forced on them" even if the person is exactly what they want. ... Things are fine if the person is good. But because they come through a "suspicious process", if they are okay but not great, then it becomes problematic'. Further, the former dean suggested that it is possible that accommodations could 'hurt women's reputations on campus when folks feel that they are "shoved" into a department. Sometimes it is better to wait for a line to open up. There is a little bit of that "weak sister type of attitude" that can take place'. At the same time, when we interviewed couples who had been accommodated, we saw very little evidence of gender-related inequality that could be linked to the dual career couple policy.

The following accounts of dual career couples' experiences may illuminate the situation at KU. Four years ago, Lorie and her husband James applied for the same position in the Department of Physics. Initially, only Lorie was invited and interviewed on campus. Very early in the course of that interview, Lorie mentioned that her husband was also interested in an academic job in physics and in fact had applied for the same position as she. Lorie very favourably impressed the faculty. She was offered the job and James too was offered an interview that also resulted in an offer of an academic appointment.

Lorie, in response to a question about her perceptions of gender relations, explained, 'One reason I was [happy about coming here] is that I knew that I wouldn't be the first woman, or first part of a couple, in the Department'. We were struck by this response because our question was intended to root out perceived *problems* in gender relations. In Lorie's view, there were no problems with departmental faculty, male or female, in relation to her being a part of a dual career couple or being a woman in an historically male field. Her biggest complaint was with male students, who sometimes referred to her as Professor X's *wife* rather than as Professor Y.

Like Lorie, James did not perceive problems related to being part of a dual career couple. James attributed this largely to the efforts of dean of the College at the time he and his wife were hired. This dean was well aware of the difficulties faced by dual career couple – perhaps because she too was married to an academic – and was instrumental in systematizing the College's dual career accommodation policy. James also commented that the process by which spouses are hired might militate against such problems as resentment and the perception of unfairness. Specifically, once he was finally invited to interview on campus, James was 'subjected to the same scrutiny as everyone else. It [the interview] was very professional. They made it as rough as, maybe rougher than, any interview I've gone on'. James explained that department faculty were asked to decide if they would like to hire him, aside from any consideration about his wife. When he eventually was offered a position, James was treated as if he were 'a completely separate hire. Instead of being treated like a "tagalong", I negotiated for startup resources just like any new hire. All along, Lorie and I were treated as two independent new hires. That made a real difference'. James's observation about the hiring process is consistent with past research indicating that accommodation of dual career couples is less contentious at institutions where the so-called 'trailing spouse' is hired only after a process that is as rigorous as that faced by any new hire (Wolf-Wendel, Twombly, & Rice, 2003).

The experience of Joan and Andrew, faculty in the Department of Psychology, is similar to that of the couple, Lorie and James, in the Department of Physics. In both cases, the female partner was the 'leading' spouse. When she came for the interview, Joan was forthright about the fact that she was married to another academic psychologist who was seeking a tenure-track job. When it became clear that Joan was the top candidate, the chair offered to bring Andrew in for an interview. The interview went well, and Andrew was also offered a tenure-track position. Andrew received tenure the year before we interviewed him, and since the time of our interview, Joan was also promoted and tenured.

From the time they decided to live their lives together after meeting in graduate school, Joan and Andrew systematically sought ways to both hold tenure-track appointments at the same institution. She devoted her research to cognitive-neurological science while he focussed his on ageing and cognition. Joan believes that the fact that her field is male dominated actually gave her an advantage in the job search process. As she reports, 'I took advantage of my gender. There aren't that many women in cognitive-neuroscience. ... To be honest, my gender helped me. And as far as our situation here, I don't see that there are any gender implications [related to being part of a dual career couple]'. Asked directly, 'Are you and Andrew treated equally?' Joan replied, 'Oh, yes. He's my program head! [laughs] He was appointed pre-tenure, so there's no question that he's valued. ... He's fully supported by the Department'. We noted with interest that Joan interpreted our question to concern Andrew's treatment rather than her own. We took her response as further indication of a lack of bias against women who are part of dual career couples.

Joan's experience at KU has not been tainted in any way by being part of an 'accommodated couple'; in fact, it has been very positive. In her words, 'KU is perfect for us. It was the right choice. ... People [at other institutions] have put out feelers since we came here, but it would have to be an unbelievable offer for us to leave. It is the right balance for us. We really enjoy the atmosphere and the collegiality. Our department is so collegial, so comfortable'.

Andrew, Joan's husband, tells of an experience that is similar to that of James. Like James, Andrew was a 'trailing' spouse who was brought in for an interview after his wife was interviewed and, like James, has had a positive experience at KU since arriving. Andrew attributes his experience to three factors. In his words, 'My personal experience is really colored by a wonderful academic environment, a good institutional culture supporting spouses, and a good personal situation in which I feel confident in my own abilities'.

When asked if he was aware of any gender bias related to the fact that he is part of a dual career couple, Andrew said, 'I know there's a lot of gender bias in academia, but I'm not sure that dual career couples play into that. I'm not even sure it comes from faculty. In fact, I'm thinking more about students' bias. For example, Joan has gotten comments of a sexual nature on her students' teaching evaluations. That would never happen to me by virtue of the fact I'm male'.

The third couple with whom we spoke had a slightly different experience from the first two. Linda, the accompanying spouse, had completed her course work and her comprehensive examination but had not completed and defended her dissertation for a PhD in history when her husband Jordan was hired by the College in the History Department. Because she had not completed her terminal degree, KU was unable to offer a tenure-track position to Linda. Instead, she was initially appointed as a part-time lecturer in the Western Civilization Program and was told that when she completed her degree a more permanent position *might* be forthcoming. In 2000, Jordan was offered a prestigious fellowship and decided to take a year-long leave of absence. Before leaving, Jordan and Linda communicated with the dean that they would like a more permanent accommodation for Linda when they returned. The dean told them, 'I promise Linda will be gainfully employed when you both return'. Gainful employment, they learned, meant a full-time non-tenure-track lecturer position, more money, and the potential for a tenure-track appointment in the future. While they were away, Linda completed her degree and applied for and was offered tenure-track positions at two research universities. At the same time, the history department at KU agreed to interview Linda for a tenure-track position. The timing was such that Linda turned down the two offers and returned to KU as a full-time non-tenure-track assistant professor. Linda held that position for two years and was then offered a tenure-track joint appointment in History and Western Civilization.

While both Linda and Jordan express frustration with the university for making them wait so long for a tenure-track position, they were also able and willing to see the issue from the University's perspective. Linda, for example, noted, 'The history department has made a lot of dual career accommodations, and once hired they treat us like any other faculty member'. Jordan noted, 'The large number of spouses in the Department creates strategic planning difficulties on one hand but loyal faculty members on the other'. When asked specifically if gender were related to the delay in offering Linda a position or in her treatment during the process, both Linda and Jordan indicated that they were unaware of gender being a consideration by the university. Linda responded, 'Non-tenure-track faculty are always treated less well than are tenure-track people, but that works similarly for both men and women. In that status, we are all second class citizens'. However, she also admitted that gender did come into play when she speculated that a man in her situation might not have turned down the two tenure-track job offers without clearer assurances from KU that a tenure-track job was forthcoming.

These three couples' experiences share several common characteristics. First, all entered departments that had previously hired dual career couples and in which faculty members and administrators accepted the process. Second, all three departments also have a very good record of hiring women, regardless of their spouse or partner status. Third, all the couples were forthright about having academic spouses who were seeking tenure-track positions. There is much debate about whether applicants should be up-front about their marital or partner status from the outset or whether this information should be shared only after a job offer is in hand. At issue is the question of whether hiring decisions will be influenced by the knowledge that there is a spouse or partner involved who will need to be accommodated. It is likely that how individual couples choose to disclose their status will depend largely on whether they are interviewing at an institution that is known to accommodate spouses and partners or one at which this is not a common practice. Fourth, in the first two cases, the accompanying spouse came to KU with an earned doctorate, ready to hold a tenure-track position. In the third case, the accompanying spouse, Linda, had to wait for a tenure-track position until she had completed her doctorate and served time in a non-tenure-track position. Fifth, before being hired for the tenure-track position, however, all three spouses went through a hiring process that was similar to the regular hiring process for tenure-track faculty appointments (e.g., interviews, giving a research presentation, etc.). The data from our three couples, combined with our more extensive institutional case studies (Wolf-Wendel, Twombly, Rice, 2003) suggests that if there is a poor fit between an accompanying spouse and an institution's needs, or if that person is deemed unqualified for a position, it is less likely that an accommodation would be offered – especially if the accommodation sought is a tenure-track position. This reality, which no doubt causes some unhappiness, distress, and inconvenience in the short term, actually works to the long-term advantage of both the institution and the partners (although neither may think so at the time). It is not good practice for universities to hire faculty members who do not meet their perceived needs, but it can also be damaging, personally and professionally, for faculty to be hired into positions that do not match their particular qualifications.

Do men and women respond differently to non-tenure track appointment? One option within KU's policy is to accommodate a spouse or partner through a non-tenure-track position, which may offer full-time employment (primarily teaching) but which does not lead to tenure. This approach is common at KU and at other universities with or without dual career couple-hiring policies. According to the dean of the College, 'Partner accommodation around here means a lot of different things. Most people want it to be "I get a tenure-track job and my partner gets a tenure-track job". That is what most people want. But accommodation can take other forms as well. It may mean that someone comes here, and they are put in a part-time position and told that we will try in the future to hire them more permanently. The upshot is that we have dozens of people who believe that there is a tenure-track position out there for them'. He adds, 'We want people to feel hopeful and we might unintentionally mislead them because we want them to be happy'. The policy itself is clear about not making promises to couples. It says, in essence, that the university will do the best that it can to find an appropriate job either within the university or to work with the couple to help them find work elsewhere. In practice, there are many instances where no accommodation is made or the accommodation offered is not what the couple had hoped for.

Administrators involved with the policy offered some thoughts about gender-based implications involved in placing the accompanying spouse in a non-tenure-track position. The former dean, for example, speculated that '[S]ome husbands who are the "trailing spouse" come in with a chip on their shoulder. Instead of getting over it, the husbands continue to grumble over their lot in life. In contrast, many women say "I will prove to them that I am good."' The former dean observed, 'Women are used to accommodation and adjust better to the situation whereas a lot of men seem less willing to be in a holding pattern. The men want the position immediately rather than going through a "soft" position first'. Other administrators also suggested that the men biding their time in non-tenure-track positions along with their wives were potentially more demanding of the administration to find a permanent position more quickly. Although it was beyond the scope of our study to conclude with any degree of certainty that gender influences whether an individual is given a non-tenure-track or a tenure-track position, the dean's comments about attitudinal differences between male and female accommodating partners raise questions about whether there may well be gender differences in the ways that the positions are perceived and experienced.

Will a policy change lead to gender inequalities? A recent policy change allows lecturers to be employed full-time for long-term contracts, to receive benefits, including raises and some research and travel support.[3] Until 2004, such full-time lecturer/instructor positions were limited to three-year appointments with the occupant having to reduce his or her appointment to less than 100% at the end of the third year. Although creation of this lecturer track received support from faculty governance, there was great concern that such a track would be overused and would become a substitute for tenure-track accommodations for dual career couples, with women more likely than men ending up in such positions. Since the policy was just implemented, we have no evidence that this will happen. When asked whether he was worried about this happening, the current dean of the College replied, 'KU recruits more women than men at the junior level. If we created a more permanent full time instructor track, I am not worried about having more women as the majority of the lecturer positions'.

The other argument is that women are slightly over-represented in lecturer and instructor ranks nationally ("Almanac Issue," 2004) and at KU (see figure 13.1) and that improving the terms and benefits of such positions will improve the situation for women who hold them. As one vice-provost commented, 'KU doesn't allow [non-tenure] people to get promoted or be full-time if they are in a lecturer position at this point. They aren't eligible for faculty development, teaching awards, sabbaticals, etc. Most of all of the teaching awards are structured for tenured faculty. You might end up with more women as lecturers, but why not make their work more palatable'. The recently passed lecturer policy seeks to improve upon the existing situation. The effects of this policy on women should and will be monitored.

Conclusion

Returning to the lens of feminist policy analysis, we ask our original questions: do dual career couple policies help women; to what extent can we label dual career couple policies as feminist? Our earlier research identified perceived problems associated with dual career couple accommodation. These perceived problems range from a concern over the basic fairness of accommodating partnered academics to the logistics of tenure and promotion decisions (Wolf-Wendel, Turombly, & Rice, 2003). We were therefore somewhat pleasantly surprised to find that in the College at KU, dual career couple accommodation is currently relatively unproblematic from the point of view of the three couples we interviewed, from the perspective of College administrators, and from an examination of the numerical data.

Although it is beyond the scope of our work at this time to statistically analyse the relationship between the dual career couple-hiring practices and the increase in the number of women faculty members in the College over the past ten years, conventional wisdom would suggest that the practice has been helpful in improving the representation of women faculty. In 2001, nearly half of the assistant professors in the College were women (61 out of 129), some of whom came to KU as either the initial hire or as an accompanying partner in a dual career relationship. In fact, approximately 40 women (not including the same-sex couples) have taken faculty positions in the last five years at KU with the assistance of this policy as either the initial hire or accompanying partner. Would they have come had a position not been offered to their spouses or partners? There is no way to know this for sure except to say that the couples we interviewed believed that they and other dual career couples they knew on campus came here because the College made it easy for them to do so. The policy is used frequently and has, as the current dean noted, become part of the culture. The fact that the dean can state in 2004 that the policy is part of the culture in and of itself is indicative of significant and rapid change in attitude. In a KU equity study conducted in 1999, faculty and administrators reported considerable animosity toward any kind of faculty search (although not necessarily hostile to any one individual beneficiary of such a hire) in which a candidate was perceived to have been 'given' a position that they presumably had not earned because they did not go through a traditional search (Office of the Provost, 2001). Although the survey has not been repeated, our interviews with faculty (all of whom were appointed around 1999) and administrators for this chapter suggest that the policy has become accepted as critical to the recruitment and retention of high quality faculty members in a highly competitive environment. In fact, gender equity per se is not the main motivation behind the KU policy or similar policies at other universities; rather, simple market economics is the driving force behind them and can explain the increased degree of policy acceptance. The policy stems from a desire to recruit the best faculty and to do so requires that institutions like KU keep up with other research institutions, many of which have implemented similar policies. This acceptance has significant gender implications to the extent that these policies exist largely because of the increase in the number of women who pursue academic careers and who are married or are in life partnerships with other academics. Continued scepticism about such policies would undoubtedly affect women negatively. No one we talked to thought that the College invokes the policy differentially for men than for women. However, the policy can be viewed as transformative to the extent that faculty in the College, by and large, have to come to accept dual career couple hiring as necessary to recruit and retain the best faculty – of both genders. In addition, the policy is transformative in that it has contributed to greater representation of women among the faculty in the College of Liberal Arts and Sciences.

While it does not appear that the College demonstrates gender bias in how and when the policy is invoked, the couples with whom we spoke identified some lingering skepticism from their colleagues about the nature of their appointment. This skepticism, however, did not seem to be based on gender but more on the concerns about what it means to be 'accommodated'. It is perhaps telling that one administrator with whom we spoke was upset to learn that her name was included among those faculty listed as having been accommodated in the College; she insisted that though her spouse is also a faculty member at KU, that she was hired in a 'legitimate' search. Both partners in a dual career couple may be perceived negatively – and treated accordingly – for having been accommodated. Our interviewees suggested that while there are implications of being an accompanying spouse or partner, no one thought they were gender-based. That is, regardless of greater acceptance, faculty members who obtain tenure-track job outside of the regular competitive process are still viewed with some suspicion.

The gendered impact that was identified was mostly subtle. For example, the couples we interviewed observed that women may be more willing to 'trail' or follow their partners or spouses and accept non-tenure-track jobs. Additionally, although the couples we interviewed did not perceive differential treatment to be gender-based (male accompanying spouses were treated the same way as female accompanying spouses), the gender dynamics of academe suggest that female and male faculty may, in fact, be treated and judged differently. For instance, women accompanying spouses or partners, especially those in traditionally male dominated fields, may be thought to have been given preferential treatment during the hiring process or to be less competent or committed than 'regular' hires while the reverse might not be true for male accompanying spouses or partners. These women will typically feel that they have to work harder to be regarded as serious scholars in their own right. Interestingly, two of the couples we interviewed indicated that it was students who seemed to have trouble accepting that the female partner was a legitimate faculty member on her own right independent of her husband.

At the same time, men who 'trail' their wives or partners may feel themselves to be, or be perceived by others, as violating the established gender norm according to which males are supposed to be heads of household and primary breadwinners. Conversely, women who are 'leading' partners may be seen as being overly ambitious or strident, whereas their accompanying partners may be seen as relative 'wimps'. Such a perception would certainly be consistent with long-standing gender-linked stereotypes, according to which the 'same' characteristics are judged negatively when possessed by a woman but positively when possessed by a man. Even though these stereotypes were not evident among the couples we interviewed at KU, they did emerge in some of the case study data we collected for the earlier study (Wolf-Wendel, Turombly, & Rice, 2003). Dual career couple policies put universities like KU in an interesting position in relation to the Affirmative Action issues raised by Judith Glazer-Raymo (see chapter 11 in this book by Judith Glazer-Raymo). Often, although not always, dual career couple hiring skirts the 'open search' process that is so essential in making sure that women and people of colour are considered for positions. In fact, it is often through search waivers that accompanying spouses or partners are hired. If used too frequently and inappropriately, women may inadvertently end up being criticized for being party to an old girl's network of their own. On the other hand, Glazer-Raymo suggests that reordering of Affirmative Action priorities may pit gender against race in faculty hiring. Exactly how this might play out in dual career couple hiring is not clear. We do know, however, that any university has a limited number of tenure-track positions. If one hires the partners or spouses of an initial hire, then positions will be unavailable for others.

Consistent with feminist approaches to policy analysis, we believe that the local context in which this policy has been implemented accounts in significant measure for its success. As noted earlier, KU has a long-standing commitment to equity and diversity to the extent that women have been students and faculty here since the university's beginning in 1865; in recent years, there has been an effort to increase the number of women faculty in fields where they have been under-represented. KU's chemistry and physics departments and School of Pharmacy have reputations nationally as having a high proportion of women faculty. Such factors provide a relatively supportive context for dual career accommodation when the topic was initially broached in the early 1990s. That the subject *was* broached can be traced to the initiative of several former College deans, including one who was a member of a dual career couple herself. Thus, she was both sensitive to the issues of dual career academic couples and, because of her position in administrative leadership, able to propose solutions for addressing the issues. Further, the College, which is the only unit with a formal dual career couple-hiring policy, is large enough to support the hiring of spouses and partners and to avoid the logistical problems encountered in many other types of academic contexts. Added to this is the procedural dimension that requires accompanying spouses and partners to be subjected to the same type of scrutiny as other applicants prior to hiring; this policy reduces the potential for animosity from faculty who are not members of academic couples.

The College's dual career couple-hiring policy was not designed as a 'feminist' policy. It does, however, have feminist implications. The fact that the policy has been accepted can be attributed as much to market economics, however, as to a commitment to gender equity. KU wants to be competitive in attracting the best and brightest faculty when its average salaries are only about 90% of the average of salaries at its peer universities. A dual career couple policy helps KU to achieve this objective. In short, a whole constellation of factors were aligned at KU in such a way as to support implementation of the College's policy. The particular constellation of factors present at KU is not the only one that appears to be conducive to gender-progressive dual career couple accommodation policies – consider, for example, the University of Illinois at U-C among others. But we are convinced that efforts to understand institutional responses to dual career academic couples will be more productive to the extent that they account for the whole complex of factors – historical, political, and personal – that bear on this complicated phenomenon. Data from our case study of College of Liberal Arts and Sciences at the University of Kansas indicate that the demographics of university faculties are beginning to change. Although dual career couple-hiring policies may help attract highly qualified women faculty, the problem of keeping them and promoting them through the ranks still remains a major challenge for KU and other U.S. research universities.

Notes

1. In the literature on dual couples in academia, one finds numerous references to 'leading' and 'trailing' (or alternatively 'primary' and 'secondary') spouses and partners. We have tried to avoid these terms whenever possible. Intentionally or not, they imply a hierarchy of value that is bound to stigmatize faculty occupying the lower rung of this two-tiered ladder. Instead of using these terms, we refer to the 'initial' and 'accompanying' members of dual career couples. We use this language because employment of the accompanying spouse or partner is contingent on the job offer to the initial hire.
2. A typical faculty search begins when a department identifies and justifies a need for hiring. The department will often establish a search committee comprised of faculty that writes a description of the position and arranges for the description to be published in various forums, such as the *Chronicle of higher education* and professional journals. Applicants are asked to provide evidence of their qualifications for the position. The search committee reviews the files and determines which are best suited for the position. Generally, three or four of the especially well-qualified applicants are invited for an interview. After all the applicants have interviewed, they are often rank-ordered in terms of perceived overall merit. The top candidate will typically be offered the position.
3. Lecturers are full-time employees whose main responsibilities are teaching. They are eligible for health and retirement benefits and for some professional development funds. Lecturers are more common in disciplines that have high undergraduate enrollments, such as English and mathematics.

References

Astin, H. S., & Milem, J. F. 1997. The status of academic couples in US institutions. In M. A. Ferber & J. W. Loeb (Eds.), *Academic couples: Problems and promises* (pp. 128–155) Urbana: University of Illinois Press.

'Almanac Issue', 2004–2005 (2004) *The chronicle of higher education, LL* (1) (August 27).

Bensimon, E. M., & Marshall, C. (1997) Policy analysis for post-secondary education: Feminist and critical perspectives. In C. Marshall (Ed.), *Feminist critical policy analysis: A perspective for pos-secondary education* (pp. 1–21). London: Falmer Press.

Loeb, J. W. (1997) Programs for academic partners: How well can they work? In M. A. Ferber and J. W. Loeb (Eds.), *Academic couples: Problems and promises* (pp. 270–298) Urbana: University of Illinois Press.

National Survey of Student Engagement Institute for Effective Educational Practice (2004) *University of Kansas Deep Report*. Bloomington, IN: NSSE, Indiana University Center for Postsecondary Research.

Office of the Chancellor, University of Kansas (2004) Executive Summary. Unpublished document. University of Kansas: Office of the Chancellor.

Office of Institutional Research and Planning, University of Kansas (2004) Profiles. Unpublished document. Lawrence, KS: Office of Institutional Research and Planning.

Office of the Provost, University of Kansas (2001) Equity study. Unpublished document. University of Kansas: Office of the Provost.

Raabe, P. H. (1997) Work-family policies for faculty: How 'career-and-family-friendly' is academe? In M. A. Ferber and J. W. Loeb (Eds.), *Academic couples: Problems and promises* (pp. 208–226). Urbana: University of Illinois Press.

Wolf-Wendel, L. E., Twombly, S. B., & Rice, S. (2003) *The two-body problem: Dual-career couple hiring practices in higher education*. Baltimore: Johns Hopkins University Press.

Chapter Fourteen
Frames, Changes, Challenges, and Strategies

Mary Ann Danowitz Sagaria and Lyndsay Agans

Envisioning gender equality measures as a dimension of university change opens new possibilities to rethink gender activism within the dominant framework of competitive markets and entrepreneurialism. Success will depend on persistent and consistent work over an extended time to adjust to external environmental change. Challenges to gender equality progress are inevitable, but good leaders and committed activists will not be daunted. Excellence in research and teaching calls for having the best talent in our universities, whatever their gender and background.

In this chapter, we extract information from the case studies information about the current conditions and status of gender equality in higher education and strategies for transforming our universities. First, we provide a brief overview of the differing conceptions of equality in the European Union and United States. Second, we identify factors influencing progress towards gender equality change drawing upon Sporn's (1999) model of university adaptation and examples from the nation-state and university case studies. Third, we present key internal organizational issues that require attention if gender equality is to become more fully part of a university change processes.

Transatlantic Perspectives

Neo-liberalism is reshaping the purposes and workings of universities in the European Union and the United States. In freeing markets from trade barriers to increase the movement of goods and generate economic opportunities and profits, the ideology is creating a culture of entrepreneurialism and competition among universities to increase their economic strength through research accomplishments and by preparing individuals for the labor market. Müller (see chapter 3 in this book) explains how within the frame of the Bologna Process, a neo-liberal economic ideology is driving structural changes in German universities, making them contested locations with contradictory opportunities and challenges for progress towards gender equality. Among these structural changes are the further decentralization of institutional autonomy, the reduced time towards degree, split of the bachelors/masters

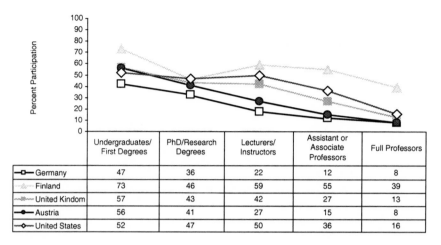

	Undergraduates/ First Degrees	PhD/Research Degrees	Lecturers/ Instructors	Assistant or Associate Professors	Full Professors
—□— Germany	47	36	22	12	8
·····▲····· Finland	73	46	59	55	39
⚫⚫⚫ United Kindom	57	43	42	27	13
—⚫— Austria	56	41	27	15	8
—◇— United States	52	47	50	36	16

Figure 14.1 Representation of Women among Students and Faculty in EU and U.S. Universities, 2002–2003

Sources: Finland, figures of 2004, KOTA database: National statistical online database updated annually on universities and higher education, http://www.csc.fi/Kota/nuts.html; United Kingdom, figures of 2001/2002 Higher Education Statistics Agency (HESA), 2003; United States, figures of 1999/2000 National Survey of Postsecondary Faculty (NSOPF); Austria, figures of 2002/2003, StatistikAustria, 2004; Germany, figures of 2002, Statistisches Bundesamt, Hochschulstatistik (Federal Bureau of Statistics, Statistics Higher Education), calculation by J. Loewen. Also, please note that Academic staff rankings were consolidated for the purposes of concise presentation in the chart and amended as follows: German academic staff at the habilitation level are included under the Assistant/Associate professor level and *C4* professors under the category of Full Professor; Austrian academic staff at the rank of university assistant are under the category of Lecturer/Instructor and assistant professors are under the category of Assistant/Associate Professor; Finnish academic staff at the rank of assistant are included under Assistant/Associate Professor and senior assistants are under the category of Full Professor; United Kingdom academic staff at the senior lecturer and researcher level are under the category of Assistant/Associate Professor; United States academic staff at the rank of associate professor are included under Assistant/Associate professor. Figures have been rounded to the nearest whole number.

degree, and increased auditing measures. Though perceived as neutral, these changes, in effect, may have adverse consequences.

Universities on both sides of the North Atlantic share very similar patterns of gender representation in their institutions. Women make up the majority of undergraduates in the European Union (58 %) and the United States (56 %), but then their presence becomes more scarce at each level of the academic hierarchy so that at the at the senior rank they are only 14% of the full professors in the European Union and 15.8% in U.S. research universities. As Morley notes (in chapter 9 of this book), because the majority of undergraduate students are women, policy makers may no longer perceive gender as an issue; hence there is a silencing of gender in policy discourse. Figure 14.1 shows the repetition of the pattern in the five nations described in this book.

Each descending line represents terrible losses, in opportunity for individual women and in institutional potential for solving pressing problems and increasing economic performance. Clearly, the lack of gender equality continues to be a serious problem.

The European Union's Gender Equality Rationale

In the European Union, the underlying principle for gender equality is that equal opportunity is a basic human right. Efforts of the European Commission (EC) have been instrumental in many EU member states' decisions to incorporate equal opportunity into their agendas. Rees's (1998) work on tinkering, tailoring, and transforming the mainstream offers an accessible vocabulary to explore differences among the underlying principles of the gender equality frameworks. The shifts in the frameworks can be seen through the various policy strategies employed in the EU: equal treatment, positive action, and transforming (mainstreaming) policy. Equal treatment (tinkering) has sought to augment equal access for women but has had limited success because of a lack of mechanisms to reinforce its application and measures to monitor effectiveness. Positive action and positive discrimination (tailoring) have sought to alter directly the status quo quantitatively and provide interventionist and active measures to ensure changes in outcome. However, while providing for equal access, unchanged structural and attitudinal barriers have continued to reinforce gender differences, placing expectations on women to assimilate into a male-dominated organizational culture in order to advance. Mainstreaming (transforming) shifts the responsibility from individual women for gender equality to organizations. Universities are expected to bring about structural and cultural changes within their organization by incorporating gender equality into all policies, procedures, and budgeting. Rees (1998) explains, 'The transforming agenda is predicated upon the argument that opportunities to participate in education, training, and employment should not be enhanced or restricted by membership of one group or another' (p. 46).

As we trace gender equality in the European Union, we recognize the inherent danger of privileging a single frame or generalizing from one distinctive nation-state to another. We also recognize that by drawing upon writings from five nations we exclude important geographical, historical, and cultural considerations in Europe. In describing shifting frames, we are referring to the formal adoption of legislation and practices of the European Union. We acknowledge that the implementation of these approaches is mediated by the historical, cultural, social, and political textures of each nation-state.

The United States' Gender Equality Rationale

Currently, gender equality in the United States is linked to diversity, which is the result of the restructuring of affirmative action through legislative and judicial processes. National social movements for civil rights in the 1960s and 1970s eventually influenced key decision makers to create affirmative action mechanisms that enforce gender equality policies. Affirmative action as a gender equality framework creates conditions that allow for equal employment opportunities and for treatment that does not discriminate on the basis of race, creed, colour, national origin, and, as of 1967, sex. Judith Glazer-Raymo points out, 'It was ultimately the leadership of women in the US Congress that resulted in passage of an omnibus higher education act in November 1971' (see chapter 11 in this book). The backlash against affirmative action that began in the 1990s along with the shift towards industry logic in university behaviour has had detrimental effects on equality in higher education in general and on women in particular. U.S. Supreme Court decisions have affirmed diversity in education as a compelling interest of the state to better prepare students for a complex labour market. The concept of diversity itself is rooted in the different cultural characteristics, such as values, language, customs, skills, knowledge, and behaviours of individuals and groups (Sagaria et al., 2003). Legal challenges, however, have established that the diversity precedent is not binding. Consequently, the current framework for gender equality rests on precarious ground. The state's dismantling of equality measures and the shifting emphasis from providing for the social good to providing for economic enterprises are causing U.S. research universities to redefine their priorities.

While the social, political, and legal contexts within the European Union and each of its nation-states differs from that of the United States, similar change strategies emerge, albeit tailored to local situations.

Factors Influencing Progress towards Gender Equality as University Change

What then are the conditions allowing effective gender equality change strategies to emerge in the cases described in this book? What factors brought about progress towards equality? To answer those questions, we employ present data that emerged from the case studies in this book with an organizing frame adapted from Barbara Sporn's (1999) model of university change. We identify five influential variables to explain changes in gender equality as part of organization adaptation.

External Environments Influence Gender Equality Change

Teresa Rees identifies the various formal governmental commitments to gender mainstreaming (see chapter 2 and table 2.1), such as policies, structures, the presence of gender studies, and institutes responsible for equality plans. The nation-state case studies of Germany, Austria, and Finland show how external demands, laws, and policies of the state can advance gender equality change at the university level. In Germany, the expectation of gender mainstreaming in the new curricula is helping incorporate gender into audit measures associated with university excellence (see chapter 3). In Austria (see chapter 5), recent legislative measures have contributed to the promotion of women in science. The University Act 2002 provides for equal treatment of men and women in university policy, incorporates a quota for female employment, requires affirmative action plans, and establishes a unit for the equal treatment and promotion of women and gender studies in each university. In Finland (see chapter 7), the creation of supportive national childcare policies, gender quotas on research councils, and the establishment of a position of Equality Ombudsman have been catalysts for progress towards gender equality within universities.

The United Kingdom and the United States demonstrate how external environments can be either adversarial to progress towards equality or null, preserving gender asymmetry. Both external conditions have similar inhibiting consequences for the progress of gender equality. For example, despite the presence of laws, policies, and structures in the United Kingdom, there is a gender silence in higher education policy, suggesting that universities have addressed equality and that they have acted to reduce inequities only when legal expectations and activism have mandated or called for change (see chapter 9). Likewise, in the United States (see chapter 11), challenges to affirmative action measures have led to policy alterations, effectively ungendering higher education and removing programmes aimed at improving gender equality.

Positive Action from University Leaders is Essential for Progress towards Gender Equality

In the five university case studies, leaders were instrumental in bringing about significant progress towards gender equality. Their universities illustrate the important role that a rector, president, chancellor, or dean have in both providing the vision and leading efforts for gender equality. They show that when a senior administrator publicly advocates for equality and visibly makes a personal and university commitment to equality, then he or she influences others by sending a powerful signal that the university is committed to equality.

At the University of Dortmund (see chapter 4), the rector and a vice-rector assumed responsibility for the Volkswagen Foundation's funded Quality and Innovation: Gender Equality Challenges Higher Education Reform Project to produce significant changes in gender equality with the governing board and administration and to improve quality and performance within faculties and departments. The Volkswagen Foundation expected the rector to lead the project, a condition generally considered critical in organizational change in higher education (Clark, 2004; Sporn, 1999).

At the Vienna University of Economics and Business Administration (see chapter 6), the rector has provided leadership to ensure policy efforts to mainstream gender equality. Two of his approaches have been to draw upon his social policy research and to support the Working Group for Equal Opportunity. His actions have contributed to the creation of a belief system within the university that supports gender equality. At the University of Helsinki (see chapter 8), a vice-rector has chaired the Equality Committee. While in that role, he gave many presentations at Finnish universities and viewed himself as an ambassador for gender equality within and outside of the university. At Ohio State University (see chapter 12), the president and provost have advocated for and overseen the development and implementation of family and women-friendly policies and have encouraged the collection of extensive gender, racial, and ethnic data as well as the creation of an internal leadership development institute for women and under-represented men. At the University of Kansas (see chapter 13), a dean has championed and implemented a dual career couple-hiring policy in which the partners of 25% of all recently hired faculty members have been accommodated.

Supportive Structures and Incentives Are Necessary to Put in Place Equality Measures

The creation of new committees, offices, programmes, and positions demonstrates tangible change for guiding and/or providing resources and activities associated with equality. The triangulation of policies, structures, and procedures dealing with a particular phenomenon often has the affect of aligning activities with espoused goals (Brown, Van Ummersen, & Hill, 2002). The University of Dortmund demonstrates efforts to mainstream gender equality through both structural and cultural change. By requiring departments to commit funds to improve unacceptably high female dropout rates and rewarding departments for progress towards gender equality, institutional leaders have encouraged behavioural and cultural changes. The University of Helsinki has succeeded in integrating gender equality into the highest management agendas and creating an infrastructure to monitor and promote gender equality. It has also utilized the position of the equality advisor to create cultural change by reducing sexual harassment. Finnish legislation and documentation of the problem of sexual harassment in the university compelled the university to develop policies, provide training, and place a well-qualified professional in the role of equality advisor. As a result, most cases have been handled properly at the faculty or unit level.

Miriam David's story of her development of the professional doctorate in Education at Keele University (see chapter 10) is an example of creating a programme that mainstreams gender into the curriculum. It shows two simultaneous change processes. One, the programme has disrupted dominant pedagogical discourses and practices and created new ones in order to better serve women students. Two, the feminist approach of the programme has created a more equitable and inclusive higher education environment and may become a catalyst for subsequent change in higher education as graduates apply their learning to practice. The case study shows how academic programme creation infusing women's personal experiences into knowledge development and the curriculum can radically reform teaching and learning.

Ohio State established a new structure, the Women's Place, to offer important resources for women. The formation of this unit has provided a senior administrative position of associate provost for women's policy initiatives. The incumbent is an equality activist who is involved with university-wide policy matters. Creating this organizational unit has occasioned a source for ongoing feedback on policy issues, a data clearinghouse, a communications hub, an advocacy base, and a source of increased visibility for the needs and contributions of women at the university.

Funding Puts in Place Equality Measures

Scarcity of resources in an increasingly competitive market gives status and priority to funding as a determinant in decision making and university adaptation. The use of financial rewards to stimulate or reinforce a practice indicates that resources have been redistributed. In an entrepreneurial university culture, financial allocations are symbolically and practically important. Similarly, budgetary increases, over time, demonstrate an institutionalized commitment to gender equality and enable activities and programmes that otherwise would not be possible.

For instance, the gender equality project, Quality and Innovation: Gender Equality and Challenges in Higher Education Reform at the University of Dortmund, demonstrates the importance of leadership and financial incentives for reform as a way of making university structures 'vulnerable and susceptible to new ideas' in order to overcome the asymmetrical gender divide in German society. At the institution level, the University of Dortmund demonstrates efforts to mainstream gender equality. Behavioural and cultural changes are encouraged by requiring departments to commit funds to improve unacceptably high female dropout rates and reward departments for progress towards gender equality. Additionally, the establishment of scholarships and programmes, including the Austrian Program for Advanced Research and Technology (APART) as well as a mentoring project for women in academe, are contributing to meaningful progress towards gender equality in Austria. In the United States at Ohio State University, the commitment of resources for the Faculty Hiring Assistance Program (FHAP) included the hiring of at least five to ten women and minority faculty members as part of the diversity strategy of the organization-wide Academic Plan. These examples demonstrate that while economic forces may marginalize gender equity measures, economic incentives can have a powerful effect on propelling gender equality programs forward.

Auditing Puts in Place Equality Measures

Increasingly, external entities have used audits to redirect financial allocations. Within an entrepreneurial environment, accountability emerges as another important variable in shaping university change. Müller (chapter 3) explains how incorporating gender as a criterion into such acts as budgeting, promoting, and evaluating has become routine. Furthermore, the German Ministry of Science and Education includes a *gender concept* in their requirements for the distribution of research funds. The United Kingdom, as Morley (chapter 9) points out, stands in contradistinction to these policies as their audits are gender-neutral. The Research Auditing Exercise (RAE), which does not incorporate gender equity measures, directly affects the amount of research funding an organization receives. Accountability and the definitions used in evaluating 'excellence' at universities in the European Union and United States are often regarded as value-free. However, socially based constructs of knowledge and excellence effectively norm the male-dominated status quo and thus devalue women in academe and the labor market. Awareness of gender within accountability and auditing, such as the inclusion of gender scorecards in reviews of the implementation of the Bologna Process, become all the more important for creating change.

Conclusion

As the aforementioned review of factors influencing progress towards gender equality indicates, nation-states and universities are engaged in significant policy changes and programme developments. Yet, it is also clear that reforms are tempered by several factors. In the external environment, universities have shifted towards an increased market orientation with finances driving the priorities of institutions (Sporn, 2003). In many nation-states, legislative measures have not brought about the anticipated progress towards equality, and policy makers no longer consider gender an issue because women now comprise more than 50% of undergraduate students (see chapter 9). Gender equality reforms in the policy sphere have set new directions for universities, but they continue as male-dominated cultures grounded in principles of meritocracy and scientific methods as well as practices of peer-review and informal networks, which often are not gender-neutral.

Changing universities to achieve gender equality ultimately means changing organizational structures and cultures, and at times, the larger policy spheres in which they function. Ideally, institutional efforts to progress towards gender equality will occur in the broader policy sphere, in the overall institutional sphere, and in decentralized faculty and department spheres. Many of the cases reported in this book show the impact of successful structural change. But as Müller (chapter 3) points out, the impact of structural changes on gender developments is important but is insufficient in itself because it fails to consider the 'androcentricity of the organization of science and of the culture of universities' (see chapter 2).

Key issues within organizations require attention for gender equality to become a part of a deeper cultural organizational change that makes transparent changes in practices, which, at best, underserve women and at worse discriminate against them. We offer five key internal factors derived from the American Council on Education's work on the experiences of U.S. university presidents as they strive to advance women in the name of equality (Brown, Van Ummersen, & Hill, 2002):

- Gender equality measures must be grounded in the university's basic values and strategic action plan.
- Various constituencies within the university must buy in or accept the proposed gender equality measures.
- Gender equality initiatives must be tailored to the particular needs of the university and must be adapted to its mission and culture.
- Gender equality initiatives must be linked to major programs and endeavors.
- A gender equality monitoring system with accountability must be put in place to assess short range and long-range outcomes.

There is no definitive end to the factors and initiatives that will advance gender equality in universities nor is there a limit on the kinds of individuals and coalitions that can bring about positive change. Achieving equality in our universities will require state policy makers, university leaders in administrative and faculty roles, and activists to be both prepared and to engage in this crucial task.

References

Brown, G., Van Ummersen, C., & Hill, B. (2002) *Breaking the barriers: A guidebook of strategies.* Washington, DC: American Council on Education Office of Women.

Clark, B. R. (2004) *Sustainng change in universities: Continuities in case studies and concepts.* Berkshire: Open University Press.

Rees, T. (1998) *Mainstreaming equality in the European Union.* London: Routledge.

Sagaria, M., Glazer-Raymo, J., Sporn, B., Pellert, A., & Subotzky, G. (2003) Gender equality and university change: Tensions and leverages. Paper presented at the Plenary Session of the Association for the Study of Higher Education International Conference, Portland, OR, November.

Sporn, B (1999) *Adaptive University Structures.* London: Jessica Kingsley Publishers.

——— (2003) Trends relating to higher education reform in Europe: An overview. In H. Eggins (Ed.), *Globalization and reform in higher education.* Maidenhead, Birkshire: Open University Press.

Index

CPSIA information can be obtained at www.ICGtesting.com
Printed in the USA
LVOW130101281212

313554LV00004B/23/A